WHEN GOOD GOVERNMENT MEANT
BIG GOVERNMENT

When Good Government Meant Big Government

THE QUEST TO EXPAND FEDERAL POWER, 1913-1933

Jesse Tarbert

Columbia University Press
New York

Columbia University Press
Publishers Since 1893
New York Chichester, West Sussex
cup.columbia.edu
Copyright © 2022 Columbia University Press
All rights reserved

Library of Congress Cataloging-in-Publication Data
Names: Tarbert, Jesse, author.
Title: When good government meant big government : the quest to expand federal power, 1913–1933 / Jesse Tarbert.
Description: New York : Columbia University Press, [2022] | Includes bibliographical references and index.
Identifiers: LCCN 2021038276 (print) | LCCN 2021038277 (ebook) | ISBN 9780231189729 (hardback) | ISBN 9780231189736 (trade paperback) | ISBN 9780231548489 (ebook)
Subjects: LCSH: Federal government—United States—History—20th century. | Public administration—United States—History—20th century. | United States—Politics and government—1913–1921. | United States—Politics and government—1919–1933.
Classification: LCC JK325 .T37 2022 (print) | LCC JK325 (ebook) | DDC 321.02/0973—dc23
LC record available at https://lccn.loc.gov/2021038276
LC ebook record available at https://lccn.loc.gov/2021038277

Cover design: Noah Arlow

CONTENTS

Introduction   1

Chapter One
Administration and Accommodation: Before 1913   10

Chapter Two
The Elite Reformers in Exile: 1913–1918   24

Chapter Three
After the Armistice: Spring 1919   42

Chapter Four
The Budget Debate: 1919–1920   52

Chapter Five
The Dark Horse: 1920–1921   65

Chapter Six
Early Success: Spring and Summer 1921   79

Chapter Seven
Equal Protection Under Law: 1921–1923   92

Chapter Eight
Backlash: Spring and Summer 1923   107

Chapter Nine
Southern Strength: 1923–1924   119

Chapter Ten
Congressional Counteroffensive: Spring 1924   128

Chapter Eleven
Low Expectations: 1924–1927   140

Chapter Twelve
The Great Engineer: 1929–1931   155

Chapter Thirteen
Dashed Hopes: 1930–1933   170

Conclusion   184

ACKNOWLEDGMENTS   193

ABBREVIATIONS   197

NOTES   201

INDEX   245

WHEN GOOD GOVERNMENT MEANT
BIG GOVERNMENT

INTRODUCTION

The title of this book brings together two well-worn phrases from the American political lexicon. "Good government" was a watchword in the late nineteenth century for genteel members of the northeastern establishment. It encompassed an avowedly moderate, bipartisan agenda aimed at rooting out official corruption and ejecting so-called grafters, boodlers, and spoilsmen from the public payroll. Often it has been pejorative, a dismissive shorthand for middle-of-the-road proposals that seemed to forestall more radical or revolutionary reforms.[1] "Big government," on the other hand, emerged as a term of derision among conservatives and moderates after World War II. Its inconsistent application has often masked the motivations of those who use it. While the label seems to imply some straightforward or principled objection to size or quantity, in most cases the actual objection has been to the kind or quality of some particular government action.[2]

Why does the United States have the government that it has? Why can the national government do some things but not others? These are historical questions. To answer them requires an understanding of the historical forces that have shaped the development of American government. This book attempts to identify some of those forces by examining a brief but crucial period when a well-connected group of moderate reformers emerged as the leading proponents of central control and national authority in debates about federal power—a period when elite advocates of "good government" promoted plans that would give rise to "big government."

1

The know-it-when-you-see-it ambiguity of the phrase "big government" reflects the difficulty of quantifying federal power. How should we appraise the size and strength of the national government? Expenditures, revenue, employees, functions? In 1913, the federal government was already "big" by all of these measures. Its reach and touch had expanded dramatically since the Civil War. In nominal dollars, federal spending increased nearly elevenfold, rising from about $66 million in 1861 to nearly $725 million in 1913. Federal receipts increased by a factor of seventeen, from about $41 million in 1861 to nearly $725 million in 1913. The number of federal employees had grown had nearly tenfold, increasing from about fifty thousand in 1861 to nearly half a million in 1913. The cabinet expanded from six executive departments to ten, adding the Department of Agriculture, the Department of Justice, the Department of Commerce, and the Department of Labor. The executive branch in 1913 also included two new independent commissions—the Civil Service Commission and the Interstate Commerce Commission—and several new offices and bureaus, including the Office of the Comptroller of the Currency, the Bureau of Education, and the Bureau of Corporations.[3]

Nevertheless, the national government in 1913 remained fundamentally weak. The bloated federal Leviathan lacked the sinew and muscle necessary to convert its reach and touch into action. The executive branch was a bureaucracy in the literal sense: a loose collection of bureaus, each budgetarily dependent upon the generosity of congressional committee chairmen and led by largely autonomous officers who owed their employment to party bosses. These bureaus were rooted within a slipshod administrative structure that allowed congressional and party leaders to intervene and frustrate the designs of the president, who had no real mechanism through which to supervise and direct the actions of his subordinates in the units supposedly under his control. The administrative incapacity of the national government allowed local officials and citizens in some corners of the nation to effectively nullify federal law.[4]

INTRODUCTION

2

In 1913, a loose-knit group of corporation lawyers, bankers, corporate executives, genteel reformers, and philanthropists launched a quest to fix these problems. They had perceived that the incapacity of the national government was in fact the biggest obstacle to good government. And they came to understand that, if they wished to eliminate public corruption in the United States, it would be necessary to strengthen the national government and transform the nation's ramshackle bureaucracy into an effective and efficient system of national public administration.

Although this movement was bipartisan, it was primarily identified with the Republican Party. Its progenitors were men such as William Howard Taft, Charles Evans Hughes, Elihu Root, Charles D. Norton, and Henry L. Stimson—leaders of the party's Wall Street–allied northeastern wing. They drew their preoccupations and preferences from their experience in the business world, which also gave them an appreciation of the mutually constitutive relationship between government and business. This group was a subsection of what has often been called "the Establishment." They liked to call themselves "public men." In this book, I will call them "elite reformers"—a phrase that conveys their status as well as the limited and decidedly unrevolutionary nature of their ambitions.[5]

During the last years of the nineteenth century, the elite reformers and their allies witnessed at close range the rise of a new American institution: the large, multiunit, vertically integrated, national-scale corporation. These new firms put into practice an array of organizational innovations. The introduction of modern budgeting solidified the ability of the corporation's chief executive to plan and coordinate the activities of disparate units according to a unified business strategy. The development of a functionally efficient administrative structure with an executive staff agency allowed the far-flung units of the corporation to implement the executive's plans. Modern accounting and auditing methods gave board members and shareholders the ability to assess the effectiveness and efficiency of executives and their subordinates. Together, these practices increased the profitability and productive capacity of the firms that adopted them.

Some observers have characterized these innovations as a "managerial revolution" in business. The elite reformers were convinced that modern administrative methods had been instrumental in the rise of modern

American capitalism, and they came to believe that the nation would benefit if lessons from business management could be applied to the administration of the national government.[6]

The elite reformers were also convinced that a strong national government was necessary to support the expansion of markets at home and abroad. From their point of view, a well-functioning society was good for business, and a nation beset by social dysfunction was bad for business. America's ineffectual national government was also bad for business. The solution, as they saw it, was not to shrink the government but rather to render it responsive and responsible. As Henry Stimson, perhaps the most articulate spokesman of this movement, put it,

> We may as well recognize that legitimate pressure on the Government to enlarge its activities will not cease. Our population is increasing; our communities and methods of business are constantly growing more complex; more government and newer forms of government are being made necessary; every year legitimate expenses are bound to increase. There can be no going backward into the simpler times of old.[7]

A national government that could enact coherent national policy to solve national problems would, the elite reformers believed, ensure general prosperity. And they believed it would serve what they conceived to be the national interest—which, thanks to their position at the center of industrial capitalism in this era, was essentially identical with their own financial interests. Unlike the regional or sectoral business leaders who were focused on the success of this or that particular firm or industry, the elite reformers' fortunes depended generally on the efficient functioning of capitalism as a system.

As a group, the elite reformers were by no means ideologically homogeneous. Their preferences varied widely on other policy questions—particularly in debates on taxes, regulation, labor, and welfare, where members of this group took positions that ranged from progressive to conservative to reactionary. Consider three leading elite reformers who have regularly appeared in histories of this period. Elihu Root is usually classified as a conservative. His protégé Henry Stimson is sometimes called a progressive and sometimes a conservative, and in his autobiography refers to himself as a "progressive conservative." Stimson's protégé Felix Frankfurter is usually classified as a liberal supporter of the New Deal, although some of the more radical members of the New Deal coalition felt that Frankfurter was a sort of crypto-conservative. On labor questions, Root was antiunion, Stimson took a middle-of-the-road position, and Frankfurter was decidedly pro-union. Nevertheless, on questions that touched the core of the elite reformers' agenda, Root, Stimson, and Frankfurter were in wholehearted agreement.[8]

3

The expansion of federal power in the mid-twentieth century is usually seen as the product of a progressive reform tradition stretching back to the late-nineteenth century and inspired by academic experts in public administration. Popular discussion of these questions tends to mix partisan mythology with platitudes about American traditions of liberty. In scholarly writing, the delays and compromises that constrained federal power are usually blamed on business interests. Well-informed readers might conclude that expanding federal power has been a project of the ideological Left, and that the American government's incapacity stems primarily from the historical power of big business.[9]

This book tells a different story. It was the elite reformers, inspired by their experience with big business, who first devised and promoted the reform agenda that underpinned the expansion of federal power in the twentieth century. And it was the elite reformers who led the movement to expand federal power during the 1910s and 1920s. *When Good Government Meant Big Government* follows their quest to expand federal power, and it shows how that quest was foiled by opponents who preferred to preserve the old system of local control over public administration.[10]

This book is not a comprehensive history of the period between 1913 and 1933. Instead, it focuses on debates about the administrative power of the national government. It focuses particularly on budget reform, executive reorganization, and antilynching—the three topics that formed the backbone of the elite reformers' agenda and which have traditionally received only passing attention in histories of this period. Antilynching was an effort to combat the most troubling kind of lawlessness in American society and one that demonstrated the dangers of federal incapacity. Budget reform and executive reorganization were the two proposals that derived most directly from the elite reformers' business experience and were central to their effort to bring what they called "business efficiency" to the federal executive branch.[11]

For the elite reformers, national budget reform was the logical first step toward improving the national government. Modern budgeting had increased the capacity of business enterprise dramatically in the preceding decades, but the national government in 1913 did not have a budget system. Spending by the bureaus, agencies, and offices in the executive branch was determined not by plans made by the president, but by ad hoc negotiations between bureau chiefs and congressional committee chairmen. The elite reformers sought to change this by endowing the presidency with budgetary authority similar to that of a corporate CEO and by creating a budget bureau that could serve as the president's staff agency. Empowered to devise and carry out the budget, the president would be able to plan and supervise the enactment of coherent national policies.[12]

The elite reformers also sought to emulate organizational innovations in business by streamlining the national government's hodgepodge administrative structure, regrouping bureaus, agencies, and offices according to function and major purpose. They called this "executive reorganization." Although the topic has not figured prominently in many histories of American politics, specialists have placed executive reorganization at the center of the history of national governance in America. Should the U.S. Forest Service be located within the Department of Agriculture or the Department of the Interior? Should the Corps of Engineers remain in the Department of War or be moved to Interior? While such topics have held little interest for most writers of American history, the resolution of these questions would shape the reach, touch, and strength of the national government. They would help determine whether a president could exert his will in Mississippi and Montana as well as in Manhattan, or whether a congressman could intervene to defend local prerogatives.[13]

4

In 1913, the elite reformers adopted budget reform and executive reorganization as their primary goals. After facing resistance from Woodrow Wilson and his allies, the elite reformers achieved some success during the administration of Warren G. Harding. However, their progress stalled in 1922 when they attempted to pass an antilynching bill.[14]

The elite reformers' dream of a government with the capacity to implement national solutions to national problems seemed more like a nightmare to white southern leaders, who had always been reluctant to endow national officials with the power to make decisions about social life in the South. White southerners and their allies had always been suspicious of the elite reformers' motivations. Reconstruction was not that long ago in the 1910s and 1920s. When the elite reformers embraced the antilynching movement after World War I, white southerners readily came to regard the elite reformers' plans as an opening wedge that would ultimately bring an end to Jim Crow.

This is not to say that the elite reformers were necessarily motivated by what twenty-first-century readers would call antiracist principles. Indeed, the ease and speed with which they abandoned antilynching in the face of a racist backlash in the mid-twenties calls the strength of their commitment into question. However, as with violations of Prohibition, lynching was a glaring example of lawlessness that troubled the elite reformers. Any open violation of law by public officials—or official toleration of such open violations—struck at the heart of good government. In the case of Prohibition, the elite reformers supported enforcement of settled law even though many personally believed that the Constitution was an inappropriate vehicle for promoting temperance. Similarly, their advocacy for antilynching legislation stemmed as much from their views about the law as from their views about racism.

At the same time, not all who preferred local control of public administration were motivated by white supremacy. White southerners did not act alone. On certain issues, representatives of various regional interests, sectoral business interests, and cultural traditions entered into situational alliances with white southern leaders to preserve local control. In some cases, these actors sympathized with southern racism. In other cases—especially on questions where, on the surface at least, white supremacy did not seem to be at issue—these allies found it convenient to overlook southern racism. For instance, on questions of education policy, politically organized Catholics sometimes found common cause with white southerners. However, within the coalition that sought to preserve local control, it was southern

Democrats in Congress who wielded the greatest political power and set the terms of debate.

The most powerful alliance for the southern Democrats in these years was the one they formed with western Republicans in the Senate. White southerners held a dominant position within the Democratic Party, which meant that other factions within the party—organized labor, social workers, agrarian populists in the West, and the Gold Democrats of Wall Street—were forced to accommodate their sensibilities on most questions. However, southern Democrats often found sympathy from traditionally Republican constituencies, such as the parochial "Main Street" business leaders and especially with white nationalists from the agricultural states of the Middle and Far West. Since Democrats were in the minority for most of the period covered in this book, the "Farm Bloc" that they formed with western Republicans provided them with the most opportunities to shape the legislative agenda. The power of this alliance would have profound consequences for the development of the American state.

* * *

The story of the elite reformers' quest intersected with many of the issues and controversies of the day. In the course of describing the movement to enact executive reorganization, for instance, this book will also describe the nation's mobilization for World War I, the creation of the veterans welfare system, debates on the role of the federal government in education, and efforts to reform the enforcement of national alcohol Prohibition. While chronicling the antilynching movement of the 1910s and 1920s, this book will revisit the history of racist violence in the United States. To understand the political factors that shaped the outcome of debates on budget reform, executive reorganization, and antilynching, this book also traces transitions from one presidential administration to the next, shifting voting blocs in Congress, and shuffling coalitions within the Republican and Democratic Parties.

The elite reformers' efforts between 1913 and 1933 helped lay the foundations for the eventual expansion of federal power in later years. Reforms enacted during the middle third of the twentieth century hewed closely to the elite reformers' pre-1933 preferences. From the creation of a presidential staff agency in 1939 to the formation of the Department of Defense and the Department of Housing Education and Welfare after World War II, and even to the Civil Rights Act of 1964 and the Voting Rights Act of 1965, most of the key reforms of the mid-twentieth century resembled the plans envisioned by the elite reformers and their allies in the years before the New Deal.

The story presented here also plumbs the origins and early development of another, longer-lasting movement. *When Good Government Meant Big Government* describes a key period in the evolution of racist and antidemocratic forces in American life. The political tools developed in opposition to the elite reformers during this period would eventually fuel the rise of a powerful antigovernment political coalition. By the twenty-first century, that coalition would become strong enough to threaten the advances of the mid-twentieth century.[15]

Chapter One

ADMINISTRATION AND ACCOMMODATION
Before 1913

The elite reformers' quest to strengthen the American state took shape during the presidency of Woodrow Wilson, as leaders of the Wall Street–allied northeastern wing of the Republican Party began to embrace an administrative reform agenda built around budget reform, executive reorganization, and antilynching. However, the transformation of the good government agenda in the 1910s was the result of the interweaving of two reform traditions that had their origins in the late nineteenth century. One thread was spun from the evolution of elite opinion about the proper functioning of governmental institutions, stretching from the civil service reformers of the 1880s to the municipal researchers at the turn of the twentieth century. The second thread was spun from the struggle to satisfy federal obligations owed to African Americans after the Civil War, stretching from Radical Reconstruction to the accommodation of Jim Crow. While these two threads unfurled separately across several decades, by 1913 the pattern that would bring about their eventual union had been cast.

1

When a new president took office in second half of the nineteenth century, he faced an onslaught of party loyalists seeking jobs in post offices and customs houses as reward for their support for the victorious candidate. This

ADMINISTRATION AND ACCOMMODATION

system—known as the "spoils system"—not only encouraged corruption, but over time it created a situation where most officers in the federal administration were unable to develop the expertise necessary to fulfill their duties. Even if they did manage to master their job, they would be replaced after the next election by another amateur administrator.

After a deranged office seeker assassinated President James A. Garfield in 1881, lawmakers attempted to place limits upon the spoils system with passage of the Pendleton Civil Service Act of 1883. The Pendleton Act required seekers of certain positions to pass a civil service exam to prove their merit—a process overseen by the newly created Civil Service Commission. However, only about 10 percent of federal positions were initially "covered in" under this new "merit system." During the ensuing decades, civil service reformers led by the National Civil Service Reform League, working through its periodical *Good Government* and through the meetings of its federated state and local affiliate organizations, led the battle against the spoilsmen by promoting the expansion of the merit system.[1]

The assassination of President William McKinley in 1901 promised to be another turning point for civil service reform. The ascension of Theodore Roosevelt to the presidency brought to the White House a reformer thoroughly committed to the cause of good government. Roosevelt first came to public notice in New York in the early 1880s as a twenty-something anti-corruption state legislator. Roosevelt's zeal for good government led President Benjamin Harrison to appoint him to a six-year term as a member of the U.S. Civil Service Commission in Washington, DC, where he helped to oversee the implementation of the merit system under the Pendleton Act. The same spirit marked his two-year term as president of the New York City Police Board, after which he returned to Washington for two years as assistant secretary of the navy. During his two-year term as governor of New York, his commitment to good government so offended the party bosses that they kicked him upstairs by arranging his nomination for the vice presidency at the Republican National Convention in 1900.[2]

Roosevelt brought his crusading vigor to the White House in 1901. However, despite broad elite support for the cause, and despite his many achievements on other fronts, by the end of his presidency there was very little to show for his efforts to expand the merit system. In 1908, only 58 percent of federal positions had been covered in under civil service requirements—42 percent remained uncovered.[3] This slow progress led some good government reformers to realize that civil service reform on its own was not enough to drive out the spoilsmen, boodlers, and grafters who haunted the federal administration.

William Howard Taft was among the leaders of this group of reformers. In popular memory, Taft is perhaps best known for his weight, which waxed and waned wildly over the course of his career, vacillating between a low point around 250 pounds and an upper range above 330 pounds.[4] But among supporters of good government in the early twentieth century, he was widely recognized as one of the most able and accomplished administrators in public life. As Secretary of War Elihu Root put it in a letter to Roosevelt in 1903, "No man in the country had recently exhibited such unusual ability both administrative and legislative."[5] Born in Cincinnati to a large family of Yale-educated lawyers, Taft earned his own law degree from the University of Cincinnati before beginning a career that saw him rise quickly to the positions of U.S. solicitor general and judge for the U.S. Court of Appeals for the Sixth Circuit under Benjamin Harrison, governor-general of the Philippines under William McKinley and Theodore Roosevelt, and U.S. secretary of war under Roosevelt.[6]

Many of the popular anecdotes about Taft's girth first entered circulation as attempts to emphasize the contrast between his physical problems and his evident energy as an administrator. For instance, Elihu Root's quip in response to a telegram from Taft about a long journey through the Philippine wilderness on horseback—"How is the horse?"—received its widest audience in a 1905 *New York Times* profile that emphasized Taft's administrative skills under the headline "Taft the Busiest Man of a Busy Government."[7] On the eve of the Republican National Convention in June 1908, the *Review of Reviews* ran an admiring profile emphasizing this record under the title "Taft, Trained to be President." The article included what was by then a seemingly obligatory joke about Taft's weight. "Secretary Taft is the most gallant man in Washington; he got up in a street-car the other day and gave his seat to two ladies."[8]

Inspired by the difficulties that Roosevelt had encountered in his attempts to expand the merit system, Taft had begun to consider how best to improve public administration at the national level. He discussed the problem with like-minded allies in government and on Wall Street, but his chief sounding boards were his brother Henry Waters Taft, George Wickersham—both men were partners at the firm of Cadwalader, Wickersham, and Taft,

13
ADMINISTRATION AND ACCOMMODATION

the oldest of the "white shoe" corporate law firms in New York City—and Elihu Root.

Taft and his allies came to believe that the necessary first step toward good government was to create a modern budget system for the federal government. Under the arrangement that had developed during the late nineteenth century, federal spending was determined through negotiation between bureau chiefs in the executive branch and the chairmen of the various appropriations committees in Congress. For Taft and his allies, this posed several problems. For one thing, it meant that the president often had less input into the activities of the executive branch than did congressional leaders or party bosses. Not only did the existing system create pressure for increasing expenditures and provide an opening for corruption, but, even worse in Taft's view, it made it difficult for the president to operate as administrator in chief of the national government. How could the president enact coherent national policies if his plans could be altered at will by bureaucratic underlings facing pressure from congressional committee chairmen?

2

His election to the presidency in 1908 provided Taft with a new platform from which he could pursue his expansive vision of good government in earnest. Outlining his plans for budget reform in his March 4, 1909, inaugural address, Taft made clear that his goal was not merely to cut spending, but to increase the managerial capacity of the national government. Much of the debate about federal spending in earlier years had focused solely on "economy," or the need to reduce expenditures. But, after acknowledging the need for thrift, Taft quickly shifted to a note of caution about the destructive effects of a pure economy approach:

> The obligation on the part of those responsible for the expenditures made to carry on the Government, to be as economical as possible, and to make the burden of taxation as light as possible, is plain, and should be affirmed in every declaration of government policy. This is especially true when we are face to face with a heavy deficit. But when the desire to win the popular approval leads to the cutting off of expenditures really needed to make the Government effective and to enable it to accomplish its proper objects, the result is as much to be condemned as the waste of government funds

in unnecessary expenditure. The scope of a modern government in what it can and ought to accomplish for its people has been widened far beyond the principles laid down by the old "laissez faire" school of political writers, and this widening has met popular approval.[9]

In the second year of Taft's presidency, congressional leaders overcame their skepticism and provided Taft with authorization and funding to create his President's Commission on Economy and Efficiency, otherwise known as the Taft Commission. Taft hoped that the commission could work to expand upon the efforts of the Roosevelt administration's preliminary Committee on Department Methods, which had been formed in 1907. That earlier commission, known as the Keep Commission and formed by Roosevelt with encouragement from Taft and Root, was intended to chart a course for improving government efficiency. However, the Keep Commission was underfunded and lacked authority. Its main achievement was to show that properly assessing the problem was beyond its own scope and capacity.[10]

The Taft Commission was meant to emulate on a national level the work of the Bureau of Municipal Research (BMR) in New York. Formed in 1907, the BMR had led the effort to bring efficiency and accountability to city government, while helping urban residents to access needed services. As its founding charter explained, the goals of the BMR were "to promote efficient and economical government," "to promote the adoption of scientific methods of accounting and of reporting the details of municipal business, with a view to facilitating the work of public officials," and "to secure constructive publicity in matters pertaining to municipal problems." Taft believed that the need for such an effort was even more pressing at the national level.[11]

To ensure that his commission could meet the goals he had set, Taft negotiated generous funding from Congress and, with the assistance of his executive secretary, Charles Dyer Norton, he assembled a team of researchers with expertise in business and government administration. Norton hailed from the wilds of Wisconsin but had been educated in New England and had forged business and family connections among the northeastern establishment. His own ancestry traced back to Puritan Massachusetts, and his wife was a granddaughter of the abolitionist William Lloyd Garrison. In 1909 Norton left a lucrative position as an insurance executive in Chicago to serve as the president's secretary in Washington. Alongside his other duties, Norton would supervise the Taft Commission's work, ensuring that it conformed to its namesake's vision.[12]

Taft and Norton selected Frederick A. Cleveland to lead the commission's team of researchers. Widely recognized as an expert in public and private accounting, Cleveland served as "technical director" at the BMR. His ideas on public administration were drawn from a dozen years working with both private corporations and municipal organizations. On the Taft Commission, Cleveland worked closely with William F. Willoughby, an expert in statistics and economics who had served as treasurer of Puerto Rico and as assistant director of the U.S. Census.[13]

While Cleveland and Willoughby gave scholarly creditability to the Taft Commission, the recommendations they produced ultimately followed the outlines set out by Taft himself.[14] They recommended the establishment of centralized control of finances through budget reform as the first step in a longer process of administrative reform. Creating a modern budget system directed by the president would bring the national government more into line with the methods used by large corporations, placing the president in a position similar to that of a corporate chief executive.

The second step would be further centralized control of public administration at the national level through reorganization of the executive branch. This vision contrasted with an older view, long favored by congressional leaders, that focused purely on legislature-imposed cost cutting as a method of increasing their own power over the executive departments and bureaus by limiting expenditures and frustrating executive prerogative. That older style of reorganization was meant to limit executive authority while increasing congressional authority in determining expenditures. The rhetorical rationale was to keep expenditures under control and avoid debt, but the result was to hobble the national executive and preserve local control of public administration.[15] The Taft Commission's plans for executive reorganization focused on improving organizational efficiency by rearranging federal bureaus and offices according to function and major purpose. This would, Taft and his commissioners hoped, make the executive branch more manageable from the top and create the capacity for enacting national policies.

The Taft Commission was meant to lay the groundwork for actually transforming the national government, and many supporters hoped the commission itself could become a permanent institution within the executive branch that could serve as the president's staff agency.[16] However, the work of the Taft Commission became symbolic soon after its formation. The Republicans were beaten soundly in the midterm elections of 1910. In 1911, a strong Republican majority in the House was replaced by a strong Democratic majority—a dramatic shift since the Democrats had been in the minority in both chambers of Congress for nearly two decades. In the Senate, the Republicans retained their majority, but their margin of control shrank considerably. This gave increased power to the so-called insurgent western Republicans, who could shape the party's agenda by threatening to join forces with their southern Democratic allies. This new Congress—at the mercy of southern and western populists who feared central power and national authority—was hostile to Taft's efforts at administrative reform. When Taft released his commission's report on budget reform in June 1912, Congress responded by limiting the commission's funding, causing several commissioners to resign in August 1912.[17]

3

By 1912, it had been more than two decades since the GOP's last bold effort to advance civil rights. The Federal Elections Bill of 1890 was sponsored in the House by Massachusetts representative Henry Cabot Lodge. Known in the North as the "Lodge Bill," white southerners and their sympathizers called it the "Lodge Force Bill." Among other provisions, it would have authorized federal supervision of elections if states were found to be in violation of the Fifteenth Amendment. The Lodge Bill passed the House of Representatives, but in the Senate southern Democrats, joined by some western Republicans, managed to block the bill with a filibuster.[18]

The defeat of the Lodge Bill marked the beginning of a new period of caution for Republicans, but that caution contrasted with a hard-boiled determination among white southerners to build durable institutions of white supremacy. During the years after the defeat of the Lodge Bill, southern Democrats gained in strength in the Senate, and most southern states succeeded in enacting an assemblage of new laws that were often outwardly color-blind but in fact designed to keep African Americans from participating in public life. To ensure that this system of laws—known as "Jim Crow"—achieved their intended end, they were buttressed by a system of

ADMINISTRATION AND ACCOMMODATION

extralegal coercion that ensured that southerners who transgressed the dictates of white supremacy faced the threat of violence. As state governments sought to refine the structure of Jim Crow, a tide of racist violence swept across the South as defenders of white supremacy murdered supporters of civil rights in large numbers.[19]

Perhaps the most effective and troubling of the various methods of defending of white supremacy was lynching, a label used to describe an assortment of atrocities involving groups of white vigilantes carrying out premeditated, ritualized murder. The victims of lynching were usually (but not always) Black men, and were usually (but not always) accused of some crime. It was early discovered that the most rancorous mobs assembled when a Black man was charged with raping a white woman, so it became common to raise this charge no matter what the actual provocation had been. Regardless of the victim's alleged crime, in every case the lynching was intended as punishment for some transgression against white supremacy.

In many cases, the lynch mob abducted victims who were in police custody. Sometimes local law enforcement officers looked the other way, sometimes they participated openly. Southern newspapers routinely published thinly veiled provocations by disclosing the whereabouts of an alleged criminal or describing officials' plans for moving a prisoner from one location to another. Newspapers sometimes published announcements for already-planned lynchings to ensure that more participants would attend. The lynching would take place in front of an assembled crowd, usually including women and children. Hanging was perhaps the most common method of murder, but other methods, such as burning the victim at the stake or dragging them behind a horse or automobile, were also widely used. In cases where the mob had become particularly incensed, the murder would be preceded by ritual mutilation. In some cases, attendees distributed the victim's body parts as souvenirs. Photographs of the proceedings were printed in bulk and kept as mementos by members of the mob. Newspapers would publish postmortem descriptions as a warning against violating the dictates of white supremacy.[20]

It was during this period that the African American educator Booker T. Washington came to national prominence. In a speech at the 1895 Atlanta Exposition, Washington described a compromise that appealed to many white leaders. The best way to achieve suffrage and civil rights in the long term, Washington argued, was for southern Blacks to tolerate Jim Crow. Rather than to fight against legal segregation or agitate for civil rights, Washington advised southern Blacks to instead focus on vocational education and self-improvement—the program pursued by the Tuskegee Institute in Mississippi, where Washington served as principal. By following this plan, Washington argued, southern Blacks would eventually prove themselves to be essential to the economic success of the South, and of the nation as a whole, without bringing on a backlash from defenders of white supremacy. "In all things that are purely social," Washington explained, in an oft-quoted metaphor, "we can be as separate as the fingers, yet one as the hand in all things essential to mutual progress." Washington's efforts won him large numbers of followers—both white and Black—in the South. In the North, philanthropists began donating large amounts to fund Washington's program of vocational uplift.[21]

The optimism of Washington's white allies belied the stark reality of life in the South during the early Jim Crow years. Many white southern leaders viewed even Booker T. Washington's accommodationist strategy as a dangerous threat to white supremacy and Jim Crow. Regardless of whether they embraced Washington's approach, southern Blacks were forced to live and survive under the omnipresent threat of lynchings and mass killings by southern whites. Racist violence in the South remained routine in these years, and this created a problem even for policy makers who preferred to avoid the issue.

This fact was given dramatic demonstration by the reaction of the white South to Theodore Roosevelt's decision to host Washington for dinner at the White House in 1901. Southern leaders publicly deplored TR, as the president was called, for putting his daughter at risk by allowing a Black man at the dinner table. South Carolina senator Ben Tillman voiced perhaps the most extreme response: "The action of President Roosevelt in entertaining that n—— will necessitate our killing a thousand n—— in the South before they will learn their place again."[22]

4

Theodore Roosevelt's dinner with Booker T. Washington reflected a measure of racial moderation. However, as his presidency proceeded, Roosevelt's moderation seemed to drift into racism. This shift should perhaps not have been surprising. While his father had come from a prominent New York merchant family, TR's mother was the daughter of a prominent slaveholding family in Georgia. Two of his uncles served in the Confederate navy during the Civil War. And in many of his writings, Roosevelt also expressed his own clear belief in white supremacy, for instance asserting that Asians were unsuited for American citizenship.[23]

Roosevelt provided an outline of his ideas about civil rights for Black Americans in a speech at the Republican Club of New York's Lincoln Dinner on February 13, 1905. Referring to the Civil War, Roosevelt was careful to praise both sides, noting that the Union and Confederate armies "both fought with equal bravery and with equal sincerity of conviction" before conceding that "it is now clear to all that the triumph of the cause of freedom and of the Union was essential to the welfare of mankind." He seemed to question whether personal liberty and voting rights for African Americans were worthy goals, saying that "it is not possible in offhand fashion to obtain or to confer the priceless boons of freedom, industrial efficiency, political capacity, and domestic morality." Indeed, as he discussed the "race problem" in more detail, he seemed to direct the bulk of his criticism at well-meaning northern whites and at southern African American citizens. "Laziness and shiftlessness, these, and, above all, vice and criminality of every kind, are evils more potent for harm to the black race than all acts of oppression of white men put together," he said. "The colored man who fails to condemn crime in another colored man, who fails to cooperate in all lawful ways in bringing colored criminals to justice, is the worst enemy of his own people, as well as an enemy to all the people."[24]

Turning to lynching, Roosevelt seized upon an apparent recent decline in incidents, despite the lack of reliable statistics in those years. "I am glad to say that during the last three months the returns, as far as they can be gathered, show a smaller number of lynchings than for any other three months during the last twenty years," he said. "Those are rather striking figures and I take a certain satisfaction in them in view of some of the gloomy forebodings of last summer." And Roosevelt approvingly cited the assertion of a white bishop in North Carolina that "there must be no confusing of civil privileges with social intercourse" and that "civil law cannot regulate social practices."[25]

Growing frustration with Roosevelt's presidency among African Americans came to a climax in 1906 after an incident at Brownsville, Texas. Late one August night, a group of armed men shot up the town, killing one white resident and injuring two others. The gunmen were unknown, but local leaders—without evidence—blamed the Black troops stationed at nearby Fort Brown. The soldiers denied the charges, and their own white commanding officers testified that the soldiers had in fact remained in their barracks at the time of the shootings. Nevertheless, Roosevelt credulously accepted the story offered by the white townspeople and ordered the discharge without honor of three companies of African American soldiers.[26]

In the weeks and months following this decision, Roosevelt rebuffed the advice of several of his most trusted advisers, including Booker T. Washington and then secretary of war William H. Taft, who both urged him to reconsider. Even in the face of clear evidence that the Black soldiers had not been at fault, Roosevelt refused to rescind the discharges. In response to this obstinance, most of the nation's prominent Black leaders, including W. E. B. Du Bois, William Monroe Trotter, and T. Thomas Fortune, publicly rebuked the Republican Party and urged their supporters to remain neutral in the upcoming 1908 election.[27]

Booker T. Washington chose to remain within the Republican Party. This decision meant that, as the election of 1908 approached, Washington was the only major African American leader operating within the Republican establishment. This gave him unprecedented influence in discussions of Republican policy on civil rights. Washington was motivated in part by his long-standing relationship with William Howard Taft. Secretary Taft had for many years supported the efforts of Washington, whom he'd come to know while serving on the boards of various philanthropic organizations that provided industrial education for African Americans in the South.[28]

This put Washington in a strong position to influence Taft and the party leadership in 1908, especially since many African Americans planned to continue their protests over Brownsville by casting a vote for the Democratic presidential candidate. Washington's correspondence in this period shows him brokering meetings between Secretary Taft and wealthy donors to Tuskegee-connected organizations. In February 1908, for instance, Washington arranged for George McAneny—New York reformer, former secretary of the National Civil Service Reform League, and a founding director of the BMR—to accompany Taft to a meeting of the trustees of the Anna T. Jeanes Foundation's Negro Rural School Fund. Making the arrangements, Washington suggested to McAneny that "perhaps it might help you in certain directions just now to get in a little closer touch with the excellent qualities of the Secretary."29

Taft's nomination at the Republican National Convention and his victory in the November general election were also victories for Booker T. Washington. In his inaugural address, Taft devoted six paragraphs—about 20 percent of his speech—to a discussion of civil rights, and his remarks signaled the Republican Party's embrace of Washington's strategy of accommodation. Referring to the decades-long effort to secure voting rights for African Americans in the South, Taft said that "the movement proved to be a failure." He explained that he would not seek to interfere with restrictive state laws that met the letter of the Fifteenth Amendment, which nominally prohibited race-based restrictions on voting. That is, under Taft's leadership Republicans would no longer oppose literacy tests and other practices that southern white supremacists had adopted to keep African Americans from voting. Rather than count on northern support, Taft advised Black southerners to "base their hope on the results of their own industry, self-restraint, thrift, and business success, as well as upon the aid and comfort and sympathy which they may receive from their white neighbors of the South." Taft explained that the Republican Party would no longer seek to intervene directly in the region's affairs, and he expressed his hope that by avoiding confrontation over racial issues, "a better feeling between the negroes and the whites in the South will continue to grow, and more and more of the white people will come to realize that the future of the South is to be much benefited by the industrial and intellectual progress of the negro."30

Taft's remarks reflected the effective merger of the GOP and Washington's "Tuskegee Machine." Since in these years there were very few white Republicans in the South, Taft was obligated to appoint African Americans to many of the federal patronage positions in the South that were still not covered in under civil service rules. The post-Brownsville boycott of the GOP by other prominent Black leaders meant that when Taft sought to fill these positions in the South, he was obliged to consult with Washington and his lieutenants at Tuskegee. As a result, Washington had effective control of federal patronage for African Americans under the Taft administration. This consolidation of Washington's power alarmed his critics. "After a time almost no Negro institution could collect funds without the recommendation or acquiescence of Mr. Washington," the Black scholar W. E. B.

ADMINISTRATION AND ACCOMMODATION

Du Bois recalled in later years. "Few political appointments of Negroes were made anywhere in the United States without his consent."[31]

Taft's embrace of Washington's accommodationist strategy, which was meant to avoid backlash from white supremacists, instead spurred a backlash from civil rights advocates. In 1909, an interracial group of men and women opposed to Washington and Taft's strategy formed the National Association for the Advancement of Colored People. The NAACP was intended to be a more confrontational advocacy organization that would use the techniques of modern "pressure politics" to push for the expansion of civil rights. While the Tuskegee Institute and other Washington-approved ventures received large donations from northern donors, the NAACP relied on membership dues and a large number of small donations.[32]

The leadership of the NAACP included several white reformers from New England who had identified with the Democratic Party since the 1880s. They faced a difficult choice in the presidential election of 1912. Given Taft's embrace of accommodation and the Tuskegee Machine, they were reluctant to support the incumbent. While they were supportive of much in the platform of Roosevelt's Progressive Party, their anger over the ex-president's handling of the Brownsville fiasco had been compounded in 1912 by TR's attempt at the Republican National Convention to nullify Black pro-Taft delegations in favor of "Lily White" pro-Roosevelt delegations. For his part, the Democratic candidate, Virginia-born and Georgia-reared New Jersey governor Woodrow Wilson, had pledged that if he were elected president, African Americans could count on "absolute fair dealing and for everything by which I could assist in advancing the interests of their race in the United States."[33]

NAACP leaders took Wilson's pledge at face value. In the weeks before the election, NAACP president Moorfield Storey, treasurer Oswald Garrison Villard, and publication and research director W. E. B. Du Bois gave their endorsement to the New Jersey governor:

> We sympathize with those faithful old black voters who will always vote the Republican ticket. We respect their fidelity but not their brains. We can understand those who, despite the unspeakable Roosevelt, accept his platform which is broad on all subjects except the greatest—human rights. This we can understand, but we cannot follow.

ADMINISTRATION AND ACCOMMODATION

We sincerely believe that even in the face of promises disconcertingly vague, and in the face of the solid caste-ridden South, it is better to elect Woodrow Wilson President of the United States and prove once for all if the Democratic party dares to be Democratic when it comes to black men. It has proven that it can be in many Northern States and cities. Can it be in the nation? We hope so and we are willing to risk a trial.[34]

* * *

At the end of William Howard Taft's presidency, the agenda of the elite reformers remained a curious mix of innovation on questions of national public administration and a cautious commitment to accommodation when it came to questions of race. Budget reform and executive reorganization had become part of the good government reform agenda through the work of Taft's Commission on Economy and Efficiency, which sought to bring business methods and municipal reform to the federal government. However, when the commission released its final reports in February 1913, after nearly two years of work, Congress simply ignored its recommendations and allowed the commission's funding to expire at the end of the fiscal year. Although the Taft Commission achieved little in the way of concrete achievements, it succeeded in sketching a general path that elite reformers would follow for the next two decades.[35]

In the early 1910s, Taft and his allies remained firmly committed to the accommodationist approach of Booker T. Washington. Above all they sought to avoid antagonizing proponents of segregation and white supremacy. Taft's timidity on questions of racism and civil rights was in part a reflection of the belief of many Republican leaders that there was little chance of reversing Jim Crow through direct federal action without reopening the wounds of the immediate post–Civil War era—something that they felt northern voters would be unlikely to support. However, as the elite reformers would discover during the course of Wilson's presidency, white southerners did not possess a similar sense of caution.

Chapter Two

THE ELITE REFORMERS IN EXILE
1913-1918

The election of 1912 was fought primarily over tariffs and the trusts. The NAACP's endorsement of Woodrow Wilson had little impact on the result. Debates over budget reform and executive reorganization had even less influence. William Howard Taft's work to advance administrative reform and his reputation as an able administrator did not sway voters, and he struggled to evade the mantle of conservatism. His third-place showing revealed how little the public cared about the efficiency of the federal administration.

However, the elite reformers' disappointment at Taft's defeat in 1912 was tempered somewhat by optimism in early 1913 that progress toward budget reform and executive reorganization might be possible with Wilson in office. The new president's reputation as an academic expert on government, his experience as president of an Ivy League university, combined with his progressive record during his two-year term as governor of New Jersey, gave reformers the sense that Wilson shared their views.

However, these hopes were quickly dashed when Wilson revealed himself to be unsympathetic to the elite reformers' expansive vision of good government. As a result, they worked to develop and define their agenda without direct access to the reins of government. As the Wilson years unfolded, the logistical challenges and domestic dislocations that accompanied the advent of World War I would help to fortify the reformers' belief

THE ELITE REFORMERS IN EXILE

in the need to improve the capacity of the national government. At the same time, the rise of racist violence in America during Wilson's presidency began to reveal the limitations of Tuskegee-style accommodation.

1

In the lead-up to the 1912 election, NAACP leaders had declared themselves "willing to risk a trial" with the Democratic Party. However, it did not take long for that trial to prove a failure. In the first weeks of his administration, Wilson and his cabinet launched an intensive effort to segregate the federal executive branch. Over the previous decades, Black employees had filled positions throughout the civil service, working alongside—and sometimes even supervising—their white counterparts. Starting in April 1913, the Wilson administration began mandating separate facilities for white and Black employees, reassigning African Americans to separate Jim Crow offices and forcing them to use Jim Crow toilets and lunch areas. Over the course of Wilson's first term, his administration fired African American officials and hired white replacements. To aid this effort, the Civil Service Commission adopted a rule requiring new job applicants to submit photographs with their applications.[1]

The NAACP's white treasurer, Oswald Garrison Villard,* complained in a letter to Wilson that the administration's policy was harmful and in obvious conflict with the president's campaign promise to help African Americans. Wilson replied that the policy was intended for African Americans' own good:

> It is as far as possible from being a movement against the Negroes. I sincerely believe it to be in their interest. And what distresses me about your letter is to find that you look at it in so different a light.
>
> I am sorry that those who interest themselves most in the welfare of the negro should misjudge this action on the part of the departments, for they are seriously misjudging it. My own feeling is, by putting certain bureaus and sections of the service in the charge of negroes we are rendering them

---

* A prominent journalist in these years, Villard was owner and editor of the *New York Evening Post* and the *Nation*. He was a grandson of William Lloyd Garrison and a cousin to Katherine Garrison Norton, the wife of Taft's executive secretary, Charles D. Norton.

more safe in their possession of office and less likely to be discriminated against.²

A few days after his reply to Villard, Wilson received another letter of complaint, this one from the author Thomas Dixon, whose novel *The Clansman: A Historical Romance of the Ku Klux Klan* had been inspired in part by Wilson's writings. Dixon wrote to protest the appointment of a Black man to the position of register of the Treasury. Wilson responded by reassuring Dixon that the departments were in the process of being segregated and that, when his administration's "plan of concentration" was complete, the executive branch would "not in any one bureau mix the two races."³

Thomas Woodrow Wilson was born in Virginia five years before the start of the Civil War. His family moved to Augusta, Georgia, during his infancy. His paternal grandparents had immigrated to Ohio from Northern Ireland and his mother came from England.* Once in the American South, however, Wilson's family adjusted to southern culture, enslaving African Americans before the war and supporting the Confederacy once the conflict began. After the war, an eight-year-old Tommy Wilson was among those who watched as Union soldiers led Jefferson Davis through Augusta in shackles. As an adult, Wilson eventually went north, graduating in the class of 1879 at the College of New Jersey (renamed Princeton University in 1896). After dropping out of law school at the University of Virginia, Wilson ended up earning a PhD in history and politics at Johns Hopkins University. While working at a series of university teaching positions, Wilson developed a reputation as an expert on the theory of government and published several popular history books before he was hired as president of Princeton University in 1902.⁴

---

*Wilson was, after Andrew Jackson and James Buchanan, only the third president to have four foreign-born grandparents. A 1921 article in the *Daughters of the American Revolution Magazine* noted that Wilson was the only president who was neither a veteran of the revolution nor a lineal descendant of a revolutionary veteran. See Mrs. Amos G. Draper, "Revolutionary Ancestry of the Presidents of the United States," *Daughters of the American Revolution Magazine*, March 1921, 134.

THE ELITE REFORMERS IN EXILE

Despite his well-known southern roots, Wilson's active racism in the White House seemed to come as a surprise to many. A more careful examination of his academic writings, however, would have made clear where his priorities lay. For instance, in his 1885 dissertation, "Congressional Government," Wilson described federal election supervisors during Reconstruction as "the very ugliest side of federal supremacy," and he complained that "the tide of federal aggression probably reached its highest shore in the legislation which put it into the power of the federal courts to punish a state judge for refusing, in the exercise of his official discretion, to impanel Negroes in the juries of his court."[5]

In a chapter on Reconstruction in his multivolume *History of the American People*, published in 1902, Wilson described a postwar South suffering under humiliating domination by ambitious Blacks and meddling northerners before being rescued by vigilantes who "took the law into their own hands, and began to attempt by intimidation what they were not allowed to attempt by the ballot." In flights of lyricism, Wilson recounted how these "roving knights errant . . . set themselves . . . to right a disordered society through the power of fear."[6]

The Birth of a Nation, the filmmaker D. W. Griffith's film adaptation of Thomas Dixon's novel *The Clansman*, drew heavily from Wilson's book. At several key points in the film, Griffith inserted title cards with quotes from Wilson's account of the formation of the Ku Klux Klan. Wilson himself evidently appreciated this touch, as well as the possibilities offered by the new medium. After a private screening at the White House in 1915, Wilson is said to have told Griffith and Dixon that the film was "like teaching history with lightning."[7]

2

Shortly after Wilson's inauguration, a delegation of Democrats visited the president to discuss the fate of the Taft Commission. The group, which included Bureau of Municipal Research director Henry Bruere and Wilson's economic adviser, Louis D. Brandeis, urged Wilson to resurrect the commission and continue its work. Wilson assured the group that he shared their interest in the project, but he denied their request. He argued that overseeing the commission would be a distraction and that his focus must be on the large issues he would be facing in trying to enact his ambitious "New Freedom" agenda.[8]

Wilson's refusal to consider the group's arguments mystified the elite reformers, who viewed budget reform and executive reorganization as essential prerequisites to enacting any coherent national policy agenda. However, as Wilson proceeded with his New Freedom agenda, it became clear that his vision differed substantially from that of the elite reformers. The president seemed intent on expanding the reach and touch of the national government without increasing its strength. Many of Wilson's major achievements, such as the implementation of a federal income tax and the creation of the Federal Reserve Board and the Federal Trade Commission, seemed to have been designed to accentuate the evils of the existing system that required reform. For instance, many elite reformers favored a national income tax—it was, after all, less prone to partisan abuse than the tariff—but the imposition of a national income tax in the absence of a national budget system seemed to invite irresponsible "raids" on the Treasury. Leading elite reformers had been involved in early discussions around a federal reserve system, but changes to that plan devised by Wilson had seemed to undercut the Fed's potential to bring order to the financial system. Similarly—as the "trust-busting" of the Roosevelt and Taft administrations attests—the elite reformers were not averse to the goals of the Clayton Act, which created the Federal Trade Commission. However, they would have preferred to pursue those goals through the Bureau of Corporations within the Department of Commerce rather than to establish a new independent commission. To the elite reformers, creation of new functions outside of the administrative structure of the cabinet simply multiplied the problems that would later need to be fixed through executive reorganization.[9]

Some remained optimistic that the scholar-president might be persuadable in the longer term and that his lack of enthusiasm for the Taft Commission was the result of a misunderstanding that could be corrected. But others concluded that Wilson was not a true friend to the good government movement after all. Not only did Wilson oppose the proposals developed by the Taft Commission, but he seemed to be actively working against civil service reform. Most of the new government positions created under Wilson's New Freedom policies—including the employees charged with administering the federal income tax, the Federal Reserve Board, and the Federal Trade Commission—were exempted from the merit system.[10] "This was a great surprise to the advocates of civil service reform," wrote William Dudley Foulke of the National Civil Service Reform League (NCSRL). "The new President had declared himself on many occasions in strong and unmistakable language as a friend of the merit system and at the time of his election he was one of the vice-presidents of the League."[11]

Civil service reformers were also frustrated by Wilson's early declaration that all fourth-class postmasters would be required to pass a civil service exam. Some hopeful observers viewed this declaration as a victory for the merit system, but that interpretation was undercut when Wilson's postmaster general announced that he would ask members of Congress for advice on the final selection of candidates.[12] The main impact of this order from Wilson was to remove Black postmasters in the South who had been "blanketed into" the merit system under Taft in favor of white replacements. A correspondent for the *Crisis*, the NAACP's official publication, noted that there were "a lot of disappointed office seekers from the South who want the civil-service bars let down long enough to let them in [through] the revocation of Mr. Taft's order placing fourth-class postmasterships upon the civil-service list."[13] In response to protest from the NCSRL, Wilson confirmed that his primary motivation was to preserve local control over federal appointments. He asked for advice from congressmen "not in their capacity as members of a political party but as representatives of their districts and of the postal communities interested in the service."[14]

Unable to exert any influence within the executive branch during the Wilson administration, the elite reformers looked for other ways to pursue reform. Some attempted to work through the United States Chamber of Commerce (USCC), which had been formed in 1912 as a membership association adjunct to the U.S. Department of Commerce and Labor. The USCC formed a special committee on budget reform, which included Harvey S. Chase, who had been a member of the Taft Commission. In January 1913, in the USCC's first national referendum, members had "almost unanimously declared in favor of a national budget." Chase published an article in the May 1914 edition of the *Nation's Business* explaining the Taft Commission's plan for a national budget in business terms. It would, he explained, "apply business principles to national finances." However, with its broad, geographically dispersed membership, the USCC was unsuited for action beyond issuing referenda and promotional publications.[15]

In 1914, several other veterans of the Taft Commission formed a new organization, the Institute for Government Research (IGR), with the goal of continuing the work of the Taft Commission as a national counterpart to the BMR in New York.* One of the primary organizers was Jerome Greene, who was secretary of the Rockefeller Foundation. In addition to Greene, the group included Charles D. Norton, the organizer of the Taft Commission, and Frederick Cleveland, the commission's director. In a letter to prospective directors, Greene explained that "a small group of men interested in [the work of the Taft Commission] have lately been considering whether there might not be a way of renewing the work on a basis that would not be dependent upon political support or congressional appropriation."[16]

During the period before the institute was incorporated, Cleveland (who was still on the payroll of the BMR) served as its acting director. However, at the board meeting at which the IGR was incorporated, William F. Willoughby, another member of the Taft Commission, was selected as director. Fully staffed and endowed with funding from the Rockefeller Foundation, the institute set about its work of trying to improve public administration at the national level. Prospects for action were slim, however, with Wilson in the White House. So the IGR focused on conducting studies and publishing books.[17]

3

In addition to working through the IGR and the USCC, elite reformers also sought opportunities to pursue their agenda at the state level during the Wilson years. The most important of these was at the New York State Constitutional Convention of 1915.

The chairman of the convention was Elihu Root.† Active in public affairs from the 1870s to the 1930s, Root was a central figure in the Wall

---

*In the late 1920s, the IGR would be merged with two other organizations to form the Brookings Institution.

†Root's singular position in American affairs in this era was reflected even in the pronunciation of his forename. Most Elihus pronounced their name as *ee-LIE-hew*, with emphasis on the long *i* in the second syllable. Root, in contrast, was *ELL-ih-hoo*, with emphasis on the first syllable and a short *i* in the second syllable. A popular name-pronunciation guide published in 1922 gave two entries for the name Elihu. In the first, general entry, they instruct the reader to pronounce it "ĕ-lī'-hū"; but in a second entry, they instruct that it is pronounced "ĕl'-ĭ-hū" for

THE ELITE REFORMERS IN EXILE

Street-allied northeastern wing of the Republican Party. Among the elite reformers, Root's preeminence was rivaled only by ex-president Taft. Root's long career as a statesman was preceded by and interspersed with intensive work as a lawyer on Wall Street, where he represented leading robber barons such as Jay Gould, and corporations such as Western Union, U.S. Rubber, and Standard Oil. Transitioning to public service near the turn of the century, Root rose to prominence alongside Theodore Roosevelt, serving as secretary of war under McKinley and Roosevelt and secretary of state in TR's administration before serving a term in the Senate starting in 1909.[18]

Root and Taft had worked closely together during the Roosevelt years as the leading proponents of administrative modernization in the executive branch. As secretary of war in the aftermath of the Spanish-American War of 1898, Root had led the effort to streamline the chain of command, creating the Army War College and the General Staff, and increasing presidential control over the army bureaucracy—an effort that Taft continued during his tenure as secretary of war. As secretary of state, Root worked to bring diplomatic positions under civil service rules and create an effective administrative organization within the department.[19]

As chairman of the New York State Constitutional Convention in 1915, Root selected many of his own allies for leadership positions, placing his most prominent protégé, Henry L. Stimson, in charge of the committee that devised the budget proposal. One decade into a more than half-century-long career in public service, Stimson had followed his mentor's career path from a lucrative practice at the corporate bar to service in the federal government. As U.S. attorney for the Southern District of New York, Stimson played a leading role in the trust-busting efforts undertaken during TR's second term. After a failed run for the governorship of New York in 1910, Stimson served as secretary of war under Taft, where he worked to extend the reform agenda initiated by Root and Taft.[20]

Stimson had first developed an interest in budget reform during the Taft administration, when, as the nominal head of the Department of War, he was alarmed to find that he was often powerless to control the activities of

---

Elihu Root. See Mary Stuart Mackey and Maryette Goodwin Mackey, *The Pronunciation of 10,000 Proper Names, Giving Famous Geographical and Biographical Names, Names of Books, Works of Art, Characters in Fiction, Foreign Titles, Etc.* (New York: Dodd, Mead and Company, 1922), 97.

his bureau chiefs, who could appeal directly to congressional committee chairman to provide funding for various projects. In his annual message as secretary of war in 1912, Stimson had advocated for executive control of budgeting as a means to ensure the coherent enactment of national policy.[21]

As he prepared for the New York State Constitutional Convention in late 1914 and early 1915, Stimson consulted with scholars of government, reviewed the reports of the Taft Commission, and discussed the problem with former commission members such as Frank Goodnow, who was now serving as president of Johns Hopkins University. Stimson also conferred with others who shared his own experience as both a corporate lawyer and federal official. This group included his mentor, Elihu Root, as well as former attorney general George Wickersham.

Although Stimson's purpose at Albany was to devise a budget system for the government of the state of New York, he immediately began to consider how his plans could be implemented at the federal level. Before long he had developed a fully-fledged general philosophy that would provide the keystone for the elite reformers in the coming years. Stimson referred to his plan for administrative reform as "responsible government"—a term that had been used in passing by scholars of government, but which Stimson transformed into a slogan for an agenda that combined the technical recommendations of the academic experts with insights drawn from his experience in corporate law and government.[22]

Stimson saw several benefits in melding business know-how with academic theory. Stimson believed that, in addition to increasing the capacity of the government, it would also improve the functioning of democracy. By making the democratically elected executive responsible for devising and enacting policy, and by removing administrative openings where the legislature and other actors could interfere with the enactment of the executive's plans, voters would more easily be able to discern who was responsible for a given policy's success or failure. Voters could then enforce that responsibility at the polls. Another advantage, as Stimson saw it, was that the reforms necessary to establish "responsible government" could be framed as "business practice" in a way that could make them appeal to traditional good government reformers as well as the Main Street businessmen whose support would be necessary to carry any policy agenda to enactment.[23]

In Stimson's view, the solution to the nation's problems was to concentrate authority in the national executive, in the same way that large national corporations had concentrated authority in their chief executive officers. Stimson became convinced that many of America's problems derived from the lack of clearly assigned responsibility, which meant that voters could not readily tell who to blame or reward for the failure or success of any policy:

> It is now not so much a question of putting limitations on the power of the sovereign from above, as it is of making it perfectly certain that when your agent acts wrongly you will know it. Instead of putting limitations on the public officer, the real problem now is to have his action as clear and as public as possible. There is no longer any real danger in giving your agent power, now that the people have power to re-place him if they find out that he has done wrong.[24]

This insight was drawn from Stimson's experience with large corporations. In the modern corporation, poor administrative organization meant lost profits. If business could not be run in such a way, Stimson reasoned, government should not either. Just as big business had gone through a managerial revolution in the preceding decades, it was now time for government to follow suit. The "business methods" of the federal government ought to conform to the best practices of private corporations.

Stimson's plan for the New York State budget echoed the recommendations of the Taft Commission: the executive would prepare the budget; the legislature would approve or disapprove of that budget. During the proceedings, Stimson invited testimony from leading members of the Taft Commission, including Frederick Cleveland, Frank Goodnow, Charles Norton, and ex-president Taft himself, who each supported Stimson's proposed budget amendment.[25]

Voters in New York, however, ended up rejecting all of the convention's amendments in November 1915. Yet Stimson's efforts had more than symbolic importance. They provided a framework for the elite reformers' plans to enact administrative reform at the national level.

However, realizing those plans would take some time. If political conditions were not yet ripe for enactment of a modern budget system in New York State, the climate seemed even worse at the national level with

Woodrow Wilson in the White House. Wilson's continued hostility to the elite reformers' agenda seemed to present an insuperable barrier to national budget reform.

Taft lamented this reality in a two-part article published in the *Saturday Evening Post* in February 1915. "One great lack in our present governmental plan for economical and responsible expenditure of money has been the absence of machinery for constructive work under responsible leadership," the ex-president wrote. "The most effective instrument that has ever been devised for locating official responsibility as to the financial condition of a Government has been what is commonly known as a budget. In this country we have never had a budget."[26] Taft saw two obstacles to enacting a budget. First, the general public was bored by such topics. Second, Wilson and his allies exploited public indifference in order to perpetuate the existing system:

> The minor political importance that President Wilson evidently assigns to this issue of economy in the business methods of the Government is probably a correct estimate. Rarely, indeed, can the people, as a whole, be roused to the benefit of a policy the discussion of which involves a tedious recital of figures or a detailed explanation of a complicated plan of governmental reorganization.
>
> Reforms of this kind are the result of the hardest kind of work in the closet. They cannot be exploited in headlines. They tire the audience. Those who effect them must generally be contented with a consciousness of good service rendered, and must not look for the reward of popular approval.[27]

4

The United States entered World War I on April 6, 1917. The logistical challenges involved in transporting two million troops to France while also coordinating the delivery of supplies and munitions were great. Geographic difficulties were made even worse by administrative snafus. The national government's hodgepodge administrative structure meant that there was no mechanism to easily coordinate the action of disparate bureaus, agencies, and offices. The difficulties encountered in the wartime mobilization provided the elite reformers with an I-told-you-so moment, demonstrating the need for increased national administrative capacity in stark terms. However, as the sometimes chaotic mobilization proceeded, Woodrow Wilson continued to resist the elite reformers' suggestions for improving the administrative capacity of the executive branch.

Wilson's inclination was to rely on informal coordination rather than formal administration. Early in the war, this coordination was managed by the Council of National Defense, which was comprised of six cabinet members—the secretaries of war, navy, interior, agriculture, commerce, and labor—plus a seven-man advisory commission. Wilson worked with Congress to create a series of wartime agencies, including the U.S. Food Administration, the U.S. Fuel Administration, and the War Industries Board, which were staffed by volunteers drawn from the private sector. These "dollar-a-year men," as they were called—most were wealthy enough that they did not require a government salary—were sometimes assisted by employees of the IGR. However, without formal administrative control, this hodgepodge collection of newly created agencies proved to be an inefficient means for carrying out wartime mobilization.[28]

By the winter of 1917–1918, wartime imperatives had forced Wilson to bend, but he did not break fully from his preferences. In February 1918, Wilson asked Democrats in the Senate for a bill that would provide him with the authority to create new agencies and combine or abolish existing ones. Elite reformers had been arguing for pursuing permanent comprehensive reorganization along the lines suggested by the Taft Commission, but Wilson stopped short. The bill drafted in response to Wilson's request, sponsored by Senator Lee Overman, Democrat of North Carolina, applied only to war-related activities and specified that any action taken under the act would be reversed six months after the conflict's end.[29]

Although many elite reformers hoped the bill might provide an opportunity to make a permanent improvement to the organization of the executive branch, some had qualms that led them to clarify their preferences. For instance, even though the bill resembled the recommendations of the Taft Commission, Taft himself argued that it was unwise—and unconstitutional—for a president to create new agencies without legislative approval.* Others feared that, given his record, Wilson might

---

* The elite reformers would henceforth include provisions requiring legislative approval for the creation of new offices in their subsequent attempts to enact executive reorganization.

use these powers irresponsibly. However, after the Overman Act became law in May 1918, Wilson stuck to his scruples and used his authority under the law only sparingly.[30]

The most consequential action taken under the Overman Act was to shift an enlarged and reorganized War Industries Board (WIB) from the Council of National Defense to the office of the president. Yet even this arrangement faced difficulties. While WIB administrators now had nominal authority over the sprawling wartime bureaucracy, the nature of that bureaucracy continued to hinder the flow of information within the system. The WIB's ability to exercise authority was undermined by an inability to get an accurate picture of what was happening in any particular bureau. Although the reins were now held in the White House, the lines of administrative control between the president and the bureaus of the executive branch remained tangled.

Edwin F. Gay, the founding dean of Harvard Business School and a trustee of the IGR, had joined the government as a dollar-a-year man on April 4, 1917, two days before Wilson's declaration of war. Through his work on the Commercial Economy Board, Gay sought to bring business methods to the wartime government agencies. His focus, especially in the early months, was on promoting modern practices such as uniform cost accounting and the compilation of accurate statistics to aid planners.[31]

In February 1918, after devising a system that dramatically increased the efficiency in the shipping of personnel and supplies across the Atlantic, Gay became head of the Shipping Board's new Division of Planning and Statistics. By the summer of 1918, the results achieved by Gay and his staff of nearly two hundred seemed to provide an obvious solution to leaders frustrated by the wartime government's lack of administrative capacity. In August, Gay took the helm of the new Central Bureau of Planning and Statistics in the WIB. During the next few months, Gay worked to create a government-wide system for planning, accounting, and administrative oversight.[32]

By the fall of 1918, after a series of halting stops and reluctant starts, the Wilson administration had finally created a wartime administrative structure that came close to fulfilling the hopes that the elite reformers had held for the Taft Commission. The Overman Act gave the president the authority to reshape the jumbled national administration, while Gay's Central Bureau of Planning and Statistics filled the role of staff agency, helping the president to oversee the rapidly growing bureaucracy and identify which branches should be pruned, grafted, or braced.³³

5

The nation's mobilization for the war in Europe coincided with a sharp rise in racist violence at home. The wartime increase in lynchings, massacres, and so-called race riots put a strain on the advocacy coalitions formed in the prewar era. When the frequency of racist atrocities had seemed to decline during the first decade of the twentieth century, many observers, in both the North and South, had hopefully concluded that "race feeling" was easing in the South. But the new wave of violence—coincident with a massive "Great Migration" of southern Blacks to the industrial North— began to undermine the notion that a policy of accommodation toward Jim Crow was a viable strategy for improving conditions for African Americans.³⁴

The election of Woodrow Wilson had already altered the landscape of civil rights advocacy. Booker T. Washington's role in directing the dispensation of federal patronage in the South during the Roosevelt and Taft administrations had been a key source of his influence. With that wellspring stoppered, the power wielded by the Tuskegee Machine began to wane. Accommodation suffered another blow in November 1915 when Washington died of heart disease at the early age of fifty-nine. Washington's successor at the Tuskegee Institute, Robert Russa Moton, was an able administrator who worked to maintain Washington's nonconfrontational approach. Yet Moton lacked Washington's charisma and close connections with wealthy northerners. This left an opening for organizations that had opposed Washington's policy of accommodation, and that void was filled by the NAACP, whose membership grew dramatically during the war, as did circulation of the *Crisis*.³⁵

While the practice of lynching was widely known in the South, in the 1910s relatively few northerners were aware of the prevalence and horror of these crimes, despite the work of pioneering African American journalist Ida B. Wells. But in 1915, news coverage of the case of Leo Frank helped to pierce the veil of northern ignorance.

A Jewish graduate of Cornell University, Frank was a supervisor of a National Pencil Company factory in Atlanta, Georgia. On April 21, 1913,

Mary Phagan, a thirteen-year-old white employee, was found murdered at the factory. In August of that year, Frank was convicted on dubious evidence and sentenced to death. On June 21, 1915, the day before Frank's scheduled execution, after a series of failed appeals, and in response to thousands of requests to reverse the verdict, the governor commuted Frank's sentence from death to life in prison. In response, a five-thousand-person mob surrounded the governor's home and groups of vigilantes began to organize.

The vigilantes found encouragement from former Georgia congressman Tom Watson, a "populist" and racist political leader who directed an army of followers through his weekly *Jeffersonian* newspaper and the monthly *Watson's Magazine*. On August 12, 1915, Watson printed in his paper an all-caps warning: "THE NEXT JEW WHO DOES WHAT FRANK DID, IS GOING TO GET EXACTLY THE SAME THING THAT WE DO TO NEGRO RAPISTS." Four days later, on August 16, a group of twenty-five vigilantes removed Leo Frank from the state penitentiary, drove him across the state to Mary Phagan's hometown of Marietta, Georgia, and murdered him by hanging. Lynchers mutilated Frank's corpse and collected pieces of clothing and rope as souvenirs. Photos of the lynching were sold. In the face of denunciations from around the nation, Watson and his allies in Georgia remained defiant. In his newspaper, Watson warned that if outsiders insisted on meddling in Georgian affairs, "another Ku Klux Klan may be organized to restore HOME RULE." Later that year, thanks in part to Watson's encouragement, the "second" Ku Klux Klan was founded at a ceremony at Stone Mountain, Georgia.[36]

In April 1916, with the support of northern philanthropists outraged by the Frank case, the NAACP launched a campaign to combat lynching. The association sent investigators to the scene of each new atrocity to gather information that would be published in the *Crisis*. NAACP leaders also began to cultivate white editors at magazines and newspapers around the nation in an effort to expand the organization's reach beyond its own membership and subscriber base.[37] After the May 1916 lynching of a mentally disabled African American boy in Waco, Texas, the *Crisis* also began printing photos showing mutilated victims and bloodthirsty crowds.[38]

Among the most shocking of the wartime atrocities was the massacre of hundreds of African Americans in East St. Louis, Illinois, on July 2, 1917.

This so-called race riot was the culmination of trouble that began around the election of 1916, when local Democrats accused Republicans of attempting to "colonize" East St. Louis with Black voters imported from the South. As the election approached, the Wilson administration gave added credence to this conspiracy theory when Mississippi-born attorney general Thomas W. Gregory launched a "colonization" investigation in the Great Lakes states of Illinois, Indiana, and Ohio. As part of this investigation, officials from the Department of Justice interviewed African Americans in East St. Louis to determine what had motivated them to move north.[39]

Woodrow Wilson indicated his personal approval of the conspiracy theory two days before the election when he warned against voter fraud in a message to Democratic state and county chairmen. Using language that was elliptical but nonetheless clear to his intended audience, Wilson told party officials that it was "our duty to take every precaution lest conscienceless agents of the sinister forces working in opposition to progressive principle and popular government resort in their desperation to industrial coercion or the evil and insidious practices of a decade and more ago."[40]

The conspiracy was forgotten by Democratic leaders after Wilson's victory. The attorney general had promised prosecutions, but no charges were brought. However, white labor leaders in East St. Louis remained in a state of agitation. In April and May 1917, tired of waiting for official action from the Wilson administration, armed whites began taking matters into their own hands, targeting African Americans in East St. Louis, whom they accused of coming north to steal jobs from white workers.

More than two months of skirmishes culminated on July 2, when thousands of armed whites invaded African American neighborhoods in East St. Louis, killing hundreds. In the days after the massacre, reports emerged that local officials had taken part in the atrocity, and that the local militia had stood idle. An NAACP investigation conducted by Martha Gruening and W. E. B. Du Bois filled nearly twenty pages of the *Crisis* with grisly descriptions and eyewitness accounts of African American citizens—men, women, and children—shot, beheaded, burned, and drowned. The article ended with a provocative question: "And what of the Federal Government?"[41]

On July 28, 1917, the NAACP organized a "Negro Silent Parade" in New York. More than ten thousand African Americans marched in silence down Fifth Avenue. On August 1, a delegation of twenty marchers from the parade visited the White House to deliver a resolution and petition to Wilson. The petition noted that "in the last thirty-one years 2,867 colored men and women have been lynched by mobs without trial," and added that "mobs have harried and murdered colored citizens time and time again with impunity, culminating in the latest atrocity at East St. Louis." The petition ended with a plea for "immediate action by the Congress and the President of the United States."[42] The delegation was forced to leave their resolution and petition with Wilson's secretary, Joseph Tumulty, but Wilson later agreed to meet with a smaller delegation on August 16. At that meeting, Wilson assured the delegation that the federal government would work to stop lynching, but he did not offer any specific action.[43]

As bad as the situation seemed in the summer of 1917, by the summer of 1918 it was even worse. The pages of the *Crisis* and other outlets in the African American press showed that the tide of racist violence in America was continuing to rise at an alarming rate. The increase disturbed even supporters of white supremacy, particularly those like Woodrow Wilson who viewed themselves as defenders of the Constitution and who hoped to assure civil rights advocates that the "race problem" was already being solved by southern leaders. And so, in the summer of 1918, when the leaders of the NAACP asked Wilson to speak out against lynching, the president agreed.[44]

However, in his speech, delivered on July 26, 1918, Wilson took care not to endorse the demand for congressional action. Wilson emphasized that lynching was not merely a *southern* phenomenon, and that African Americans were not the only victims of lynching. In identifying his topic, Wilson said, "I allude to the mob spirit which has recently here and there very frequently shown its head among us, not in any single region, but in many and widely separated parts of the country." Still, Wilson gave an apparently heartfelt denunciation of lynchings, saying that "every one of them has been a blow at the heart of ordered law and humane justice." Further, he said that "no man who loves America, no man who really cares for her fame and honor and character, or who is truly loyal to her institutions, can justify mob action while the courts of justice are open and the governments of the States and the nation are ready and able to do their duty." After warning would-be lynchers that their actions served to "emulate" Germany's "disgraceful example," Wilson ended his address by urging citizens to refrain from lynching:

> I therefore very earnestly and solemnly beg that the governors of all the States, the law officers of every community, and, above all, the men and women of every community in the United States, all who revere America and wish to keep her name without stain or reproach, will cooperate—not passively merely, but actively and watchfully—to make an end of this disgraceful evil. It cannot live where the community does not countenance it.[45]

However, Wilson's disapproval of lynching apparently did not cause him to reevaluate his beliefs about the importance of local, not national, authority in such matters. The subtext of Wilson's message was that responsibility lay with leaders in each state, and in particular with members of "the community" where a lynching occurred. Most observers agreed that lynching was bad. The question was what to do about it. Wilson pointedly did not endorse federal action to stop lynching.

* * *

For the elite reformers, the U.S. experience in World War I created a heightened recognition of the mismatch between the administrative capacities of business and government. The dollar-a-year men had seen firsthand how the federal government worked, and when they compared government to business, they found government lacking. As one writer put it, "Compared with our great business concerns, the United States Government has been extremely weak in central administration."[46] The temporary, grudging compromises made by Wilson only exacerbated this, and his decision to call an end to the experiment in wartime administration—to, in effect, return the national government to a state of normalcy—led many members of the northeastern business community to embrace the administrative reform agenda of the elite reformers. At the same time, the troubling increase in lynchings and "race riots" helped focus attention on Wilson's deplorable record on civil rights. The wartime experience and the rise of racist violence thus solidified the reformers' understanding that President Wilson was himself perhaps the biggest impediment to increasing the capacity of the national government.

Chapter Three

AFTER THE ARMISTICE
Spring 1919

Woodrow Wilson's triumphal announcement of the armistice on November 11, 1918, came at a pivotal political moment, just six days after his party had suffered a decisive defeat in the midterm elections of November 5. After six years of dealing with a Congress controlled by his own party, Wilson would have to contend with Republican majorities of 49–46 in the Senate and 240–192 in the House during the second half of his second term.[1]

The elite reformers hoped that a Republican-led Congress might provide an opening in which to advance their agenda. In the immediate postwar months, they were preoccupied by the nation's rapidly ballooning war debt and the continuing wave of racist violence. The effort to finance the war had seemed to provoke a new awareness of the nation's place in the global order and a new sense of patriotism among investors. The war debt seemed to provide a rationale for leveraging that patriotism to enact budget reform. At the same time, the postwar rise in lynchings and race massacres had convinced many that, if they wanted good government—that is, if they wanted to fight corruption and create an efficient and effective national public administration that could enact coherent national policies—they must confront racist violence and ensure equal protection under the law. In order to seize the opportunity created by the armistice and the midterm results, the elite reformers created a new advocacy organization to make progress on budget reform. In order to meet the problem of racist violence, they abandoned the old strategy of accommodation and formed a new alliance with the NAACP.[2]

1

During the winter that followed the armistice, the leading elite reformers were focused on budget reform. When the United States entered the war in April 1917, the national debt stood at just over $1 billion, but in less than two years, that amount had grown to more than $20 billion. The nation's war debt seemed to present an opportunity. Perhaps, the reformers reasoned, with the carrot of good government now accompanied by the stick of possible debt-triggered tax increases, they could leverage the sense of fear and alarm that surrounded the war debt into popular support for some of their old plans.

William Howard Taft led a series of conversations at the Metropolitan Club, the Down Town Association, and the Recess Club about ways to take advantage of the new situation. Joining the ex-president in leading these post-armistice budget discussions were Charles D. Norton and William F. Willoughby, two old allies from the days of the Taft Commission. In the six years since Taft had left the White House in 1913, Norton, Taft's former secretary, had moved to New York and served as vice president of the First National Bank of New York, which was part of the banking network affiliated with J. P. Morgan and Co. Willoughby, director of the Institute for Government Research, had written a series of scholarly books on budget reform and executive reorganization that drew on the experiences of the Taft Commission, state-level budget reform efforts, and the wartime mobilization.[3]

The first step toward enacting budget reform, Taft, Norton, and Willoughby decided, would be to form a new advocacy organization to supplement the activity of the Institute for Government Research. The IGR had proven to be an effective research organization, but the limitations imposed by its funders restricted its activities. For instance, John D. Rockefeller Jr. was willing to fund a series of books written by Willoughby, but only if they focused on the "scientific" study of administrative problems and refrained from advocating specific governmental reforms.[4] What the budget movement required, Taft, Norton, and Willoughby decided, was a respectable "propaganda organization" that could build political support for administrative reform.

The new organization would be called the "National Budget Committee." To lead it, Taft, Norton, and Willoughby chose John Teele Pratt. A corporation lawyer, financier, and one of the wealthiest men working on Wall Street, Pratt was one of a select few in this era who could comfortably address letters to John D. Rockefeller Jr. with the greeting "Dear John," although he was not nearly as wealthy as his correspondent. John T. Pratt's father was Charles Pratt, one of the original nine trustees in the Standard Oil Trust. One of John's brothers was a director of Standard Oil of New Jersey and another brother was head of Standard Oil of New York.* During the war, Pratt worked for the American Red Cross in Paris. After the armistice, he settled back into his law practice on Wall Street and started a new firm specializing in management consulting and corporate reorganization.[5]

In March 1919, Pratt produced a self-published pamphlet that would serve as a prospectus for the National Budget Committee (NBC). Titled *An Executive Budget System: What the Country Has Done, What the Country Can, and Should Do*, it was essentially a summary of the ideas that Henry Stimson had developed at the New York State Constitutional Convention in 1915 and which had been elaborated upon in the meantime in several books on budget reform written by IGR director William Willoughby. Pratt reminded readers that the existing budgeting system remained essentially unchanged from the nineteenth century, with bureau chiefs and congressional committee chairmen negotiating expenditures without any formal oversight from the president. And he warned his readers that if the nation continued without modern budgeting, the war debt would inevitably lead to higher taxes. The solution, Pratt argued, was to run the federal government "on a plan that is sound and businesslike."[6]

By "businesslike," Pratt had in mind the analogy promoted in previous years by Taft and Stimson, with government modeled on the basic structure of corporate governance, with the executive in charge of planning and implementing policy, a board of directors in control of the purse strings but without direct authority in administration, and an independent auditor to

---

* In the 1920s, his wife, Ruth Baker Pratt, would become the first female member of the New York City Board of Aldermen and the first congresswoman elected in New York.

ensure that the executive had carried out that policy responsibly. Describing how this would look when applied to the federal government, Pratt argued that the president should be responsible for preparing a budget. Then, a single Senate committee should approve or disapprove of the budget devised by the president. Once Congress had approved the president's budget, Congress would use "a system of audits and reports ... to supervise the work of the Administration."[7]

Shortly after his pamphlet appeared, Pratt worked with Taft, Norton, and Willoughby to bring in four others to form a five-man organization committee, with Pratt himself serving as chairman. The men who filled out this committee—Benjamin Strong, Paul M. Warburg, Joseph P. Cotton, and Henry L. Stimson—were all well-known, both on Wall Street and in the nation's capital, and their selection reflected how closely administrative reform had come to be identified with Wall Street during the war. Strong and Warburg were two of the most important bankers in New York; Cotton and Stimson were two of the city's most respected corporate lawyers. Benjamin Strong was governor of the Federal Reserve Bank of New York, which at that time meant that he was effectively the nation's central banker. Before joining the Fed, Strong had been president of the Morgan-dominated Bankers Trust, and during the war he had served as chairman of the Liberty Loan Committee.[8] Paul Warburg had played a leading role in formulating the original, Wall Street–friendly "Aldrich Plan" for the Federal Reserve system. Born into a prominent Jewish banking family in Hamburg, Germany, he had settled in New York in 1902, joining Kuhn, Loeb and Co., the banking firm founded by his wife's father, Solomon Loeb, and her uncle, Abraham Kuhn, and run by her brother-in-law, Jacob Schiff.[9] Joseph Cotton, formerly a partner at the preeminent Wall Street law firm of Cravath and Henderson, was considered to be among the most talented lawyers of his generation.[10] During the war, he had been Herbert Hoover's right-hand man at the U.S. Food Administration.[11]

The member of the committee with the most experience in government was Henry Stimson, the former U.S. attorney for the Southern District of New York and secretary of war. A partner at the law firm of Winthrop and Stimson, his reputation as an expert in budgetary matters had been solidified at the 1915 New York State Constitutional Convention. Throughout the 1910s, he had been a prominent advocate of universal military training. In 1917, after declining Herbert Hoover's request that he serve as Hoover's chief deputy at the Food Administration during the war—the position eventually filled by Joseph Cotton—the fifty-year-old Stimson instead volunteered and served in the army as an artillery officer, rising to the rank of colonel shortly before the armistice.[12]

During the spring of 1919, the NBC drafted articles of incorporation and made plans for its "propaganda" campaign and a membership drive modeled after the wartime Liberty Loan drives. The first step was to secure the services of a research director. At the first official meeting of the committee, held March 4, 1919, at the Metropolitan Club, the five organizers decided to retain the research services of Samuel McCune Lindsay, professor of political science at Columbia, secretary of the Bureau of Municipal Research, and president of the Academy of Political Science of New York.[13]

The leaders of the NBC spent the spring months of 1919 preparing for action at the end of the summer. They hoped to capitalize on the dollar-a-year men's newfound awareness of the importance of administrative reform, and they hoped to use the fear of rising taxes to convince the national business community to support their proposals and put pressure on Congress and President Wilson.

The moment seemed ripe. "I think this is really a psychological time to push through a budget system," Stimson wrote to Pratt in April. "The country is facing a financial burden incomparably greater than anything it has ever had before and the pressure which this burden produces will create a demand for better financial methods. That demand ought to be steered at once into the right channels."[14]

2

While the debt crisis had led Taft and his allies to look for ways to revive and refine policy proposals developed during the previous decade, the recent increase in racist violence led them to adopt a new approach to civil rights issues. Before the war, wealthy northerners and mainstream Republicans interested in contributing to greater civil rights for African Americans had tended to support the accommodationist policies of Booker T. Washington. But that approach had not prevented the wartime wave of violence and, in the months following the armistice, many prominent northeastern Republicans who had been Tuskegee loyalists in the prewar era decided to support the efforts of the NAACP.

This shift coincided with the NAACP's publication of a 105-page pamphlet, *Thirty Years of Lynching in the United States, 1892–1918*, in April 1919. The pamphlet was the culmination of the antilynching campaign begun by the association in 1916 and was based on an exhaustive analysis of newspapers in the Library of Congress. It listed the name, sex, age, and race of 3,224 Americans who had been lynched during the previous three decades—2,522 African Americans and 702 whites—along with the date, location, and details of each lynching.[15]

To capitalize on the publication of *Thirty Years of Lynching*, NAACP leaders began making plans for a national antilynching conference, to be organized in cooperation with the Association of the Bar of the City of New York. The leadership of the New York Bar had long been the domain of elites who had traditionally supported the Tuskegee model and who had previously been wary of the NAACP's more confrontational approach. However, the NAACP did not have to work very hard to convince the leading elite reformers. Most had readily agreed by late February 1919 to sign the NAACPs call for an antilynching conference and committed to attend before the date and location had been finalized. Elihu Root explained his own reasoning in a letter of acceptance to NAACP president Moorfield Storey: "I have always felt that such a practice as lynching necessarily implies serious defect in administration of law, so that it is an evil which calls not merely for a vigorous negative, but for a counter affirmative."[16] Charles Evans Hughes, in his acceptance letter, wrote, "I agree with you that public attention should be arrested and the matter put in a strong light."[17]

In a sign of how far the elite reformers had shifted away from the nonconfrontational Tuskegee approach since 1913, NAACP leaders secured the attendance of these men before they had even consulted Tuskegee principal Robert Russa Moton. In a letter to NAACP secretary John Shillady in early March 1919, after the NAACP's plans were underway, Moton urged the NAACP to reconsider. Moton argued that holding an antilynching conference in the North would only make the problem worse, and that in order to avoid further white backlash, the antilynching conference ought to be held in the South and organized by the Tuskegee Institute. Ignoring Moton's advice, however, and with the support of the elite reformers, the NAACP proceeded with its plans to hold the conference in Manhattan.[18]

On April 13, 1919—just two weeks before the conference scheduled to take place—the organizers' resolve was bolstered when news arrived of a "race riot" in Jenkins County, Georgia. Like most such incidents, the details filtered to the national press in a confusing haze of contradictory fragments. The violence apparently began during a festival at a Black church, with a traffic incident involving two white police officers and a Black man named Edmund Scott, who was transporting a minister to the revival and had apparently rebuked the officers for their reckless driving. The officers' response was to place Scott under arrest. As Scott was being led away, he shouted for help from Joe Ruffin, a well-respected Black farm owner and Mason. As Ruffin talked with the officers, surrounded by a crowd of onlookers, the situation veered out of control. Gunfire erupted. Ruffin was shot and wounded. Scott was shot and killed. Both police officers were shot and killed, likely at the hands of Ruffin's two sons.[19]

News of the white officers' deaths spread quickly and white vigilantes from the surrounding area raced to the scene. Ruffin, bleeding from his gunshot wound, fled to the nearby home of Jim Perkins, a prominent white farm owner. After the vigilantes discovered he was harboring Ruffin, Perkins, with the aid of the county sheriff, concealed Ruffin in the backseat of his car and drove almost sixty miles north to Augusta, Georgia, where Ruffin was placed in the city jail for safekeeping. Meanwhile, a white mob burned the church where the deaths had occurred and burned one of Ruffin's cars. They abducted two of Ruffin's sons and lynched them. Moving to the nearby town of Millen, the mob burned three Black Masonic lodges and destroyed Black property. The mob found and killed one of Ruffin's friends, Willie Williams, who was being hidden in a stable under guard of a sheriff's deputy. While it would be some time before NAACP leaders could discover the facts of the case, news reports about the destruction of a church and Masonic lodges helped to underline the need for urgent action.[20]

Held May 5 and 6, 1919, at Carnegie Hall, the National Conference on Lynching drew 2,500 attendees. In the preceding months, the NAACP had secured the signatures of 119 "distinguished citizens of the United States— white and Black, Northerners and Southerners, statesmen, judges, college presidents, congressmen, ministers, reformers, authors, men and women"— for a "Call for an Anti-Lynching Conference." After the conference, 141 attendees signed the conference's "Address to the Nation."[21]

The conference's keynote speaker was Charles Evans Hughes, who had been the Republican presidential nominee in 1916. After two decades as a corporate lawyer on Wall Street, Hughes had been elected governor of New

York in 1906. In Albany, Hughes developed a reputation as a progressive champion of good government. Reelected in 1908, Hughes resigned the governorship in 1910 when President Taft appointed him to a seat on the U.S. Supreme Court—from which he then resigned in 1916 before accepting the Republican nomination for the presidency.[22]

Hughes's keynote address at the antilynching conference illustrated the elite reformers' evolving views about the appropriate response to racist violence. "We have come here to do our utmost to create public sentiment in support of the most important duty of the citizens of the United States," Hughes announced, "and that duty is to enforce the guarantees of the Federal Constitution. In any community where the courts are open and the processes of justice are available, lynching is murder of the foulest sort." This language pointedly echoed Wilson's speech a year before. In a further jab at Wilson, Hughes alluded to the negotiations then proceeding at the Paris Peace Conference and argued that the United States had little claim to advocate for international peace and justice while lynching remained a problem at home. "We can never properly appear as the exemplar of justice to the world as long as the black man, because he is a black man, is denied justice within the United States." Hughes also cautioned against northern complacency, arguing that, although lynching was primarily a southern problem, its continuation harmed the cause of justice throughout the nation. "You cannot dethrone justice in the South and let lynching go unpunished there and expect to be secure in this great metropolis of New York."[23]

What set Hughes's speech, and the conference as a whole, apart from previous antilynching activism was that it was paired with a bold call for federal action. During the conference, attendees resolved (among other motions) "that in the opinion of the National Conference on Lynching an attempt should be made to secure Federal legislation against lynching."[24]

The list of signers to the post-conference "Address to the Nation" illustrates how the postwar violence had begun to erode the prewar wall separating supporters of the Tuskegee and NAACP approaches. The most prominent of the former "accommodationist" signers of the address was ex-president Taft himself. The list included several eminent corporate lawyers, most notably Elihu Root (senator and former secretary of state and war), John G. Milburn (of the firm Carter, Ledyard and Milburn), former U.S. attorney general George Wickersham (of the firm Cadwalader, Wickersham, and Taft—the oldest white-shoe law firm in New York City and the firm of the ex-president's brother), and former secretary of commerce Charles Nagel. The signers also included several prominent clergymen and liberal academics, as well as numerous other prominent businessmen, current and former presidents of several Ivy League colleges, and the current or former governors of Alabama, Arizona, Connecticut, Georgia, Idaho, Illinois, Iowa, Indiana, Kansas, Maryland, Nevada, Rhode Island, South Dakota, Tennessee, and Utah. (New York governor Alfred E. Smith notably declined the NAACP's invitation.) Perhaps most importantly, the list also included two Republican legislators, Representative Leonidas Dyer, of Missouri, and Senator Charles Curtis, of Kansas, who were both preparing to introduce antilynching bills in Congress.[25]

* * *

The elite reformers' sense of urgency was tempered by pessimism. Although their collaboration with the NAACP had resulted in plans for antilynching legislation, there seemed to be little chance of enacting that legislation while Woodrow Wilson remained in the White House. This pessimism was compounded by worries about whether the antilynching bill would be vulnerable to charges of unconstitutionality. Given the Supreme Court's record in upholding Jim Crow, NAACP president Moorfield Storey was not optimistic. Still, he and others felt that it was worth a try. If—sometime after the next presidential election—the court were to strike down an antilynching law, perhaps that decision would arouse public support for more durable reform. "The feeling seemed to be that it would be worth while to try legislation and let the Supreme Court, if it must, decide that it was unconstitutional," Storey explained to Hughes. "I have always felt that unless the constitution is amended, Congress lacks the power to legislate, and certainly with a Democratic Congress and President Wilson in the White House, there has been no chance of getting any law passed."[26]

That urgency and pessimism were both heightened as the postwar surge in racial violence continued in the weeks and months after the conference. The lynchings and atrocities in the summer of 1919 surpassed the already high levels of violence seen in 1918, and the violence in Jenkins County, Georgia, turned out to be merely the first atrocity of what became known as the "Red Summer" of 1919. By summer's end, the bloody wave had swelled and breached the barriers that had previously confined such brutality to the

South. So-called race riots erupted in Chicago, Omaha, and Washington, D.C.[27]

Northern reformers were particularly alarmed when John Shillady, the white executive secretary of the NAACP, barely survived a severe beating by local officials in Austin, Texas, in late August. "Mr. Shillady is a gentleman of training and experience, known to social workers all over the land," W. E. B. Du Bois explained in his column in the October edition of the *Crisis*. "He was set upon by a judge, a constable and other officials, who have openly boasted their lawlessness and have been upheld by the Governor of the State." The leader of the Austin mob, county judge Dave Pickle, explained himself to the local newspaper: "We can handle the Negro question without interference by these Northerners, who come down here and preach social equality."[28]

Chapter Four

THE BUDGET DEBATE
1919–1920

Reformers' pessimism about lynching contrasted with optimism about budget reform. With the National Budget Committee, they had formed an advocacy organization that could fight to enact a budget system—the first step toward ensuring that authority and control over national policy would rest with the presidency rather than with local officials like Judge Pickle.

By the end of the summer, the NBC was ready to launch its campaign. The committee had anticipated opposition from advocates of the existing congressional budget system, but they were caught off guard by the opposition that emerged from the Wilson administration. The leaders of the NBC had been hopeful that the experience of wartime mobilization might have left Wilson open to their ideas. But it quickly became apparent that the president's own vision for budget reform clashed with that of the NBC. From the fall of 1919 through the spring of 1920, the directors of the NBC would repeatedly debate the wisdom of compromise while engaging in an extended tug-of-war with Wilson's deputies, who doggedly attempted to convince the NBC that reform would be impossible without the president's backing.

1

On September 1, 1919, the NBC published the first issue of its twice-monthly newsletter, the *National Budget*. The public relations firm of John Price Jones produced the newsletter, working under the supervision of NBC research director and Columbia professor Samuel McCune Lindsay. The go-to publicity man for elite endeavors in this era, Jones had previously worked with the McCann advertising firm. He came to the NBC's attention through his work as director of publicity for the Liberty Loan drives and as general manager of the Harvard Endowment Fund.[1] The first issue of the *National Budget* included articles on the background of the NBC, plans for the committee's membership drive, and assessments of the various budget bills that had been introduced in Congress.[2]

The NBC's plans received their widest hearing through a two-part article written by Henry Stimson that appeared in the August and September issues of the popular magazine the *World's Work*, which was edited by Arthur W. Page. In the article, Stimson presented a clear case for a presidential budget system: the president would devise the budget, Congress would approve or disapprove of that budget, and then an independent auditing agency responsible to Congress would assess whether the president had faithfully carried out his plans.[3]

Stimson took the opportunity to reiterate the vision for "responsible government" that he had developed during the New York State Constitutional Convention four years earlier. By "fixing the responsibility" for public administration in the president's office, by clarifying Congress's role as critic of the president's program, and by ensuring that debate and criticism of that program was conducted in public, Stimson believed the NBC's proposed budget system would help voters discern who was responsible for the success or failure of a given policy. In this way, he argued, his plan would strengthen central authority at the national level while also strengthening democracy.[4]

While, at certain points, Stimson emphasized budgetary savings as a major justification for budget reform, he took care to argue that cutting expenditures was not an end in itself. He cautioned his readers that big government was here to stay. The real challenge, Stimson argued, was not to shrink the government but rather to ensure that big government was rendered effective and efficient. "We may as well recognize that legitimate pressure on the Government to enlarge its activities will not cease," Stimson wrote. "There can be no going backward into the simpler times of old."[5]

Stimson also took care to couch his argument in business terms. The wisdom of the NBC's proposed budget system, he insisted, should be clear to "every business man who is acquainted with corporate activities." He emphasized this point when he explained his preference for placing budgetary authority directly under the president. "How long would the president of a corporation stay in office if he failed to present a plan of work for the coming year to his Board of Directors and left it to them to worry out of him the facts and reports which he should present," Stimson asked. "Such a work-programme must normally come from the executive head of any organized human activity."[6]

Besides being derived from basic business principles, the decision to place the budget officers directly under the president would have the more profound benefit, Stimson explained, of providing "the necessary expert and clerical assistants who will serve as the machinery with which the President renders easily and intelligently his decisions." Placing the budget officers directly under the president, in other words—rather than within the Treasury or somewhere else within the executive branch—would allow the Budget Bureau to fill the role of a presidential staff agency, which in turn would provide the president with the necessary "machinery" to efficiently enact national policy.[7]

Shortly after Stimson's *World's Work* article appeared, Samuel McCune Lindsay, research director for the NBC, and William F. Willoughby, director of the Institute for Government Research, began to organize hearings for the House Select Committee on the Budget on a bill drafted by Willoughby at the NBC's request. The bill was sponsored by the chairman of the committee, James W. Good, Republican of Iowa. The "Good Bill, " as it would be known, provided for a budget bureau in the office of the president and the creation of an independent auditing agency.[8] In planning the committee hearings, Lindsay and Willoughby helped arrange things so that the majority of witnesses favored the NBC's approach.[9]

In their testimony at the hearings, the leaders of the NBC and their allies continued to emphasize that their ideas were derived from business methods. Stimson elaborated on the arguments from his *World's Work* article. "The thing that impressed itself upon me more than anything else was that in common public matters we were not following the principle which we were in our private business," he told the committee. "When you get into private business, and you want to get something done," he explained, "the first principle is to focus the responsibility for doing it upon someone whom you know . . . and [provide] him with the proper machinery and power to do it." Moreover, budget planning must be done by "that branch of the Government which has charge of the doing of the work," Stimson said. "It must, therefore, be done by the Executive, just as in the case of any large corporation."[10]

Taft's former secretary, Charles D. Norton, agreed that the budget "should be initiated and submitted by the executives who are to carry the projects out" because "it is the way it is done in business generally." Norton observed that "there is not a single business corporation that I have observed closely that is not run along the lines of the Good bill prepared by your committee."[11]

One incredulous congressman questioned whether Norton's business analogy could be usefully applied to the U.S. government, asking, "Do you know of any business organization that has three heads?" Norton replied, "I know of many businesses where the executive, after he has made a given plan, is content to abide by the judgment of his board, even if it is negatived or partially negatived, or is content to abide by the advice of his counsel, without feeling that his usefulness has been impaired."[12]

The House hearings served their intended purpose and helped the NBC and the IGR to build consensus within the House in favor of some form of budget reform. Supporters of the NBC's proposal had largely drowned out the protests of the southern and western congressmen who had argued in favor of the existing budget system.

2

On October 21, 1919, just days after the House hearings adjourned, the Good Bill passed easily by a margin of 283–3, with 143 abstaining. Although passage of the Good Bill was a victory for budget reformers, this victory sparked new opposition from advocates for the budget bill introduced by Senator Medill McCormick, Republican of Illinois.[13]

The McCormick Bill differed significantly from the Good Bill. In contrast to the Good Bill, which placed its proposed budget bureau in the office of the president, the McCormick Bill would create a budget bureau in the Department of the Treasury. From the point of view of the NBC, placing the bureau directly under the president would help to correct the problems of the existing system. The McCormick Bill seemed designed to preserve and institutionalize aspects of the old pattern. Since the Treasury was traditionally the department with the closest relationship to Congress, the McCormick plan would help to maintain a congressional role in the budget process, which would ultimately limit the Budget Bureau's ability to serve as a presidential staff agency.

Also, in contrast to the Good Bill, which called for creating an independent auditing agency, the McCormick Bill would leave the auditing function within the Treasury. Henry Stimson had argued that an independent audit would help to move execution of the budget beyond the realm of petty politics, thus further strengthening the president's administrative power. Placing the auditing function within the Treasury would accomplish the opposite aim. Rather than focus public debate on the merits of policies themselves, as Stimson had advocated, maintaining the audit within the Treasury would open the audit—and, by extension, the president's authority to devise and execute the budget—to political criticism.

The two bills also differed in their origins. Where the Good Bill had been written by William F. Willoughby of the IGR and had embodied the preferences of the NBC, the McCormick Bill was written by Charles Wallace Collins, at that time a researcher employed at the Library of Congress, at the direction of Carter Glass, the secretary of the Treasury.[14]

Glass was a Virginian, an ex-newspaperman, and an old friend of Woodrow Wilson. Well-known for his long career in Congress, Glass's thirteen-month tenure in the Treasury came after sixteen years in the House and before twenty-six years in the Senate. Glass was a fiscal conservative and a critic of big business. He was also an unapologetic defender of white supremacy and segregation who led the movement to disfranchise African Americans in his home state in the 1890s.[15]

During House hearings on the Good Bill, Glass justified his preference for giving budgetary responsibility to the secretary of the Treasury by insisting that a president in the modern age would be too busy to handle responsibility for the budget. "The President of the United States has not the time," he insisted. He also warned that a bureau chief under the president would lack the prestige necessary to gain cooperation from the members of the cabinet.[16]

Glass, who was one of Woodrow Wilson's most faithful allies, did not seem to intend this as a knock against the incumbent. But Senator

McCormick, who was one of the president's fiercest opponents on the issue of U.S. membership in the League of Nations, seemed to take delight in discussing the inability of the president to handle too much extra work. Glass and McCormick of course clashed on many other issues, and their curious alliance here underscores the ways that the budget debate cut across the traditional fault lines of early twentieth-century politics.[17]

While the directors of the NBC and other advocates of a presidential budget repeatedly cited the creation of a presidential staff agency as the ultimate benefit of their proposal, advocates of the Treasury budget instead insisted that placing a budget bureau directly under the president would create a dangerous concentration of central administrative control in the government. Charles Wallace Collins, author of the McCormick Bill, alluded to this danger in his House testimony when he warned that the director of a presidential budget bureau would "become, in effect, more powerful than a Cabinet officer."[18]

Mindful of the influence that NBC leaders could exert within the establishment wings of both parties, Secretary Glass and Senator McCormick spent considerable energy in late 1919 and early 1920 attempting to convince the NBC to support the McCormick Bill rather than the Good Bill. Glass had some leverage over NBC director Benjamin Strong, who, as chairman of the Federal Reserve Bank of New York, was in regular contact with the Treasury secretary. Several times after the House passed the Good Bill, Glass and McCormick were able to convince Strong and John T. Pratt that backing the McCormick Bill was the only way to ensure passage of a budget bill.

The first of these cycles came in the initial weeks after passage of the Good Bill. In response to Strong and Pratt, Henry Stimson vetoed the suggestion and expressed his aversion to the idea of placing the Budget Bureau within the Treasury. "I cannot join in any suggestion to change the Good bill, so as to place the new machinery in the Treasury Department," Stimson explained in November. "It has always been my view that the responsibility should rest directly upon the President, and the new machinery for that purpose should be directly under him." Stimson also questioned the tactical wisdom of seeking an alliance with the Wilson administration, particularly if it meant accepting a bill that did not conform with the committee's own preferences. "I think it would be a serious mistake," he warned. "It might result in giving opponents of budget reform an excuse for sidetracking the whole effort."[19]

In response the NBC's refusal, the Wilson administration and its allies shifted to coarser tactics to try to win support for the McCormick Bill. Some supporters of the Treasury plan attempted to sow public suspicion about the NBC's purposes and tried to win converts from among advocates for a congressional budget by claiming that the Good Bill was part of a corporate conspiracy to take over the national government. This idea had been raised at the House hearings by William H. Allen, a former codirector of the BMR who had resigned in 1914 to protest the BMR's association with John D. Rockefeller Jr. Referring to the NBC, Allen asserted that the Good Bill would put power "in the hands of a permanent nonpartisan organization of banking and business experts."[20]

During a press conference on Thanksgiving Day 1919, Senator McCormick elaborated on Allen's critique of the Good Bill as an opening wedge for corporate domination by adding a layer of antisemitic innuendo. "The truth," McCormick said, "is that when the original plan of the House bill was conceived, and before Mr. Good fathered it, it was the intention of the bill's progenitors to create the position of Director of the Budget, under the President, to be filled by Mr. Paul Warburg of New York."[21] Warburg, a director of the NBC, was of course one of the nation's most prominent Jewish investment bankers. In this age when open antisemitism was not uncommon in public life, the NBC's only response was to deny the senator's assertion that Warburg had ever been slated for the position of budget director.[22]

Even after this episode, Pratt and Strong remained open to compromise with Glass and McCormick. A budget bureau in the Treasury was better than no budget bureau, they reasoned, and they still hoped to capitalize on the president's avowed opposition to the existing congressional budget system. The McCormick Bill seemed like an opportunity to secure the support of fiscally conservative southern Democrats such as Glass, as well as that of western Republicans who were distrustful of their party's Wall Street wing. These were, after all, the groups that had killed the budget reforms proposed by the Taft Commission.

Woodrow Wilson's endorsement of the McCormick Bill in his annual address to Congress in December prompted the NBC to reconsider a compromise, with the directors holding a vote on which bill to support. A majority of the NBC board voted to stick with the Good Bill, with Pratt and Strong favoring the McCormick Bill. It is unclear whether Pratt and Strong really thought endorsing the McCormick Bill was a good idea in itself, or if they were simply trying to show Secretary Glass that they were making a genuine effort to convert their fellow board members.²³

The deliberations within the NBC continued even after the Senate hearings on the McCormick Bill adjourned in mid-January. The directors of the NBC prepared to reconsider the whole question again and agreed to employ a freelance researcher to investigate the situation on Capitol Hill. However, that report—written by William O. Heffernan, a Kentucky-born accountant with connections to supporters of the McCormick Bill—leaned heavily toward endorsing the McCormick Bill, drawing mainly on information provided by Charles Wallace Collins, that bill's author.²⁴

Collins seemed to use Heffernan's investigation as an opportunity to try to turn the directors of the NBC against Representative Good and the IGR. Heffernan relayed Collins's warning to the NBC that the Good Bill itself was not what it seemed. He argued that, although the bill appeared to call for an executive budget system, there were flaws in the bill that would make the system unworkable. And, he seemed to suggest, these flaws had been inserted purposefully. The directors responded to Collins's conspiracy theory with bafflement.

In 1920, Collins was a relatively unknown expert in banking regulations and administrative questions who often performed research for Carter Glass. An Alabama-born lawyer, Charles Wallace Collins would become prominent after World War II as a theorist of white supremacy.* His views on the proper relationship between federal power and local control were outlined most clearly in his 1947 book, *Whither Solid South? A Study in Politics and Race Relations*, where he inveighed against what he saw as the interrelated dangers of "state capitalism" and desegregation.²⁵

3

On February 1, 1920, Carter Glass resigned from the Treasury to take a seat in the Senate. Glass's replacement at Treasury was David Franklin Houston,

---

*Charles Wallace Collins's name might sound familiar to readers of the popular children's novel *A Wrinkle in Time*. Collins's niece Patricia was close friends with the author Madeleine L'Engle, who used "Charles Wallace" for the name of the younger brother of the book's protagonist. See Leonard S. Marcus, *Listening for Madeleine: A Portrait of Madeleine L'Engle in Many Voices* (New York: Farrar, Straus and Giroux, 2012), 35–38.

who had been Wilson's secretary of agriculture. Like the majority of Wilson's cabinet members, Houston also hailed from the South. Lacking Glass's connections in financial circles, Houston seems not to have continued Glass's efforts to maintain the administration's alliance with Senator McCormick or to cultivate the leaders of the NBC.

The willingness of John T. Pratt and Benjamin Strong to repeatedly entertain the idea of compromise with the Wilson administration seems to have stemmed largely from their relationship with Glass's primary deputy, Russell Leffingwell, who was a former associate at the Cravath law firm (and a future executive at the Morgan banking firm). However, where Glass had come to trust and rely on Leffingwell, the new Treasury secretary did not get along with Leffingwell. And, as Leffingwell's influence within the Wilson administration waned, the connection between the Treasury Department, Senator McCormick, and the NBC also weakened.[26]

The termination of the Treasury's influence campaign created space for the NBC to launch its own counteroffensive against the Wilson administration. The McCormick-Wilson alliance had been unstable to begin with, but with Glass's exit, Senator McCormick was now vulnerable to persuasion by the NBC. In January 1920, McCormick had told the NBC that reforming the audit system would be "too great a thing to undertake at present" and that this was a rationale for leaving the auditing function within the Treasury. To justify this assertion, McCormick told the NBC that Treasury Secretary Glass agreed with this assessment.[27]

By mid-February, however, with Glass gone from the Treasury, the NBC leaders were able to convince McCormick to shift his position on the issue of an independent auditing agency. McCormick dropped Glass's insistence on leaving the audit within the Treasury and revised his bill to instead provide for an independent auditing agency. The McCormick Bill still placed the Budget Bureau within the Treasury, but its provision for an independent audit now meant that both the House and Senate bills were in conflict with the preferences of the Wilson administration.[28]

In March 1920, the members of the NBC were faced with an awkward situation when they received a book manuscript that had been commissioned from Frederick A. Cleveland at the height of the NBC's wrangle with the Wilson administration. Viewed by many as an authority on budgeting and other administrative matters, Cleveland had been research director for the Taft Commission and had served as an interim director of the

IGR before its board selected William Willoughby to lead the new organization. Cleveland had not been directly involved in the movement for several years, but memories of his work with the Taft Commission meant that he was still viewed as a leading expert. More importantly, Cleveland was viewed with particular respect by Senator McCormick and Secretary Glass. However, while the leaders of the NBC had hoped when they commissioned Cleveland's manuscript that the book would help settle debate over which bill to support, the text delivered by Cleveland actually threatened to reopen the question as the new McCormick Bill neared passage in the Senate.[29]

The main problem was that Cleveland's text was sharply critical of the Good Bill. "One may read it time and again and still be in doubt as to what it does aim to accomplish," Cleveland wrote. Echoing Charles Wallace Collins's assessment, Cleveland questioned Representative Good's motives and dismissed the bill as "essentially a well-camouflaged legislative budget device." Cleveland focused his critique on the wording of several specific clauses and referred to "the framers of the bill" with disdain, which suggests he may have been motivated in part by his long professional rivalry with the Good Bill's author, William F. Willoughby.[30] It is not clear whether Cleveland himself had drafted a bill, but his generous assessment of the bill sponsored by Representative James A. Frear, Republican of Wisconsin, suggests that Cleveland may have had some role in its development. Regardless, the intensity of Cleveland's opposition to the Good Bill in early 1920 sits awkwardly with his initial assessment—provided to the directors of the NBC in June 1919—that the Good Bill was "a long step in the right direction," and it suggests that he had been influenced in the meantime by Glass.[31]

Forging ahead with publication, the NBC counterbalanced Cleveland's critique of the Good Bill by inserting several chapters on state and municipal government written by Arthur Eugene Buck, a researcher at the BMR in New York, and an introduction written by William Howard Taft.

In his introduction, Taft offered his own unequivocal support for the Good Bill. Drawing on his experience in office, Taft lamented the evils of the current system. "Except in the very early days of the Republic, when Hamilton, with his wonderful genius, was inaugurating the business side of our Government, we never had anything like a proper budget," Taft wrote.[32] He also dismissed the avowals of Treasury advocates that "the President has not the time" to manage the budget. "The preparation of the budget is going to be one of the most important functions that the whole Administration performs," Taft insisted. Noting that disputes were "certain to arise between his Budget Bureau and the departments whose estimates are to be subjected to a pruning," Taft argued that it was necessary to put the president in charge of this process in order to resolve such disputes. The president, the ex-president suggested, "can do it with his power—I doubt if the Secretary of the Treasury can."[33]

To smooth over the stark contrast between Cleveland's text and Taft's introduction, the NBC also included an editor's note, dated March 17, 1920, from the committee's research director, Samuel McCune Lindsay, explaining how the NBC finally resolved the question of which bill to support. "In the ranks of the National Budget Committee," Lindsay wrote, "there developed differences of opinion almost from the start concerning the relative merits of the proposals for a national budget system, especially with respect to the location of the budget bureau and the concentrating of responsibility for the initiation of the budget." Lindsay summarized the ex-president's position: "Mr. Taft is primarily interested in seeing executive responsibility fixed and strengthened and therefore naturally prefers the Good plan." And he dismissively summarized Cleveland's position: "Dr. Cleveland is so much attracted by other features of the McCormick plan . . . that he seems to prefer it as a whole." Finally, Lindsay outlined the new official position of the NBC, which he said was now in favor of "a combination of the two plans in a McCormick-Good bill, which may finally be enacted by Congress."[34]

Of course, McCormick had changed his bill's treatment of the auditing question while Cleveland was still writing his manuscript. The Senate approved the revised McCormick Bill on May 1, 1920, and, two days later, a conference committee began the three-week process of reconciling the conflicting Senate and House bills. The resulting compromise bill, produced on May 26, called for a budget bureau within the Department of the Treasury, as specified by the McCormick Bill, and matching the preference of the Wilson administration. It also called for an independent audit, following the recommendation of the Good Bill and the revised McCormick Bill but contrary to the preference of the Wilson administration. The conference committee's version of the bill was approved by the Senate on May 27, and by the House on May 29.[35]

Having spent more than half a year insisting that the audit must remain within the Treasury, leaders in the Wilson administration were predictably troubled by the bill's provision for an independent audit. In the days following passage in the House, as the bill sat on Wilson's desk, administration officials focused on this provision's apparent blurring of the separation of powers. The officers in charge of the independent audit, the comptroller general and assistant comptroller general, were to be appointed by the president, but were "removable only by concurrent resolution of Congress or by impeachment."[36]

This provided a pretext for Wilson to reject the bill. Over the course of two harried days near the end of the congressional session, administration officials composed a series of letters outlining their rationale for killing the bill. On June 2, four days after the bill was passed and only three days before Congress was scheduled to adjourn, the president's secretary formally asked Treasury Secretary Houston for his opinion on the budget bill. Houston, in his reply, pointed out the separation-of-powers issue and suggested that the attorney general review the constitutionality of this provision, which could be interpreted as an infringement on presidential prerogative.[37] After receiving the attorney general's reply, which stated that the act was "clearly unconstitutional," Houston wrote a veto message for Wilson, who returned the bill to Congress on June 4, the second-to-last day of the session.[38]

* * *

Advocates of budget reform insisted that Woodrow Wilson's veto reflected a mere technicality that could be easily resolved. But this glossed over the Wilson administration's long record of opposing the creation of an independent audit. Elite reformers such as Taft and Stimson viewed the independent audit as a source of real power and prerogative for the presidency, a view drawn from their understanding of corporate governance. An independent auditor's seal of approval strengthened the authority of a corporate CEO to enact the plans embodied in their organization's budget without interference from their board of directors. Similarly, having an independent, nonexecutive actor assess the president's actions would solidify the presidency in its role as administrator in chief and the legislature in its role as critic. The elite reformers viewed such a system as an essential prerequisite for carrying out national policy.

Wilson and his supporters framed the veto as a defense of executive prerogative and the result of the president's strict constitutionalist scruples. But Wilson's persistent opposition to an independent audit suggests that his actual motivation was to avoid limiting Congress's role to that of mere critic of a powerful executive. Similarly, Wilson's insistence that a budget bureau should be located within the Treasury seems to reflect his desire to preserve a congressional role in the budget process, maintaining a check on executive power. The NBC's business-derived vision of a presidential budget system with Congress confined to an oversight role clashed with Wilson's vision of collaboration between Treasury and Congress that would preserve openings where local elites could intervene to frustrate the implementation of national policy.[39]

Chapter Five

THE DARK HORSE
1920-1921

Wilson's veto was a setback for budget reform, but it helped to put the stakes of the 1920 election into relief. The National Budget Committee and its allies had come very close to achieving their objective. Passage of the budget bill by both the House and Senate in 1920 was an unqualified victory. If the NBC could help ensure that a supportive president was in the White House, there was nothing to stop the committee's eventual success.

Going into the Republican National Convention in 1920, delegates were split among three major candidates and several minor ones. Very few of the delegates gave any serious thought to the chances of the man who would eventually be crowned the party's nominee, Ohio senator Warren G. Harding. The elite reformers were initially disappointed with Harding's nomination, which carried more than a whiff of the smoke-filled room. However, to the surprise of many, as the campaign progressed, Harding proved himself to be an effective proponent of good government, combining an interest in administrative reform with advocacy for moderate progress on civil rights. After his victory in November, a crisis involving medical care for ex-servicemen came to underscore the need for central control and national authority.

THE DARK HORSE

1

On June 8, 1920, four days after Woodrow Wilson vetoed the budget bill, the Grand Old Party held its quadrennial gathering to choose its nominee for the presidency in Chicago. This was the fifth consecutive time the party had held its convention in the city, but any nostalgia delegates may have felt as they filed into the Chicago Coliseum was likely tempered by memories of the fiasco of 1912, when the party split after ex-president Theodore Roosevelt's unsuccessful challenge to the incumbent, President William Howard Taft. In 1916, party leaders had tried to strike a conciliatory tone, from the platitudinous keynote delivered by the relatively unknown Senator Harding to the selection of the ideologically ambiguous Charles Evans Hughes as the party's nominee. Yet in 1920, with Wilson on his way out of office and a Republican victory in the presidential race seemingly within reach, the old schism between "insurgent" progressive and "stand-pat" conservative Republicans threatened to reopen.

In the months leading up to the convention, the race for the Republican presidential nomination had developed into a three-way contest between California senator Hiram W. Johnson, Illinois governor Frank O. Lowden, and Major General Leonard Wood. Lowden was a favorite of the conservatives, while Johnson and Wood sought the support of progressives. The latter two both claimed heirship to the legacy of Theodore Roosevelt: Johnson as the vice presidential nominee for the Bull Moose Party in 1912; Wood as the commanding officer of the Rough Riders.[1]

However, the issues at hand in 1920 cut across the old battle lines between progressive and conservative Republicans. On the question of whether the United States should join the League of Nations, the two progressive candidates were at odds. Johnson was a leading "Irreconcilable" opposed to joining the league on any terms, while Wood joined the conservative Lowden in the "Reservationist" camp—both thought that the United States should join the league if certain conditions were met. On the issue of the budget, Wood followed the lead of his campaign adviser, Henry Stimson, and supported the Good Bill and a presidential budget system. In contrast, the conservative Lowden and the progressive Johnson both favored the McCormick Bill and a Treasury budget system.[2]

The reshuffling of internal debates within the Republican Party after 1912 was perhaps most dramatic on the issue of civil rights. As the National

Conference on Lynching had illustrated in 1919, the power of the "Tuskegee Machine" had waned, and "accommodation" was no longer the watchword for those who sought leadership positions in the party. However, none of the three frontrunners had distinguished themselves on issues relating to civil rights.

Early in 1920, the NAACP had sent questionnaires to "17 men mentioned for the presidency," soliciting their opinions on seven issues of concern to its membership: lynching, "Jim Crow" railcars, disfranchisement, U.S. policy toward Haiti, national aid to African American common schools, the status of African American army officers, and segregation of the civil service. By the time of the convention, only three candidates had replied. "Fourteen gentlemen have announced by their silence that they have no convictions or policy toward the greatest social problem facing America," W. E. B. Du Bois wrote in the convention-eve edition of the *Crisis*. "We will forget these gentlemen neither in our prayers nor in our votes." Of the three candidates who did reply, Senator Miles Poindexter, Republican of Washington State, made the most forceful statement, affirming that he was "in favor of maintaining the legal rights and opportunities of all our citizens, regardless of color or condition." Leonard Wood replied "only to statements of his reported attitude toward colored army officers," saying, "The reports concerning colored officers are not true." The third candidate to respond was Senator Warren G. Harding. While Harding demurred from a definite statement on any of the NAACP's questions, Du Bois reported the candidate's affirmation "that he would stand on the party platform."[3]

Entering politics after a successful career as an editor and publisher in Ohio, Warren G. Harding was endowed with a newspaperman's flair for alliteration and wordplay. As a mainstay on the northeastern lecture circuit in the 1910s, it was Harding who coined the term "founding fathers" to refer to the framers of the Constitution.[4] (Harding himself was an ardent admirer of Alexander Hamilton.) "Normalcy," the word perhaps most closely associated with Harding's career, was introduced in a speech titled "Back to Normal," given by Harding less than a month before the convention and reprinted in a collection published by the Republican Party after his nomination. The word appears a quarter of the way through a sentence that strung together a sonorous series of eight alliterative pairings:

America's present need is not heroics, but healing; not nostrums, but normalcy; not revolution, but restoration; not agitation, but adjustment; not surgery, but serenity; not the dramatic, but the dispassionate; not experiment, but equipoise; not submergence in internationality, but sustainment in triumphant nationality.[5]

Harding's relative obscurity in 1920 meant that he had not yet offended any of the major factions within the party, and his crowd-pleasing-but-evasive manner of speaking meant that few had any idea of his stand on most issues. It was this cypher-like quality, combined with his statesman-like bearing, that led party leaders to see Harding as the ideal candidate to bridge the old schism between the "regulars" and "insurgents." As the three-way race between Johnson, Lowden, and Wood remained deadlocked at the Republican National Convention, and as leaders began to cast around for a compromise candidate, the Ohio senator's name quickly rose to consideration. When the delegates cast their tenth ballot, on June 12, Harding secured the presidential nomination.[6]

2

The Republican platform in 1920, as it turned out, included a strong statement against lynching, drafted by a committee led by Herbert Parsons, a Wall Street lawyer and close ally of Henry Stimson. "We urge Congress to consider the most effective means to end lynching in this country, which continues to be a terrible blot on our American civilization." The first five words of this sentence—"We urge Congress to consider"—were the most important, as they signaled party leaders' support for congressional action.[7]

And, after securing the nomination, Warren G. Harding did in fact "stand on the party platform," as he had promised the NAACP before the convention. In his acceptance speech at the convention, among his list of "specific proposals," Harding declared,

> I believe the federal government should stamp out lynching and remove that stain from the fair name of America. I believe the Negro citizens of America should be guaranteed the enjoyment of all their rights, that they have earned the full measure of citizenship bestowed, that their sacrifices in blood

on the battlefields of the republic have entitled them to all of freedom and opportunity, all of sympathy and aid that the American spirit of fairness and justice demands.[8]

The opening phrase of this declaration—"I believe the federal government should"—was unprecedented for a major-party nominee.

Harding's statements on lynching and African American civil rights provoked a range of responses. The leaders of the NAACP, justifiably cautious after their endorsement of Woodrow Wilson in 1912, remained skeptical in the absence of further details about Harding's plans—especially since the candidate was a relative newcomer to the national stage. "Neither candidate is a friend of the Negro nor of democracy," a post-convention analysis in the *Crisis* explained. "Neither convention was fair to us. The Democratic platform said nothing that favored us; the Republican made a half-hearted remark on lynching. We are, therefore, under no obligations."[9]

White southerners were alarmed by what they heard from the Republicans. Arkansas governor Charles H. Brough (pronounced "Bruff") explained the dangers of a Harding presidency in a circular letter to his fellow southern governors in mid-September:

> On my arrival in Columbus, Ohio, in connection with the speaking tour through Ohio and the Middle West, I was astonished to learn . . . that a negro journal, the *Toledo Pioneer*, (copy of which is enclosed) is urging race equality and urging the negroes to unite at the polls.
>
> This, of course, strikes at the very heart of *White Supremacy*, and it is current knowledge here in the Middle West that if Senator Harding and the Republicans triumph, an effort will be made to pass a Force Bill, which will mean Federal bayonets to supervise Southern elections . . .
>
> This Presidential election means everything to the South and I urge you as a high-minded and splendid representative of your great commonwealth to become active in explaining to your people just what Senator Harding's triumph would mean in robbing the South of her most cherished birthright, Anglo-Saxon supremacy.
>
> You will remember that Senator Henry Cabot Lodge introduced the Force Bill in the House of Representatives in 1889 and secured its passage in that body, but it was defeated in the Senate by the filibuster of great Southern and some fair minded Western Senators.

Please urge the Democracy of your State to be thoroughly alive as to the seriousness of the situation.[10]

Harding's statements also provoked a revival of old rumors about his family tree. A Democratic operative from Ohio produced a one-page flyer that was widely distributed throughout the southern and border states. The flyer showed a Harding pedigree chart with the candidate's father, George Tryon Harding, listed as a "mulatto" and his grandfather, Charles A. Harding, listed as "Black." The Democratic candidate for the presidency, Ohio governor James M. Cox, did his part to spread the rumor. A longtime newspaperman in Dayton, Ohio (about ninety miles from Harding's hometown of Marion), Cox was familiar with the rumors about the Harding family. Cox told an official in West Virginia that "either the grandmother or great grandmother of Senator Harding was a Negress."[11]

The Republican National Committee responded by distributing copies of Harding's official genealogy, emphasizing the candidate's descent from seventeenth-century Puritans. In the weeks after the Chicago convention, Harding hastily completed and submitted an application for membership in the Ohio chapter of the Society of the Sons of the American Revolution, the male adjunct of the Daughters of the American Revolution, based on his descent from Abraham Harding Jr., who had been a second lieutenant in the New York militia in 1778.[12]

The air of scandal surrounding Harding's presidency has long dominated assessments of his career. This was in part the candidate's own doing, as there were plenty of scandals in both his private and professional life.* His rhetorical style didn't help matters either. He tended to string together a succession of agreeable phrases devoid of any definite meaning. Harding liked to call it "bloviation"—a nineteenth-century word that he helped to repopularize in the 1920s.[13]

---

*Recent DNA evidence has shown that he did, in fact, father a child with one of his mistresses. The same DNA test revealed no evidence of African ancestry. See Peter Baker, "DNA Is Said to Solve a Mystery of Warren Harding's Love Life," *New York Times*, August 12, 2015, and "DNA Shows Warren Harding Wasn't America's First Black President," *New York Times*, August 18, 2015.

Although Harding seemed to speak and act like a creature of the party bosses, this masked what turned out to be a firm commitment to the goals of the elite reformers. Shortly before the election, Harding adopted a mellifluous catchphrase that would encapsulate the policy agenda of his administration: "less government in business and more business in government." This was actually a slightly revised version of a motto that John T. Pratt had tried to popularize through the National Budget Committee, although Harding substituted "government" where Pratt had used "politics."[14]

Harding's adoption of this slogan was a sign of his effort to endear himself to the elite reformers. The candidate spent the late summer of 1920 in consultation and negotiation with leaders from the party's Wall Street wing, and he received weekly tutoring in governmental theory from NBC research director Samuel McCune Lindsay, who was also serving as policy advisor for the Republican National Committee. Near the end of August, Harding met with NBC president Pratt and assured him that, if elected, he would support the NBC's budget reform and executive reorganization proposals. Harding's first use of the "less government in business and more business in government" phrase came weeks later, as the title of an article that appeared under the candidate's own signature in the election-eve edition of the *World's Work*—intended as a signal that a Harding administration would pursue the agenda of the elite reformers. The article itself was filled with the sort of banal blandishments that exasperated Harding's critics, but among the few clear statements in the text was Harding's pledge to enact a national budget system.[15]

As the election approached, a number of prominent Republicans became alarmed over Harding's dissembling vacillations about U.S. membership in the League of Nations, and they publicly endorsed the Democratic candidate, James Cox. Worried that this might put the election—and their administrative reform agenda—at risk, a group of thirty-one leading Republican elite reformers signed a statement affirming their support for Harding on October 14, 1920. "The statement," the *New York Times* noted, "is signed by nearly every prominent Republican who has been considered friend to the [League of Nations], except ex-President William H. Taft, who has already indicated his intention of supporting Senator Harding."[16]

The group, known as the "Thirty-One," included Elihu Root, Charles Evans Hughes, Henry Stimson, Nicholas Murray Butler, Paul Cravath, Samuel McCune Lindsay, William F. Willoughby, George Wickersham,

Herbert Hoover, and Henry W. Taft. Harding's evident commitment to the agenda favored by these men on issues such as budget reform, executive reorganization, and antilynching seems to explain why they were willing to attest to Harding's commitment to the League of Nations when there was clear evidence that he would abandon the league if it became politically expedient to do so. The prospect of having a champion for many of their causes in the White House made them willing to take a risk on the question of the League of Nations.

The result of the November 2 presidential election was a dramatic victory for the Republicans. In the Electoral College, Harding won every state in the North and West, plus the border states of Oklahoma, Missouri, West Virginia, Maryland, and Delaware—and he secured an unprecedented southern win for the Republicans in Tennessee. GOP majorities increased dramatically in both the House and Senate.[17]

In an era before modern polling methods, and when the idea of "public opinion" had yet to be fully theorized, the meaning of the election results was open to dispute. Various advocacy groups debated whether the Nineteenth Amendment—ratified on August 18, 1920—had benefited one cause or another. Notably, opposition to woman suffrage had been strongest in the Jim Crow South. Each of the eight states that had voted to reject the amendment required segregation of education: Alabama, Delaware, Georgia, Louisiana, Maryland, Mississippi, South Carolina, and Virginia. However, despite the hopes of many activists, enfranchised white women did not vote as a bloc, and ratification of the Nineteenth Amendment did not have a measurable impact on the election.[18]

For their part, the elite reformers confidently viewed the Republican landslide in November 1920 as a solid mandate for enacting their agenda. With the prospect of an unequivocal proponent in the presidency, and solid Republican majorities in Congress, the elite reformers prepared to spring into action to enact budget reform, executive reorganization, and antilynching after Harding's inauguration. In the meantime, however, their attention was diverted by another pressing policy emergency.

3

The United States' relatively sudden entrance into World War I meant that plans for assisting veterans and their dependents were made in haste, and the equally sudden end to the war meant that policy makers had little time to improve or refine these plans. One result was that responsibility for the provision of benefits for veterans in 1920 was haphazardly divided among three agencies. The newly created War Risk Insurance Bureau (part of the Treasury Department) administered a social insurance program. The Rehabilitation Division of the Federal Board for Vocational Education (an independent agency) provided vocational training and prosthetics. The U.S. Public Health Service (also part of the Treasury Department) ran veterans hospitals. As a researcher for the Institute for Government Research observed, "the administration of these services" by these three agencies "constituted one of the most complicated and difficult tasks ever undertaken by the Federal Government."[19]

This dispersal of authority was partly by design. Democrats during the war had purposefully created an arrangement that would bypass the existing pension system, which had been created after the Civil War and had been closely identified with the Republican Party and blighted by scandal.[20] In October 1917, Sam Rayburn—then in his third term as a Democratic representative from Texas—introduced the bill creating this new system. In debate on the House floor, Rayburn touted the advantages that would accrue from this new, separate benefits system for veterans of the world war. Chief among these was the system's planned automatic destruction. After the death of the last beneficiary, Rayburn explained, the new system would cease to exist.[21]

Once this system was put into action, however, veterans who required services from two or three of the responsible agencies faced considerable delays in receiving needed treatment. Outrage over this arrangement grew steadily after the war, finally erupting into crisis during the winter months between Harding's election and inauguration after a series of exposés in the popular press and extended hearings in Congress.

The disorganized tangle of national veterans agencies quickly became a target for the elite reformers, who characteristically viewed the problem through an organizational lens. Earlier in 1920, Henry Stimson had added to his list of commitments by assuming the chairmanship of a new organization: the Joint Committee for Aid to Disabled Veterans. This was—like the NBC—a well-connected group. Among the members of its executive committee were Edward C. Delafield, president of Bank of America; Franklin K. Lane, former commissioner of interstate commerce (under Taft) and secretary of the interior (under Wilson); and Arthur W. Page, editor of the *World's Work*.[22]

The committee's stated mission was "to help discharge the Nation's debt to its disabled veterans." To this end, the group lobbied legislators and administrators, but this put the genteel committee members in an awkward position. To avoid what they viewed as the overly moralistic tone of most social reformers, the committee adopted a general policy to avoid attributing ill intent to policy makers, even when complaining about policies that were harming veterans. Stimson's mild message to a New York State senator was typical: "I have been tremendously impressed at the real neglect and suffering which the disabled men have been going through at the hands of their government in spite of the best intentions in the world."[23]

The committee's activities ranged from lobbying to fact-finding. In cooperation with the Rockefeller-funded National Committee for Mental Hygiene and the National Tuberculosis Association, they conducted a survey "to determine the number of existing buildings suitable for conversion into hospitals for the treatment and care of the patients of the Bureau of War Risk Insurance."[24] When, in September 1920, the comptroller of the Treasury changed his interpretation of the Rehabilitation Act and began requiring veterans to pay the cost of services from the Federal Board of Vocational Education, the Joint Committee for Aid to Disabled Veterans successfully petitioned the comptroller to resume the established policy of having the federal government pay for such services.[25]

The joint committee's concern for effective and efficient provision of services to veterans, as well as its focus on untangling the disorderly jumble of veterans agencies, was shared by other elite organizations. An NBC pamphlet suggested a solution that struck most of the elite reformers as obvious:

> It hardly requires more than a superficial knowledge of these arrangements to convince the most casual observer of the necessity of taking action to concentrate in a single department, so far as practicable, all those services which deal with the several aspects of the general problem of affording compensation or relief to ex-service men.[26]

At congressional hearings in early January 1921, the psychiatrist Thomas Salmon testified about the impact that delayed and substandard care could have on veterans.[27] Salmon was a professor at Columbia University and had served as chief of the Psychiatric Service of the American Expeditionary Forces during the war. As medical adviser to the Rockefeller Foundation's National Committee for Mental Hygiene, he had assisted Stimson's joint committee in conducting its hospital survey. In his congressional testimony, Salmon warned that "unless something is done within the present year to improve conditions under which insane ex-service men are receiving treatment, hundreds, who now stand a fair chance of being cured, will be doomed to permanent insanity."[28]

Three weeks later, Salmon penned a dramatic article for the *American Legion Weekly*. He noted that, as of December 1920, there had been more than 5,500 psychiatric patients hospitalized in the care of the Bureau of War Risk Insurance and that "at least as many men with mental disorders remain in their homes, losing time of the utmost value to them." Drawing on the data collected by the joint committee, Salmon explained that there were only four existing government-run hospitals capable of serving psychiatric patients. The problem, he argued, was that "the Government has not yet provided a single neuro-psychiatric hospital which surpasses in standards of scientific work some of the Army neuro-psychiatric hospitals a few miles behind the firing line in France."[29]

Based on Salmon's report, the American Legion made two requests of Congress: "Money for the building of adequate hospitals" and "coordination of the bureaus responsible for the care of the disabled."[30]

On the final day of his presidency, March 4, 1921, Woodrow Wilson signed into law an act appropriating $18.6 million for the construction of new veterans hospitals and authorizing the incoming Treasury secretary, Andrew W. Mellon, to convene a committee of experts to study the problem of veteran hospitalization.[31]

4

That committee—which would be known as the "Consultants on Hospitalization"—was assembled on March 16, in the second week of Harding's presidency. To fill the position of chairman, Mellon selected Dr. William Charles White, an expert on tuberculosis from the secretary's hometown of Pittsburgh. Mellon and White had been acquainted before the war, when White had worked with the Mellon Institute on its investigation of the health effects of smoke and soot.[32]

Aided by an eight-member advisory committee chaired by Thomas Salmon, the consultants immediately began compiling information about the problem of hospitalization for veterans. As if to illustrate their commitment to the elite reformers' ideal of organizational efficiency, their first order of business was to create organizational charts showing what they felt would be the ideal structure for the administration of veterans services.[33] These charts, which envisioned the consolidation of existing veterans agencies under a single, unified agency, echoed the NBC's recommendations and embodied the consultants' feeling "that in order to get adequate and proper care for the disabled men a centralization of authority, if it could be brought about, would materially assist in establishing a broad Federal hospital program."[34]

The organizational charts were completed in less than three weeks and were available for use on April 5, 1921, by another committee, which President Harding had appointed one week after Treasury Secretary Mellon assembled the Consultants on Hospitalization. This second committee was meant to develop legislation that would enact the first committee's recommendations. It became known as the Dawes Committee, after its chairman, Chicago banker General Charles G. Dawes. The committee included a son and sister of the recently deceased Theodore Roosevelt, two representatives of the American Legion, several prominent businessmen, and two anticommunist labor leaders.[35]

Although Dawes hailed from Chicago, he was well-known in the northeastern business community. He had grown close to the Morgan banker Thomas Lamont in the years before the United States joined the war in Europe, after Dawes's bank provided crucial support for the Morgan-led effort to fund the Allied governments. As Lamont later recalled, "the Central Trust Company under Charles G. Dawes as President, was the only institution in Chicago that had the courage to come out for the Anglo-French Loan." In Europe during the war, where General Dawes was in charge of the purchase and distribution of supplies for the American Expeditionary Forces, Lamont and Dawes met each morning for breakfast at the Ritz Hotel in Paris. A pianist and composer, Dawes wrote the melody for the popular song "It's All in the Game." He was also renowned for his use of coarse language and, after some particularly spirited congressional testimony after the war, he acquired the nickname "General Hell 'n' Maria."[36]

The Dawes Committee issued its report on April 7, just two days after its first meeting. This report recommended creating a new, unified veterans agency, largely following the outlines of the consultants' organizational charts. The committee altered the consultants' plan slightly, however, by making the new agency an independent bureau whose chief would report directly to the president rather than to the Treasury secretary, as the consultants had suggested. Dawes himself recommended this change after securing Harding's agreement, and it reflected the prevailing view among reformers that the Department of the Treasury already had too many nonfinancial functions within its domain. As part of his effort to obtain the American Legion's endorsement of the plan, Dawes explained the rationale behind this decision to a Legion commander in Chicago: "The great thing our committee contended for was the consolidation of the present uncoordinated services under a directing authority."[37]

The report of the Dawes Committee makes clear that its members viewed the question of how best to provide services for veterans primarily as a question of administrative organization. "It cannot be too strongly emphasized that the present deplorable failure on the part of the government to properly care for the disabled veterans is due in large part to an imperfect organization of governmental effort," Dawes wrote. "There is no one in control of the whole situation." While Dawes acknowledged that there had been some informal cooperation between agencies, he lamented that "in such efforts the joint action is too often modified by minor considerations, and there is always lacking that complete cooperation which is incident to a powerful superimposed authority."[38]

* * *

Since the Consultants on Hospitalization were in the early stages of their investigations and had only drafted preliminary plans (their final report would not be published until 1923), the Dawes report was silent on the details of medical care. The Dawes Committee and the Consultants on Hospitalization treated organizational questions as an emergency to be solved immediately, and they left medical questions for an extended investigation. Proper medical staffing and treatment were simply technicalities to be worked out by experts after Dawes's "powerful superimposed authority" had been established. This sensibility was shared even among medical experts such as William Charles White and Thomas Salmon, who also emphasized the general problem of poor administration, lack of coordination, and inefficiency.

The House Committee on Interstate and Foreign Commerce held hearings on the recommendations of the Dawes Committee and the Consultants on Hospitalization in late April 1921. Representative Sam Rayburn asked Ewing Laporte, assistant secretary of the Treasury in charge of war risk insurance and public health, to assess the two options under consideration: a proposal to consolidate veterans activities into a single agency under the secretary of the Treasury (as recommended by the Consultants on Hospitalization), or the proposal to consolidate veterans activities into a single agency reporting directly to the president (as recommended by the Dawes Committee). Laporte was a holdover from the Wilson administration, but he was also a Pittsburgh lawyer with close ties to Secretary Mellon. (In later years he would be Mellon's tax consultant.) Laporte told Rayburn that either proposal would be acceptable. "I do not think it makes very much difference," he said. Whether the new agency reported to the secretary of the Treasury or directly to the president, Laporte explained, "the important thing—consolidation—is accomplished by both."[39]

Chapter Six

EARLY SUCCESS

Spring and Summer 1921

After eight frustrating years of evasion, delay, and compromise under Woodrow Wilson, the bold action taken by the Dawes Committee raised hopes for the elite reformers. The first months of Warren G. Harding's presidency unfolded in a flurry of activity. Harding succeeded in enacting budget reform, and he secured passage of the Dawes Committee recommendations for consolidating the veterans agencies. He also began laying the foundations for bold action on executive reorganization and antilynching.

1

On April 12, 1921, a little over a month after he took office and five days after the Dawes Committee issued its report, Warren G. Harding delivered a speech before a joint meeting of Congress in which he carefully outlined the agenda for his presidency. Press accounts focused on Harding's statements against U.S. membership in the League of Nations. However, those comments came at the end of a long speech detailing the president's plans on a dozen other topics. A close reading of the speech reveals the depth of Harding's commitment to the elite reformers' vision of increased central power and national authority in government.[1]

After introductory remarks, Harding began by affirming his dedication to the elite reformers' keystone proposal: budget reform. "I know of no more pressing problem," the president said.[2] After a brief rehearsal of the traditional Republican defense of a protective tariff, Harding segued to his third priority: executive reorganization. Harding described his vision for improving administrative efficiency by streamlining the hodgepodge arrangement of federal agencies and bureaus in terms appropriate for the business-friendly postwar era. "A very important matter," he said, "is the establishment of the Government's business on a business basis."[3]

After a brief call for limits on business regulation—while also acknowledging legitimate fields for regulation—Harding transitioned to the topic of federal aid to states for transportation. He inveighed against no-strings-attached federal block grants to states, an idea that had gained popularity during the Wilson years. Harding acknowledged that "the Federal Government can place no inhibition on the expenditure in the several States." But he argued that the federal government had a natural interest in supervising the expenditure of federal funds in the states. "Since Congress has embarked upon a policy of assisting the States in highway improvement, wisely, I believe, it can assert a wholly becoming influence in shaping policy." He amplified this statement with a forceful defense of federal power:

> Large Federal outlay demands a Federal voice in the program of expenditure. Congress can not justify a mere gift from the Federal purse to the several States, to be prorated among counties for road betterment. Such a course will invite abuses which it were better to guard against in the beginning.
>
> The laws governing Federal aid should be amended and strengthened. The Federal agency of administration should be elevated to the importance and vested with authority comparable to the work before it. And Congress ought to prescribe conditions to Federal appropriations which will necessitate a consistent program of uniformity which will justify the Federal outlay.[4]

Harding also addressed recent technological advances in radio and air travel. The first commercial radio stations had begun broadcasting during the previous year, and commercial airlines had emerged as well. These advances, he argued, warranted increased federal regulation, and he explained that a lack of federal action would actually hinder the ability of businessmen to exploit these new technologies. "Practical experience demonstrates the need for effective regulation of both domestic and international radio operation if this newer means of intercommunication is to be fully utilized," Harding said, adding moments later that "it has become a pressing duty of the Federal Government to provide for the regulation of air navigation; otherwise independent and conflicting legislation will be enacted by the various States which will hamper the development of aviation."[5]

Turning to veterans issues, Harding endorsed the recommendations of the Dawes Committee. "This committee has recommended, and I convey the recommendations to you with cordial approval, that all Government agencies looking to the welfare of the ex-service men should be placed under one directing head, so that the welfare of these disabled saviors of our civilization and freedom may have the most efficient direction."[6]

This provided a natural transition to Harding's recommendation to consolidate the government's various welfare agencies into a single federal department of welfare. Harding commended existing government action on social issues "in the realms of education, public health, sanitation, conditions of workers in industry, child welfare, proper amusement and recreation, the elimination of social vice." He endorsed the enactment of the Sheppard-Towner Bill—a bipartisan proposal to provide medical assistance to mothers and children in order to reduce infant mortality. The bill had passed the Senate in December 1920 but had not yet come to a vote in the House. Explaining his rationale for creating a federal department of welfare, Harding noted that "these undertakings have been scattered through many departments and bureaus without coordination and with much overlapping of functions which fritters energies and magnifies the cost." Harding then made clear that his goal in consolidating these functions was not merely to save money, but to increase the effectiveness and impact of federal action. That is, he viewed the frittering away of energy as more worrisome than the magnifying cost. "To bring these various activities together in a single department, where the whole field could be surveyed, and where their interrelationships could be properly appraised, would make for increased effectiveness, economy, and intelligence of direction."[7]

Before concluding with his statement rejecting U.S. membership in the League of Nations—the remarks that drew the most attention from news reporters—Harding drew applause from the chamber by raising the subject of antilynching legislation. "Congress ought to wipe the stain of barbaric lynching from the banners of a free and orderly, representative democracy," he said.⁸ This contrasted with Wilson's statements against lynching in 1918, which had urged action from state leaders, local communities, and individual citizens rather than from Congress. After further musings on the "race question," Harding endorsed a proposal to create "a commission embracing representatives of both races, to study and report on the entire subject."⁹

If the elite reformers had any lingering doubts about Harding's commitment to their agenda, those doubts were swept away by this speech. A *New York Times* analysis identified the general theme of the speech in a subheading claiming that Harding had "Assert[ed] Executive Prerogative."¹⁰ Later that day, Robert S. Brookings, the St. Louis industrialist and chairman of the Institute for Government Research, wrote to John D. Rockefeller Jr. about the prospects for enacting executive reorganization under the Harding administration. "As you have probably noticed from the President's statements," Brookings wrote to Rockefeller, "although the detail will probably take several years to work out, our ultimate success seems to be within sight."¹¹

Civil rights advocates were also encouraged by Harding's remarks. W. E. B. Du Bois applauded the speech in the *Crisis*: "This is the strongest pronouncement on the race problem ever made by a President in a message to Congress," Du Bois wrote. "It offers hope that during this Administration we will not need to spend all of our efforts in protest and opposition, but that we shall be able to put through some constructive work and measures."¹²

One reason for Du Bois's uncharacteristically hopeful tone was that Harding's speech came just one day after the reintroduction in the House of an antilynching bill sponsored by Representative Leonidas Dyer, Republican of Missouri. In Dyer's congressional district in St. Louis, 12 percent of the voters were African American. Many of Dyer's constituents had moved into the district after the East St. Louis atrocity of July 1917. Dyer cited his own outrage at the violence of those riots as his chief motivation for sponsoring the antilynching bill. He had first introduced it in April 1918, and reintroduced it in May 1919, but it had never been brought to a vote. In 1921, however, with solid Republican majorities in both houses, and a president who was evidently committed to its passage, prospects for the Dyer bill seemed strong.¹³

Another reason for optimism was that by early 1921 the NAACP had developed an argument for the constitutionality of the antilynching bill. Several commentators had argued that the bill granted to the federal government police powers that were constitutionally reserved to state and local governments. NAACP president Moorfield Storey had initially been reluctant to back Dyer's bill because he feared that it was vulnerable on those grounds.[14]

Storey, by this point in his eighth decade, had been in his younger days one of the original "Mugwumps" who left the Republican Party to support the Democratic candidate Grover Cleveland in 1884. In addition to his work on civil rights, he had been active throughout his career in causes such as anti-imperialism and civil service reform. A well-respected Boston lawyer and a former president of the American Bar Association, Storey had cultivated long-standing friendships with other leaders of the bar. During the two years following the 1919 National Conference on Lynching, Storey consulted with several jurists about the constitutionality of the Dyer Bill. These consultations culminated in an intense back-and-forth with former attorney general George Wickersham during the first three months of 1921. By the end of March, although Wickersham still worried that a majority of the Supreme Court would disagree, Storey was convinced that the problem of lynching warranted an expansive interpretation of the Fourteenth Amendment, and that under such and interpretation the bill was indeed constitutional.[15]

Not long after Harding's address to Congress, the resolve to take action against lynching increased still further after perhaps the worst massacre of African Americans in U.S. history. As is usually the case, the details of the incident that sparked the violence are unclear. On Monday, May 30, 1921, a young Black shoe shiner named Dick Rowland stepped into an elevator in the Drexel Building in downtown Tulsa, Oklahoma. As he did so, he apparently trod on the foot of the white elevator operator, Sarah Page. Within twenty-four hours, Rowland was being held in the Tulsa County Courthouse, charged with raping Page. On the evening of Tuesday, May 31, alerted by the *Tulsa Tribune*, whites began to gather outside of the courthouse. News of the gathering mob quickly reached residents of the nearby Greenwood District, a prosperous neighborhood home to more than ten thousand Black citizens. A group of about seventy-five armed African American men, many of them veterans of the world war, went to the courthouse and offered to help protect Rowland. The sheriff declined their offer, and as they began to return to Greenwood, a member of the white mob attempted to disarm one of the African Americans. A shot was fired and the white mob erupted in violence. As Tuesday evening turned into Wednesday morning, thousands of armed whites—including uniformed police—rampaged through Greenwood, burning, shooting, and looting as armed African Americans attempted to defend their homes.[16]

By 9:00 a.m. on Wednesday, June 1, the white mob had burned the entire neighborhood to the ground, killing between one hundred and three hundred African Americans. Northern reformers were horrified at the news. Greenwood was widely admired as a relatively wealthy Black neighborhood known as the "Negro Wall Street."

While some northern politicians credulously repeated Tulsa officials' claims that the massacre was the fault of "radical" Blacks, President Harding gave an indication of his own sympathies on Monday, June 6, one week after the initial incident in Tulsa. On that day, Harding was scheduled to make a morning drive to Washington, D.C., returning from a "pilgrimage" to Valley Forge in Pennsylvania. The president and First Lady had spent the weekend at the farmhouse of Republican senator Philander C. Knox, which was located less than a mile from the house where George Washington had set up his headquarters during the winter of 1777–1778. As the four cars in presidential procession headed south, Harding made an unscheduled stop to give an extemporaneous commencement address at Lincoln University, a historically Black college in southeastern Pennsylvania, about twenty-five miles west of Wilmington, Delaware.

In his remarks, Harding praised the assembled graduates, alumni, and faculty. "It is a very great pleasure to stop here for a few moments to offer a word of greeting to such an institution on such an occasion," Harding said. "The colored citizens of America in the World War earned the right to be memorialized. I am glad to pay tribute to an educational institution like this one." At the end of his remarks Harding addressed the news from Tulsa. Notably, the president gave no credence to the version of events favored by leaders in Oklahoma:

> The colored race, in order to come into its own, must do the great work itself, in preparing for that participation. Nothing will accomplish so much as educational preparation. I commend the valuable work which this institution is

doing in that direction. It is a fine contrast to the unhappy and distressing spectacle that we saw the other day out in one of the Western States. God grant that, in the soberness, the fairness and the justice of this country, we shall never have another spectacle like it.[17]

2

While administration officials and NAACP leaders worked to devise their strategy for advancing the Dyer Bill, Harding took quick action on the budget question. In May 1921, the House again passed the Good Bill, the Senate again passed the McCormick bill, and the competing budget bills were sent, once again, to a conference committee, which once again produced a compromise bill.

The conflict that marked the budget debate in late 1919 and early 1920 was largely absent this time around. After Wilson's veto—and after the national debt continued its alarming rise—proponents of the competing bills focused on cooperating to ensure that the bills would pass again to be signed by the new president. To this end, advocates of the McCormick Bill joined forces with the National Budget Committee. McCormick himself joined the NBC's board of directors.[18] Charles Wallace Collins— the author of the McCormick Bill who had attacked the Good Bill on behalf of McCormick and Carter Glass in late 1919 and early 1920—was employed in 1921 producing research reports for Representative Good.[19]

The new budget bill that reached Harding's desk in June 1921 differed from the one passed the previous year in two ways. First, in repudiation of Wilson's rationale for his veto, the new bill actually made the new comptroller general even harder to remove. It provided that officer with a fifteen-year term, with removal possible only through a joint resolution of Congress. Second, the new bill clarified the lines of responsibility between the president and the Budget Bureau. The 1920 version had made the secretary of the Treasury the director of the budget, to be supported by an assistant director of the budget, leaving it up to the president to decide which of these two officers should exercise actual authority. The new version also specified that the director of the Budget Bureau would in fact be the director of the budget, and it made the director responsible directly to the president, thus bypassing the secretary of the Treasury entirely.[20]

On June 9, 1921, the day before signing the Budget and Accounting Act, Harding offered the job of director of the budget to Charles Dawes. The general had been Harding's initial choice for the position of Treasury secretary. Back in January, a day after declining the president-elect's Treasury offer, Dawes had written again to say that he would be "willing to help if you want me in your efforts to unify our government business system," and that he would be open "even to accepting some subordinate position in any organization which you might call into being in this effort."[21] Upon offering Dawes the budget directorship in June, Harding told the general that the budget post was the most significant office in the administration and "probably the most important appointment I am to be called upon to make." Dawes accepted Harding's offer on the condition that he serve for only one year.[22]

Although the provisions of the Budget and Accounting Act did not officially take effect until fiscal year 1923, Harding and Dawes decided to proceed as if the law had become operative immediately. They quickly set about strengthening the position of the Budget Bureau as a presidential staff agency. Harding signed nine executive orders creating new offices devised by Dawes to provide what he called "coordinating machinery" to facilitate the work of the bureau. These new offices included the Federal Purchasing Board, the Federal Liquidation Board, the corps area coordinators, the Federal Real Estate Board, the federal motor transport agent, the Federal Traffic Board, the Federal Board of Hospitalization, the Federal Specialization Board, and the Interdepartmental Board of Contracts.[23] These new offices helped to fill the administrative gaps in the organizational structure of the executive branch, enabling the president to more effectively supervise the spending activities of various bureaus and offices in the government. One result was that, within a few months of its passage, the implementation of the Budget Act even more closely resembled the president-centered vision of the Good Bill than it did the Treasury-centered vision of the McCormick Bill.

As they implemented the Budget Act, Dawes and Harding held strongly to the business analogy that had emerged during the previous decade of budget advocacy. Dawes's memoranda to Harding were typically filled with phrases playing on this theme. "The government as a business organization must function as a business organization," Dawes wrote in one memo, "with the lines of authority proceeding as they do in the ordinary corporation."[24]

Although Dawes and Harding often emphasized in their public statements the monetary savings that had been achieved through the budget system, in their private statements they affirmed their view that managerial rationalization would be the bureau's most important legacy. For instance, ten months into his tenure, in April 1922, in a personal letter to the editor of the *Saturday Evening Post*, Dawes summarized what he viewed as the chief contributions of the Budget Bureau. These included "the imposition of central policy in routine business"; the creation of "the superimposed coordinating machinery in the hands of the President"; and the clarification of the role of Cabinet members, who "as the administrators of routine business . . . must be subordinate at all times to the President and to the coordinating machinery created by him for the transmission of a unified business program."[25]

3

The leaders of the NBC and the IGR were thrilled at such statements from Dawes, but the creation of the national budget system was meant to be only the first step in the postwar drive to align the national government with the principles of business efficiency and good government. After giving the president authority over the budget, elite reformers hoped to further consolidate the president's administrative authority by reorganizing the executive branch. By shuffling the arrangement of departments, bureaus, and agencies to create clearer lines of command, they would remake the government in the image of a large corporation, with strong central executive power and a functionally efficient managerial structure.

Even before the passage of the Budget Act, the IGR and the NBC had each begun to shift their sights to executive reorganization. Back in March 1919, just as the postwar budget reform movement was getting started, the IGR had begun a study of "the organization and activities of the administrative branch of the national government" in preparation for devising a comprehensive plan for reorganization.[26]

Many of the elite reformers had hoped that the wartime Overman Act could provide the legal mechanism through which to achieve executive reorganization, so as the act's May 1919 expiration date approached, Woodrow Wilson's apparent disinterest in extending its powers was a source of frustration. Many agreed with the assessment of the Cleveland-based corporate lawyer James R. Garfield—whose interest in reorganization dated back to his membership on the Roosevelt administration's Keep Commission—that "a very great opportunity for making the needed changes was lost when President Wilson did not take advantage of the Overman law."[27]

After the expiration of the Overman Act, the NBC worked to leverage concern about the nation's war debt to bring executive reorganization back onto the national agenda in the same way they had used fiscal worries to win support for budget reform. In an August 1920 fundraising pitch to a select group of potential donors, John T. Pratt explained the NBC's "plan to follow up our budget work and make it effective by urging an efficient and economic reorganization of our financial government."[28] The next month, at the height of the 1920 presidential campaign, Pratt reported on his discussions with key Republican policy makers in a letter to NBC members. "As a corollary of budgetary reform the question of reorganization of the executive departments of the Federal Government is now uppermost in the minds of public men everywhere, and particularly of the leaders in Congress," Pratt said, adding that "after conferences with Senators Harding and McCormick," the committee had agreed to undertake an investigation and recommend a plan for executive reorganization.[29]

Just after Harding's nomination, the NBC published a book outlining its plan. Executive reorganization would, the NBC explained, increase the managerial power of the presidency by "giving to the President the machinery which he must have in order to perform effectively the functions of the chief administrative officer of the Government."[30] Among other proposals, the committee members suggested abolishing the Department of the Interior and replacing it with a "department of public works," which would include nonmilitary activities transferred from the Department of War.[31] They also advocated the creation of a "department of education and health," which would "combine in a single jurisdiction the health work, the educational work, and the work of providing for our veterans," and they proposed shifting responsibility for enforcing alcohol Prohibition from the Department of the Treasury to the Department of Justice.[32]

As in the budget debate, reformers interested in executive reorganization viewed the transition from the Wilson to the Harding administration as a boon for the cause. Raymond Fosdick—attorney and adviser to John D. Rockefeller Jr., as well as a trustee of the IGR—was optimistic in his assessment of the chances for enacting reorganization during Harding's term in office. Writing to Rockefeller about the IGR's plans, Fosdick said, "the opportunity which we have before us in Washington under the Harding administration is immense, and we are looking forward to four or five years of great service."[33]

The efforts of the IGR and NBC coincided with renewed congressional interest in executive reorganization in response to the postwar debt crisis. The rising war debt had inspired congressional leaders to revive the long tradition of Congress-centered reorganization that focused purely on budget cuts as a way to assert legislative control over the executive. In pursuit of this goal, Congress created the Joint Committee on the Reorganization of Government Departments in December 1920. The committee included two Republicans and one Democrat from the House, and two Republicans and one Democrat from the Senate. The chairman of the committee was Reed Smoot, Republican of Utah, who had been a staunch supporter of a congressional budget—and an opponent of the NBC's plans—during the debates of the previous year.[34]

Although the joint committee was intended as an assertion of congressional prerogative that would curtail the power of the executive branch, Harding turned the tables on congressional leaders. Soon after his inauguration, Harding convinced Smoot to allow a presidentially appointed representative to serve on the committee and to allow that executive representative to serve as chairman. Placing a presidential representative in charge of the committee would allow Harding to direct the project and ensure that the resulting plan would reflect his own vision—and that of the elite reformers. Harding's choice to fill this position was Walter F. Brown, a Toledo attorney who had been a leader of the Roosevelt wing of the Ohio Republican Party.[35]

Harding outlined his plans for reorganization on May 23, 1921, when he appeared in New York as the headline speaker at a conference devoted to the subject of "National Expenditures and Public Economy." The gathering was sponsored by the Academy of Political Science, which was run by Columbia University professor and NBC research director Samuel McCune Lindsay—the man who had tutored Harding in governmental theory during the 1920 campaign. Other speakers at the event included John T. Pratt, Frederick Cleveland, and William Howard Taft. Before Harding delivered his remarks, Elihu Root led a warm toast to the president and First Lady:

You are among friends. You are facing men who both admire and respect and trust you, who look to you for the preservation of that liberty and justice which will be essential to the happiness and the opportunities of their children and their children's children; and they stand ready to hold up your hands, to support you and to go with you in all efforts for the improvement, the elevation and the progress of the government of our beloved country.[36]

In his speech, titled "Business in Government and the Problem of Governmental Reorganization for Greater Efficiency," Harding explained the reformers' rationale for reorganizing the federal executive branch, and he made it clear that he shared their commitment to the cause. "To bring economy and efficiency into government is a task second to none in difficulty," Harding acknowledged. However, he noted that "the present organization is so bad that the insistent application of a few established principles of sound business organization will result in immediate economies and provide a margin of available means to meet new demands." Harding said that, although the Taft Commission had laid the groundwork with its investigations and reports, "the problem has been vastly complicated and increased" as a result of the war. However, Harding promised, the newly formed joint committee would soon address these complications.[37]

Soon thereafter, Congress approved an amendment appointing Walter Brown to the joint committee as the president's representative, despite complaints from Democrats wary of executive encroachment. In late July 1921, however, a resolution providing for Brown's salary sparked a brief filibuster led by Democratic representative Finis J. Garrett of Tennessee. Brown "ought never to have been appointed and given the authority given him as a representative of the Executive," Garrett argued. "I am pleading if I can to try and maintain not only the theory but the fact of severance between the legislative and Executive branches."[38]

However, Garrett's protest stood no chance of derailing Brown's appointment. With Brown safely installed as the leader of what was now essentially the president's reorganization committee, the Harding administration began to make plans to overhaul the structure of the executive branch. During the second half of 1921, Brown began a survey of the executive departments with the help of staff in the Bureau of Efficiency, and

Harding asked each cabinet member to provide an outline of their department's favored plan.

* * *

Shortly after Brown took charge of the joint committee, Harding took a preliminary step toward comprehensive reorganization by consolidating the nation's disorganized veterans relief agencies. After House hearings in May, a bill embodying the Dawes Committee's recommendations was sponsored in the House by Republican representative Burton E. Sweet of Iowa. The Sweet Bill, as it was called, passed unanimously in the House and cleared the Senate "in record time," the *Times* observed. Signed by Harding on August 9, 1921, less than two months after the Budget and Accounting Act, the Sweet Act created the United States Veterans Bureau. This amalgamation of three previously separate agencies created one rather large bureaucracy and achieved the "powerful superimposed authority" for which the Dawes Committee had advocated in its report.[39]

At the end of the summer of 1921, then, after four months of Warren G. Harding's presidency, the elite reformers could look with satisfaction on three major accomplishments: the passage of the Budget Act, the establishment of the Veterans Bureau, and the formation of the Joint Committee on Reorganization. However, while they celebrated these victories, trouble loomed. The relative ease with which Republicans had secured these achievements gave reformers an inflated sense of their agenda's bipartisan support. The nearly unanimous support for the Sweet Bill masked contentious and racism-infused behind-the-scenes negotiations. The emerging opposition to the elite reformers' larger plans could be discerned in the complaints about Harding's appointment of Walter F. Brown to head the joint committee, and the filibuster against the bill providing for his salary.

Chapter Seven

EQUAL PROTECTION UNDER LAW
1921–1923

During the fall of 1921, Warren G. Harding's administration turned toward fulfilling the commitments he had made on civil rights during the campaign and in his early statements as president. Already at this point in his presidency, the loudest voices against Harding were those of southern lawmakers such as Senator Pat Harrison, Democrat of Mississippi.[1] But the alarm among watchful white southerners intensified as the Harding administration began to work with the NAACP to advance a federal antilynching law. This seemed to confirm fears that Harding and the northeastern Republicans were intent on—as Arkansas governor Charles Brough had warned during the 1920 campaign—"robbing the South of her most cherished birthright, Anglo-Saxon supremacy."[2]

1

In the months after Harding's inauguration, prospects seemed good for the antilynching bill sponsored by Representative Leonidas Dyer, Republican of Missouri. Solid Republican majorities controlled the House and Senate, and now the White House was occupied by a president evidently committed to the bill's passage. The Dyer Bill's chances seemed to solidify even further when William Howard Taft was sworn in as chief justice of the Supreme Court on July 11, 1921. With the ex-president on the bench, decisions about civil rights legislation would be tried in a court led by someone who had publicly endorsed federal antilynching legislation by adding his signature to the National Conference on Lynching's "Address to the Nation" in 1919. Shortly before his confirmation to the bench in 1921, Taft confidentially assured Representative Dyer that he believed the antilynching bill was, in fact, constitutional. Dyer passed along this confidential assurance to leaders of the NAACP. Taft was, of course, only one member of a court of nine that had leaned heavily conservative on race questions for decades. However, since many lawmakers had defended their opposition to antilynching legislation by asserting that the Supreme Court would eventually strike down the law, knowledge of Taft's position gave the bill's proponents extra ammunition as they attempted to sway reluctant congressmen.[3]

The Dyer Anti-Lynching Bill would have made lynching a federal crime and provided district courts with jurisdiction wherever a "mob or riotous assemblage" committed a lynching. A "mob or riotous assemblage" was defined as "three or more persons acting in concert for the purpose of depriving any person of his life without authority of law." Any state or municipal officer who allowed a prisoner to be lynched or who failed to prevent a lynching would be guilty of a felony and could be imprisoned and fined up to $5,000—about five times the annual wages of the average full-time manufacturing worker. Any state or municipal officer who was found to "conspire, combine, or confederate" with a mob or riotous assemblage would be guilty of a felony and could face imprisonment of at least five years. If these officers "failed, neglected, or refused to proceed with due diligence to apprehend and prosecute the participants in the mob or riotous assemblage," the federal government could recover $10,000 from the county where the lynching occurred. If a victim was removed from one county and lynched in another, both counties would be fined $10,000. The money collected through these fines would then be given to the lynching victim's family.[4]

The House Judiciary Committee issued its report on the Dyer Bill on Friday, October 21, 1921. The report included a rare supporting opinion from the assistant U.S. attorney general, as well as an unprecedented two-page personal letter from U.S. Attorney General Harry Daugherty himself. "While under the statutes governing my office I am not authorized to give an official opinion to your committee relative to the bill," Daugherty wrote, "my interest in securing to persons within the jurisdiction of every State the equal protection of the laws, especially with reference to lynching, is so great that I feel warranted in submitting to you as my personal and not official opinion certain thoughts which have occurred to me as the result of a somewhat hasty examination of the bill."[5]

Five days later, Harding delivered a major speech in Birmingham, Alabama. Coming so soon after the report on the Dyer Bill, and with Republicans in the House preparing to bring the bill to a vote, Harding's speech provided observers with an opportunity to gauge the president's intentions.

Months earlier, a group of Birmingham businessmen had visited Washington and invited Harding to attend their city's fiftieth anniversary celebration. A promotional flyer advertised the festivities as the "Greatest Pageant Ever Staged in the South."[6] Leaders of the Birmingham Semi-Centennial Committee hoped Harding might speak about the rapid industrial progress that had accrued in the "Pittsburgh of the South" during the previous half century.

Delivering his remarks on Wednesday, October 26, 1921, the president obliged, at least for the first portion of his speech. Speaking from a platform at Woodrow Wilson Park in front of a segregated audience of white and Black citizens, Harding marveled at the region's mineral wealth and the city's commercial success.[7]

But then Harding segued to the topic of race. The city's dramatic industrial transformation showed that anything was possible, he said. If such progress was attainable in industry, perhaps similar progress was within reach on other issues—even racism. "Is it not possible, then," he asked, "for the Nation to lay aside old prejudices and old antagonisms and in the broad, clear light of nationalism enter upon a constructive policy in dealing with these intricate issues?"[8]

Harding struck what he intended to be an evenhanded tone. The nation, he said, should strive to establish "political and economic equality between the races." But he counterpoised this with an acknowledgment that "men of both races may well stand uncompromisingly against every suggestion of social equality." He declared, "let the black man vote when he is fit to vote; prohibit the white man voting when he is unfit to vote." And he called for "equal educational opportunity" for Blacks and whites while also asserting that "racial amalgamation there cannot be."[9]

Such statements were not much different from the platitudes offered by Republicans and northern Democrats over the previous decades. However, after these careful introductory formulations, Harding shifted to bolder remarks. He argued that the still ongoing Great Migration of southern Blacks to the industrial North meant that the nature of the "race problem" had changed. "I can say to you people of the South, both white and black, that the time has passed when you are entitled to assume that this problem of races is peculiarly and particularly your problem," he said. "More and more it is becoming a problem of the North."[10]

Carrying his logic further, Harding argued that this meant that conditions for African Americans *in the South* had become a national problem, suggesting that northern intervention in southern affairs was now justified. "It is a matter of the keenest national concern," Harding said, "that the South shall not be encouraged to make its colored population a vast reservoir of ignorance, to be drained away by the processes of migration into all other sections."[11] Exercising this new northern prerogative, Harding proceeded to effectively call for the end of Jim Crow. He suggested to southern leaders that they should treat southern Blacks so well that Blacks could "believe that, under the rule of whatever political party, they would be treated just as other people are treated, guaranteed all the rights that people of other colors enjoy, and made, in short, to regard themselves as citizens of a country and not of a particular race."[12]

On the issue of education, Harding abandoned the old accommodationist approach focused on promoting vocational instruction for African Americans and instead endorsed the philosophy that W. E. B. Du Bois had advocated in his writings on the "talented tenth." "I would like to see an education that would fit every man not only to do his particular work as well as possible but to rise to a higher plane if he would deserve it," he said. "For that sort of education I have no fears, whether it be given to a black man or a white man."[13]

Near the end of his speech, Harding explained to the crowd that it would serve the South's own economic interest to respect the civil rights of African Americans. The Immigration Restriction Act of 1921, passed in May, had imposed strict quotas on immigrants from eastern Europe. With the supply of immigrant laborers diminished, Harding predicted, employers around the nation would increasingly turn to African American workers.

This would accelerate the wave of Black migration to the North, thereby leaving southern employers in a vulnerable position. "If the South wishes to keep its fields producing and its industry still expanding," Harding warned, "it will have to compete for the services of the colored man."[14] The value of their service, Harding also argued, had been proven by the 350,000 African American soldiers who had served the nation in World War I.[15]

The segregated audience responded in predictable ways. "Parts of the speech appealed to the negroes in the audience and they gave vent to loud and lusty cheers to evidence their approval," a *New York Times* correspondent observed. "On the other hand only once or twice was there any applause from the white section and in both instances it was scattered." When Harding asserted that Blacks should have the right to vote, "the black element in the audience again shouted their approval of the sentiment in unmistakable fashion. The whites were silent."[16]

Writing in the *Crisis*, W. E. B. Du Bois gave grudging praise to Harding's speech. Du Bois criticized Harding's statements on "social equality" and "racial amalgamation," but commended Harding's demand for equality of voting rights, education, and economic justice. "The sensitive may note that the President qualified these demands somewhat, even dangerously, and yet they stand out so clearly in his speech that he must be credited with meaning to give them their real significance."[17]

In contrast to the guarded approval of Du Bois, the response from white southern leaders was unequivocal—and often unhinged. Harding's message struck them as especially brazen, coming while the Dyer Bill was under consideration in the House, and delivered to an interracial crowd gathered at a spot that had been, decades earlier, the site of a notorious lynching. The Birmingham address removed any doubts among southerners that the president's agenda threatened white supremacy in the region. Harding's assurances that he favored only political and economic equality, and not social equality, did not mollify segregationists who understood that the former could easily create conditions favorable to the latter.[18]

Senate minority leader Pat Harrison of Mississippi, already the Harding administration's fiercest critic, issued an extended statement on behalf of southern Democrats:

> To encourage the negro, who, in some States, as in my own, exceeds the white population, to strive through every political avenue to be placed upon

equality with the whites, is a blow to the white civilization of this country that will take years to combat. If the President's theory is carried to its ultimate conclusion, namely, that the black person, either man or woman, should have full economic and political rights with the white man and white woman, then that means that the black man can strive to become President of the United States, hold a Cabinet position and occupy the highest places of public trust in the nation.[19]

Inevitably shifting to the topic that pro-lynching apologists typically raised to incite fear among their followers, Harrison warned that Harding's call for political and economic equality would mean that "white women should work under black men in public places, as well as in all trades and professions," and that such an outcome would be "impracticable, unjust, and destructive of the best ideals of America."[20]

2

Despite the blustery response from Senator Harrison and other white southern leaders to Harding's Birmingham address, proponents of the Dyer Anti-Lynching Bill remained confident. However, when Republicans finally brought the bill to the floor of the House in mid-December 1921, it sparked a filibuster led by the Tennessee Democrat Finis Garrett. Earlier, when Garrett had led his summer filibuster against the bill for Walter F. Brown's salary on the Joint Committee on Reorganization, he said he was motivated by a constitutionalist desire to "maintain not only the theory but the fact of the severance between the legislative and executive branches."[21] In the antilynching debate, Garrett and his associates supplemented their constitutional objections with straightforwardly racist assertions. At one point in his remarks, Garrett proclaimed that the Dyer Bill ought to be titled "A bill to encourage rape." Acknowledging that his constitutional arguments would not sway proponents of the bill, Garrett made clear that his ultimate motivation was to maintain white supremacy. "You gentlemen do not know what it is to live in a section where a wife dare not travel alone in the fields," he said to the Republicans. "Whenever you put these ideas in the heads of those few black beasts of the ten million of their race, you are increasing the commission of crime."[22]

The filibuster was broken when Republicans agreed to delay consideration of the bill until January 1922, after the holiday recess. The *New York*

Times reported that "the Democrats admit that the bill will be passed, but are counting upon its being buried in the Senate Judiciary Committee, on the grounds of unconstitutionality because it infringes the police powers of the States." The delay would give the southern representatives time to coordinate with their counterparts in the Senate.[23]

In the final rounds of debate, southern Democrats pleaded on behalf of white supremacy. "I would rather the whole black race of this world be lynched," one representative from Mississippi said, "than for one of the fair daughters of the South to be ravished and torn by one of these black brutes."[24] A representative from Texas issued a final warning to his fellow congressmen, casting Representative Dyer as the leader of a mob. "Today the Constitution of the United States stands at the door, guarding the governmental integrity of the States, the plan and the philosophy of our system of government," he said, "and the gentleman from Missouri, rope in hand, is appealing to you to help him lynch the Constitution."[25]

On January 26, 1922, the House approved the Dyer Bill by a vote of 242–129.[26] The next day, the bill was sent to the Senate Judiciary Committee. Meanwhile, the NAACP and the Harding administration worked to rouse public opinion. In mid-February, a Republican representative from a heavily African American district in Chicago gave a series of speeches in which he relayed a message to his constituents from President Harding. "If the Senate of the United States passes the Dyer Anti-Lynching Bill, it won't be in the White House three minutes before I'll sign it," Harding said, "and, having signed it, I'll enforce it."[27]

The bill's chances in the Senate seemed solid on paper. The Republicans held a 59–37 majority—just five votes shy of the 64 needed to overcome a filibuster. Since the Dyer Bill had been approved by seven out of fifteen northern Democrats in the House vote, supporters were hopeful that, with a modest amount of support from northern Democrats, a filibuster could be avoided in the Senate. Among the optimists was W. E. B. Du Bois, who argued in his April 1922 column in the *Crisis* that the likelihood of this bipartisan support placed "a double responsibility upon the Republicans because the Democratic help of which they are sure makes their ability to pass the bill beyond any question." He assured his readers that a filibuster was unlikely because "the Republicans with Democratic support can command a two-thirds majority in the Senate for this bill." He ended his note on the Dyer Bill with an italicized warning: "*If then the Senate does not pass* the *Dyer Anti-Lynching Bill, any Negro who votes for the Republican Party at the next election writes himself down as a gullible fool.*"[28]

The bill languished in the Senate Judiciary Committee for six months until June 30, when it was finally approved by an 8–6 vote. While this was a step in the right direction, the debate within the Judiciary Committee revealed a problem. NAACP leaders had initially been confident that they could secure the support of William E. Borah, Republican of Idaho and the leader of the five-man subcommittee charged with assessing the merits of the bill. Borah, the "Lion of Idaho," was known as a progressive and claimed to oppose lynching. However, during the spring of 1923, as his subcommittee began its work, he revealed that he would support the Dyer Bill only if he was convinced "beyond a reasonable doubt" that it was constitutional. As the subcommittee's deliberations proceeded, Borah remained unconvinced, despite an extended correspondence with NAACP president Moorfield Storey, who outlined his own argument that the injustice of lynching was so great that it justified an expansive reading of the equal protection clause of the Fourteenth Amendment.[29]

However, even after this extended influence campaign, Borah remained convinced that the Dyer Bill represented an unconstitutional usurpation of local police powers on the part of the federal government. Borah argued, in opposition to Storey's position, that the Fourteenth Amendment did not authorize the federal government to intervene to prosecute individuals for violations of civil rights. When the subcommittee reported the bill to the full Judiciary Committee, Borah voted against the bill, siding with the Democrats on the subcommittee. When the full committee voted, Borah also joined the Democrats in opposition.[30]

Although the bill's supporters remained optimistic, Borah's opinion helped to establish rhetorical ground on which the bill might be defeated. By asserting that the bill was unconstitutional, Borah—a self-styled constitutional expert—gave cover to fence-sitting Republicans and northern Democrats who wished to oppose the bill without seeming to embrace southern white supremacy and lynch law.[31]

Borah's perfidiousness raised the troubling likelihood that other western Republicans would follow his example and join the Democrats who opposed the bill. Supporters of the Dyer Bill had overcome Democratic parliamentary maneuvers in the House, but Senate rules gave many more opportunities for a determined minority to block a bill. Since the

Republicans already needed five Democratic votes to reach the two-thirds threshold to overcome a filibuster, the defection of any additional western Republicans would place the bill on much shakier ground.

Even more disturbing to astute proponents of the bill was the likelihood that Borah had been actively coordinating with the Democrats since December, when leaders of the House minority had confidently assured journalists that the bill would be buried in the Senate Judiciary Committee.[32]

Southern and western senators had joined together on a number of issues over the years—particularly those pertaining to farmers—forming the legislative coalition sometimes referred to as the "Farm Bloc." But agriculture was not the only topic that brought the Farm Bloc together. On some occasions these senators came together on questions of race. Perhaps the most notable case was the Federal Elections Bill of 1890—or, as white southerners still called it, the "Lodge Force Bill"— which had been, as Arkansas Governor Brough had reminded his fellow Democrats during the 1920 campaign, "defeated in the Senate by the filibuster of great Southern and some fair minded Western Senators."[33]

Concerned over wavering western Republicans, party leaders considered their strategy for shepherding the bill through the Senate. The bill had first been introduced in the Senate by the majority whip, Charles Curtis of Kansas. Curtis hailed from Topeka. An enrolled member of the Kaw Nation, he was the first Native American member of Congress. Despite his western roots, "Indian Charley"—as he was often called—was known as an economic conservative and an ally of the northeastern business interests routinely demonized by western populists and progressives.* To introduce the bill this time around, Republican leaders selected Samuel Shortridge, a freshman senator from California. Although Shortridge lacked experience, proponents of the bill were so concerned about the need to appeal to Senator Borah's allies that they decided Shortridge's western bona fides were more important than procedural acumen.[34]

The Dyer Bill's path through the Senate was hobbled by missteps. In perhaps the most serious tactical error, Republican leaders in the Senate

---

*Seven years later, Charles Curtis would serve as vice president under Herbert Hoover. Curtis's career provides a good example of the limited explanatory power of ideological labels in this era. In addition to introducing the antilynching bill, the "conservative" Curtis also introduced the Equal Rights Amendment in the Senate in 1923. Over the course of the next century, that amendment would face resistance similar to that faced by the antilynching bill.

compounded the already lengthy delay in reporting the bill out of the Judiciary Committee by dithering through August and most of September, uncertain about when to bring the bill to the floor.

The moment would not arrive until Thursday, September 21, 1922—the last full day of business before Congress was set to adjourn for the November midterms. At 2:00 p.m., Shortridge secured the floor and prepared to introduce the bill. At that point, Pat Harrison and the Democrats were apparently still unaware of the Republicans' plans. However, as one eyewitness reported, "as soon as Senator Shortridge arose they at once knew that it meant an effort to take up the Anti-Lynching Bill." As he was about to formally introduce the bill, and while the Democrats in the chamber began to organize, Shortridge paused, yielding the floor to two other Republicans for routine business. As the second Republican spoke, Democratic leader Pat Harrison interrupted with a point of order. This, one observer noted, "gave rise to a long and complicated parliamentary wrangle." Harrison held the floor for two hours before Shortridge could regain it and move for consideration of the Dyer Bill. By that time, however, many members had left the chamber for the evening, leaving the Senate without a quorum.[35]

Since the Senate was scheduled to adjourn the next day, this meant that the vote would be postponed until after the midterm elections. This new delay was especially frustrating to leaders of the NAACP. By holding the vote on the bill after the election, supporters of the bill would lose their only real source of leverage on wavering senators. Their only hope now was for the pro–Dyer Bill coalition to gain ground in the midterms, making the bill's passage inevitable and taking the steam out of the filibusterers. However, the opposite scenario occurred. The Democrats made significant gains on Election Day. The Republicans would retain their majority in the next Congress, but their margin in the Senate would shrink from 59 to 53, dashing any hope of patching together a filibuster-proof majority.[36]

When the Senate reconvened on Monday, November 27, Shortridge again moved to take up the bill, but Democrats—quite prepared this time—immediately launched their filibuster. After the first full day, news reporters marveled at the skill of the maneuvers led, once more, by Pat Harrison. "The Democratic filibuster, engineered by Senator Harrison, of Mississippi, was classified as 'airtight,'" a *New York Tribune* correspondent wrote. "Old timers said it was the most effective they had seen for years."[37] The *New York Times* special correspondent observed that "it was not a dull filibuster."

After speaking with the southern senators, the *Times* correspondent was moved to offer the following historical analysis: "As a matter of fact it was the liveliest affair of the kind the Senate has known since the days of the Lodge Force bill," he wrote. "Even the Republicans admitted that the filibuster was practically 'perfect,' and Senate attachés commented on it as one of the most scientifically conducted filibusters that had been seen in recent years." The reference to the "Lodge Force Bill"—echoing Arkansas governor Charles Brough's campaign warning from 1920—was apt. Southern Democrats had not mobilized with this level of alarm in decades.[38]

The next day, November 28, the Senate was in complete deadlock. According to the *Times*, "No business of any kind has been transacted, and the Democratic leaders announce that none will be transacted until the Republican leaders withdraw the measure."[39] Later that evening, members of the Republican caucus voted 27–1 to keep fighting. On December 1, reporters at the White House were told that "President Harding personally favors the enactment of the Dyer Anti-Lynching bill" and that he still viewed lynching as a "very sore spot on our boast of civilization."[40] However, after the results of the midterm elections, Harding had no leverage on senators during the lame-duck session of Congress.

When they weren't busy reading from the *Senate Journal* and raising obscure points of order to continue the filibuster, the southern Democrats vacillated, as their counterparts in the House had done, between offering constitutional analyses of the bill's provisions and making passionate pleas in favor of white supremacy.[41] Over the course of a week, they made it clear that, if pressed, they were prepared to sustain the filibuster until the last day of the sixty-seventh Congress, on March 4, 1923.

On the evening of Saturday, December 2, the Republican caucus met again and voted to surrender. When senators met on the floor on Monday, December 4, Majority Leader Henry Cabot Lodge—who had sponsored the 1890 Federal Elections Bill that still burned so brightly in the memory of white southerners—accepted Pat Harrison's demand that the Republicans not raise the issue again during this Congress.[42]

3

On January 9, 1923, a little over a month after the defeat of the Dyer Bill, civil rights advocates received an unexpected cause for hope when the

Supreme Court heard arguments in the case of *Moore v. Dempsey*, which marked a key turning point for the elite reformers' participation in the civil rights movement.[43]

The case concerned the aftermath of an incident in Phillips County, Arkansas. On September 30, 1919, a group of white law enforcement officers and vigilantes attempted to break up a meeting of Black tenant farmers by firing shots into the rural church where the farmers had convened. Allegedly, someone inside the church fired back. In the shoot-out that ensued, a stray bullet killed one of the white men outside.[44]

Shocked by the spectacle of armed African Americans defending themselves, white leaders in Phillips County called on vigilantes from surrounding counties to provide assistance in stopping what local officials described as an organized plot to kill local whites. Thousands of armed whites poured into the county, and Governor Brough asked for federal troops to put down the imagined Black insurrection. In the two days of rioting that followed the initial incident, white vigilantes ran wild. Estimates of the number of African Americans killed have ranged from 250 to 856. Five whites were killed. Meanwhile, the story of the planned insurrection was reported credulously by newspapers throughout the South and North, most prominently by the *New York Times*.[45]

Local authorities interrogated and tortured dozens of African Americans, eventually arresting twelve men. A lynch mob surrounding the jailhouse threatened to abduct the prisoners, but local officials calmed the crowd by promising that the accused would meet their death through the law. To ensure that promise was kept, a large mob surrounded the courthouse during the trial. Those inside the courtroom understood that the accused would be lynched if they were acquitted, and they understood that any white citizen found to have helped the accused would face the same fate. The all-white jury quickly returned guilty verdicts and the court issued sentences of death.[46]

After the trial, the NAACP sent Assistant National Secretary Walter F. White to investigate. White, a light-skinned African American who routinely passed as white, was unable to learn much in Phillips County before his identity was discovered and he was forced to flee while a lynch mob prepared to apprehend him.[47] It was not until after he interviewed a friendly white attorney in Louisiana, however, that White learned that the official narrative of a Black insurrection stopped in the nick of time was a deliberately contrived cover story. In fact, the incident had begun when local officials intercepted a white attorney from Louisiana on his way to meet with a group of Black sharecroppers intent on forming a union. The armed whites had then travelled to the church intending to stop those sharecroppers from obtaining legal counsel.[48]

After White's investigation, the NAACP began providing legal assistance to the twelve accused men through a series of trials and appeals. Eventually, the Supreme Court agreed to hear the case—the first major civil rights case to come before the Taft court. On February 19, 1923, the court returned its decision. Writing for an 8–2 majority, Oliver Wendell Holmes argued that the trial had indeed violated the Fourteenth Amendment rights of the accused. The court ruled that a trial of African American defendants by an all-white jury that included citizens who had helped to apprehend the defendants, while a threatening mob surrounded the courthouse—with, as Holmes put it, "counsel, jury and judge . . . swept to the fatal end by an irresistible wave of public passion"—did not constitute a fair trial.[49]

Coming so soon after the defeat of the Dyer Bill, the victory in *Moore v. Dempsey* led the NAACP and its allies to reevaluate their civil rights strategy. Rather than risk resources in pursuit of legislative action, which was blocked by the inescapable threat of a southern filibuster in the Senate, the NAACP began to devote its energy to pursuing a legal strategy to win civil rights for African Americans. The NAACP's legal effort was soon joined by several northern philanthropic foundations.[50]

4

Even if the Harding administration had wished to avoid racial questions in the aftermath of the Dyer Bill debacle, there was no practical way to do so when implementing national policy in a nation that included the Jim Crow states. Moreover, simply avoiding new civil rights legislation was not enough to avoid stirring up racist backlash in the South. Many laws touched on race, and any effort by Republicans to avoid offending white southerners risked alienating Black voters and their allies in the North. This dilemma was revealed in the difficulties faced by the Harding administration as it worked to establish the veterans hospital system in 1923. Racial issues emerged frequently as officials in the Veterans Bureau and members of the

Consultants on Hospitalization sought to carry out the provisions of the Sweet Act.[51]

In World War I, the Allied Expeditionary Force had included more than 350,000 African American soldiers. In 1921, the plans of the Consultants on Hospitalization and the Dawes Committee to consolidate the administration of veterans policy raised concern among white southerners who feared that officials in Washington could be put in a position to dictate local arrangements for the treatment and rehabilitation of African American veterans. As the published report of the Consultants on Hospitalization describes, in a section titled "Problems of Race" (part of a chapter titled "Fundamental Principles"), "Very early in the work of the consultants one of the great American problems—that of race—obtruded itself more and more."[52]

Faced with the challenge of accommodating African American patients in veterans hospitals without stirring opposition that might scuttle the whole project, the committee decided to create a single, separate hospital for Black veterans in the South. This decision was made within the first two weeks of the consultants' work and was firmly established by the time of the Dawes Committee meeting. After considering several locations, the consultants chose a site in Tuskegee, Alabama, adjacent to the Tuskegee Institute.[53]

African American observers were rightly suspicious of this plan. Later in 1921, a delegation of African American veterans from the National Committee of Negro Veteran Relief visited the chairman of the consultants to register their opposition to placing the hospital in Tuskegee and to lobby instead for a location in Washington, D.C., near Howard University. They also protested against the policy (which had been mistakenly described in news reports) that all African American veterans, even those who lived in the North, would have to go to Tuskegee to receive treatment from the Veterans Bureau. In response to the African American veterans' complaints, the chairman defended the consultants' reasoning and explained that the Tuskegee hospital was intended to serve only African American veterans who resided in the South.[54]

During congressional debate over the Sweet Bill in 1921, Treasury officials had mollified white southerners by assuring them that the hospital in Tuskegee would be operated under white control.[55] However, the dispute over how the hospital would be run reemerged in the early weeks of 1923. As the Harding administration made final preparations to open the veterans hospital at Tuskegee, southern leaders sought reassurance that the facility would in fact be run by white administrators and staffed by white doctors.

Instead, Harding and Veterans Bureau director Charles Forbes sided with leaders at the Tuskegee Institute and the NAACP, who argued that the hospital ought to be run and staffed entirely by African Americans. Harding believed that such an arrangement would "afford the colored race opportunity to show its capacity for service and prove exceedingly helpful in that direction."[56] This echoed the president's remarks in Birmingham, where he had argued that the Black soldiers' service in the war justified an expansion of civil rights, and that the patriotic sacrifice of African Americans in uniform ought to lead southerners to reassess the wisdom of segregation and Jim Crow.[57]

Despite the strength of white southern forces after the defeat of the antilynching bill, the Harding administration resisted pressure to compromise with southern lawmakers and advocates of white supremacy on the issue of the Tuskegee hospital. Even after members of the Ku Klux Klan marched through Tuskegee to protest the arrival of Black employees at the hospital in July 1923, the director of the Veterans Bureau arrived two days later and informed local whites that Harding intended to follow through on his promise that the hospital would be staffed by Black Americans.[58]

* * *

Although Harding and his allies went to considerable lengths to secure passage of the antilynching bill, they lacked the means to overcome the power of southern senators to block any legislation that threatened white supremacy. Although it was still possible to pursue progress on civil rights through executive action and through the courts, the result of Harding's foray into civil rights advocacy was a serious setback. While the Harding administration seemed to momentarily regain the upper hand in Tuskegee, debate over the hospital's management only reinforced southern worries about the danger posed by the "powerful superimposed authority" that Charles Dawes had advocated in his committee's report for the consolidation of federal veterans agencies.[59]

Chapter Eight

BACKLASH

Spring and Summer 1923

On February 13, 1923, a week before the *Moore* decision, Warren G. Harding submitted the final version of his executive reorganization plan in a letter to the Joint Committee on Reorganization. Harding and Walter F. Brown had devised their plan over the course of the previous year, incorporating suggestions collected from the National Budget Committee, the Institute for Government Research, and members of the cabinet. The plan was bold, designed as it was to increase presidential control over public administration at the national level. However, while many elite reformers were optimistic that Harding's vision of "more business in government" was near fruition, the defeat of the Dyer Bill had made an already delicate situation much more difficult.[1]

The letter from Harding, accompanied by a long memo from Brown, was the first official communication the congressional members of the committee had received from either man since the summer of 1921, when—after the joint committee's second meeting—congressional members of the committee had agreed to transfer the task of designing a reorganization plan to the executive branch. In early 1923, however, the president and his "reorganization aide" needed congressional support if the plan was to be enacted.

1

The chief source of political difficulty for the Harding-Brown reorganization plan was that it emphasized increasing central control and organizational efficiency, which were the priorities of the elite reformers, while largely ignoring the question of budgetary savings, which was the priority of the congressional members of the committee. This might not have been a problem if Harding had been in a stronger position, but in the aftermath of the antilynching debacle, the Democratic members of the committee were in no mood to defer to the president. This was especially true for one particular member of the committee: Senate Minority Leader Pat Harrison, who had spearheaded the antilynching filibuster. Harrison and his allies on the committee planned to use the year-and-a-half delay in communication from Harding and Brown as justification for delaying consideration of the plan.[2]

In his memorandum, Brown explained that the plan's overall goals were "to reduce duplications of activities and to bring about more effective administration," and he described three "fundamental faults" in the government's existing organization that the plan was meant to address.[3] First, he explained, some units "perform functions having little or no relation to the major departmental purposes." Second, some agencies perform "work in the same or analogous fields of activity" as that performed in another department. Third, "too many governmental agencies exist outside the ten executive departments, virtually free from coordinated control or supervision."[4]

To solve these problems, the Harding-Brown plan featured six "outstanding recommendations":

1. Consolidate the army and navy to create a "department of national defense"
2. Move the nonmilitary functions from the army (including the Corps of Engineers) and navy to the Departments of Interior and Commerce
3. Eliminate "nonfiscal" functions from the Treasury
4. Form a new "department of education and welfare"
5. Add the Radio Bureau to the Post Office and change the latter's name to the "department of communications"
6. Eliminate most of the independent establishments in the government by folding them into existing executive departments[5]

Several aspects of this plan sparked controversy. The creation of a "defense department" had first been suggested by the Taft Commission, and it was also part of a plan published by the IGR, but it—along with the proposal for moving the Army Corps of Engineers to the Department of the Interior—put in jeopardy the existing system for allocating military infrastructure projects to congressional districts. Traditionally, congressmen had negotiated directly with army and navy bureau chiefs with no formal input from the president or the departmental secretaries. Representatives and senators were reluctant to tinker with the existing system since the allocation of military projects was a major source of political capital in Congress.

Also controversial was the proposed "education and welfare department," which resembled the "education and health" department recommended by the NBC and reflected the prevailing view among elite reformers—especially clear in the wake of the so-called Spanish Flu pandemic of 1918–1919—that the nation's health was a key component of national strength. It was also similar to a proposal in the plan proposed by the IGR. The education and welfare department would also absorb the Veterans Bureau, which was at that time the government's largest independent establishment. While this appealed to elite reformers, white southerners were especially fearful of putting officials in Washington in charge of education and welfare policy.[6]

The plan also included a particularly provocative proposal—one that seems to have been added at Harding's own insistence—to remove the Bureau of the Budget from the Treasury and place it directly under the president, fulfilling the vision of a pure presidential budget system advanced by Taft and the NBC and bypassing the compromise that had been hatched in 1920 between the elite reformers and the Wilsonians. Harding's plan also identified the need for continuing presidential reorganization authority, and recommended giving the president discretion to continue reorganization in the future without consulting Congress.[7] Together, these two proposals promised to finally create the presidential staff agency that had been envisioned a decade earlier by the Taft Commission, and by the IGR and NBC after World War I.[8]

Attempting to preempt questions about his nine-month delay in releasing the plan, Harding explained in his February 13 letter that the holdup was "caused solely by the difficulty which has been encountered in reconciling the views of the various persons" in the cabinet. The proposals submitted by the departmental secretaries had each clashed with those submitted by several others—which led the cabinet members to vie with each other since most preferred to gain rather than lose administrative territory through reorganization.⁹

The deadlock within the cabinet was still firmly in place on October 13, 1922, when the NBC held a dinner at the Waldorf-Astoria Hotel in Manhattan to honor former budget director Charles Dawes. The climax of the evening was a provocative speech from Dawes on the subjects of the budget and executive reorganization. Playing to his popular image as "General Hell 'n' Maria," the Chicago banker puffed on a corncob pipe and, the *New York Times* reported, "stamped and shook his fists and let out an occasional 'damn,' to the evident enjoyment of a few women at the tables." Dawes directed most of his criticism toward Congress—"a nest of vipers"—but he also directed substantive criticism toward Harding's own cabinet. "They are advisers," Dawes said. "They are entitled to be dignified, but in the business organization of the Government they are nothing but Vice President managers of the business, and they must take their places." He continued by telling the crowd how bureaucratic jealousies among the department heads had stymied Dawes's own efforts as director of the budget. "You don't know how President Harding was threatened with a revolt because of this imposition of central control," Dawes charged. "You don't see any of that in the papers. I tell you that the Cabinet officers are the natural enemies of the unified business control of the Government."¹⁰

However, not all of the cabinet officers were opposed to the Harding-Brown plan. The department head with the strongest commitment to the elite reformers' vision of executive reorganization was Secretary of Commerce Herbert Hoover. Not yet fifty years old, but already a wealthy man after a career as a mining executive and consultant, Hoover came to public prominence during World War I when he led an international effort to deliver food and other supplies to people in Belgium—earning various nicknames, including "the Great Engineer" and "the Great Humanitarian."¹¹ His training as an engineer made him sensitive to questions of mechanical efficiency and sympathetic to the mechanical analogies often employed by reformers. His time as an executive and consultant gave him an appreciation of the importance of managerial efficiency. Closely allied with leading elite reformers, Hoover's commitment to their agenda had been solidified during his tenure as U.S. food administrator, where he was responsible for marshalling the nation's food supply during the war.[12]

In 1921 and 1922, as Harding and Brown worked to refine their comprehensive reorganization plan, Hoover emerged as their chief ally within the cabinet. Hoover's involvement was such that other department heads began to fear that the Harding-Brown plan was part of an effort to enlarge the secretary of commerce's own administrative portfolio. However, while some aspects of the plan did benefit Commerce, most of Hoover's input had little to do with his own department. His attention to the issue illustrates his shared commitment with Harding, Brown, and the elite reformers to building central administrative control under the president.[13]

2

After the executive reorganization plan was submitted in February 1923, it remained in the hands of the Joint Committee on Reorganization through the first half of the year. One key hurdle was the skepticism of western senators such as Reed Smoot of Utah, who was the leading Republican congressman on the joint committee. In this period, in addition to their role in blocking the Dyer Bill and stalling executive reorganization, the western Republicans were also obstructing several of the Harding administration's other initiatives, including the president's proposal for U.S. membership in the World Court.

Hoping to neutralize this western opposition, Harding and his advisers spent the spring devising a plan to capitalize on the president's popularity with voters in the West to put pressure on congressmen to support the administration's initiatives. On June 21, 1923, Harding embarked on what was intended to be a forty-six-day, fifteen-thousand-mile tour of the American West and Far West. The "Journey of Understanding" was scheduled to take the president from St. Louis to Alaska, by train and boat, voyaging through Colorado, Wyoming, Utah, Idaho, Montana, Oregon, and Washington. Then, after traveling down the Pacific coast through California, Harding was to return to the White House by sea, passing through the Panama Canal and stopping at Puerto Rico.[14]

Throughout the trip, Harding was greeted by large, enthusiastic crowds and delegations of local officials. Harding made a point to spend time in the company of the senators who had been hindering his agenda in the months before the trip. For instance, in Utah, Harding took a horseback tour of Zion Canyon with a group that included Senator Smoot. When the Presidential Special passed by rail from Utah into Idaho, Senator William Borah came aboard Harding's car.[15]

The journey was cut short, however, on August 2, 1923, when Warren Harding died of a heart attack in San Francisco. The sudden death of the seemingly robust fifty-seven-year-old raised rumors of sinister conspiracies, some of them involving his personal homeopathic physician, Charles W. Sawyer, who had treated Harding for many years. However, his heart troubles seem to have stemmed from a case of influenza that he had contracted earlier in the year—possibly a late wave of the 1918–1919 pandemic.*

As the president's body was carried eastward, and as the new president, Calvin Coolidge, assessed the task that lay before him, the elite reformers sought to ensure that the Harding-Brown executive reorganization plan would not be forgotten. Perhaps, some reasoned, Harding's death could even serve as inspiration for reform, much in the way that President James A. Garfield's assassination had helped to build support for civil service reform in the early 1880s.

Walter F. Brown himself gave voice to this thought on the day after Harding's death. A short news story atop the front page of the *New York Times* quoted Brown's assertion that "there was no doubt but the exactions of the office hastened the death of President Harding." Arguing in favor of creating a presidential staff to aid the president in his administrative duties, Brown said that "faulty construction of the Government organization is the primary cause of the breakdown of all our Presidents."[16]

The next day, a longer story appeared in the *Times* elaborating on Brown's call for a presidential staff and connecting Harding's death with the executive reorganization movement. The story quoted Elihu Root, who said that "it is not the larger questions of state which constitute the chief strain upon a president's health, but the routine and added administrative tasks." These tasks, Root argued, had increased dramatically since the days of Presidents Cleveland and McKinley. "The country has become so large that this is a

---

* Another leading elite reformer, Taft's former secretary Charles Dyer Norton, had died of "complications following an attack of influenza" on March 6, 1923. See "Charles D. Norton, Banker, Dies at 53," *New York Times*, March 7, 1923.

serious question," Root said. "The President is called upon to take care of so many matters that a great many times he is left with a tired brain to attack the larger questions which come up for solution."[17]

3

On the day Harding died, a Senate Select Committee had entered the sixth month of an investigation of corruption in the U.S. Veterans Bureau, but the details of the scandal would not be made public until Senate hearings in November 1923. The initial stirrings of scandal in the bureau had reached the public in February 1923, just as the bureau was engaged in the controversy about staffing at the Tuskegee hospital.

On February 25, the *New York Times* had reported—on page 3 of the extra edition—on calls for the formation of a Senate committee to investigate allegations of fraud and corruption within the bureau. This initial story did not accuse any individual of wrongdoing, but merely outlined general charges of inefficiency and "waste." The story noted that "there have been many questions asked about sales of surplus property, including $3,000,000 of surplus hospital supplies sold from the Perryville (Md.) depot at 20 cents on the dollar."[18] By this time, Harding had already made a change in leadership at the Veterans Bureau, accepting the resignation of its director, Charles R. Forbes, on February 15.[19]

By all accounts, including his own, Forbes's hiring was the result of his previous personal acquaintance with President Harding. Forbes had relevant experience as an engineer, served as commissioner of public works in Hawaii Territory during the Wilson administration, and won a Distinguished Service Medal in the war. But he was viewed with distrust by many Washington observers, who—based on his lack of connections in established circles—dismissed him as an incompetent member of President Harding's "Ohio Gang," even though Forbes had never lived in Ohio. Since he wasn't actually part of the "gang," Forbes was also viewed with suspicion by administration insiders, partly due to his previous service under Wilson.[20]

Forbes had a very brief honeymoon in the first months of his tenure as director of the Veterans Bureau. Two and a half weeks after the bureau's formation, the *Washington Post* observed that "Col. Forbes has the real human touch with the men." The article cast Forbes as the model of an up-to-date, pragmatic administrator: "Col. Forbes impresses one with his sincerity, his clear, logical mind, his executive force and directness of thought and action."[21] A month later, the *New York Times* noted—in language that reads even more like a press release from the administration—that this new "vast bureau" was "one of the largest organizations in the world in terms of money controlled." The *Times* described the consolidation using the business analogy favored by the elite reformers: "now, like any well organized business institution of a corresponding size, the Veterans Bureau has its executive power invested in one head with authority... complete and thoroughly co-ordinated."[22]

Press accounts in the chaotic days of February and March 1923 largely cast Forbes as a hapless amateur unprepared for the job. A March 9, 1923, exposé in the *American Legion Weekly* was largely supportive of Forbes, describing him as a man who had been placed in "one of the most trying and difficult situations in the government service" and who had been "kept in ignorance of many evils." The story attributed the bulk of the problems in the bureau to a "triumvirate" consisting of Dr. Hugh Scott, an executive officer, Charles F. Cramer, chief counsel for the bureau, and Colonel Robert U. Patterson, head of the bureau's Medical Division. "They were the Big Three," the article explained. "They were reputed to be the powers behind the throne."[23] A few days later, one of the "Big Three" committed suicide. The *New York Times* reported that Chief Counsel Cramer had been found dead with newspaper clippings about the American Legion's allegations near his body.[24]

As the Senate investigative committee set to work, the narrative shifted over the course of the spring and summer of 1923. By the time Senate hearings began in October 1923, suspicion had come to center squarely on Forbes, who found himself without friends in Washington after Harding's death in August. Forbes was now accused of masterminding a conspiracy to defraud veterans and the government, in cooperation with Cramer, who was dead, and a man named Elias H. Mortimer, the prosecution's central witness.

Mortimer's testimony before the Senate committee in October, November, and December 1923 provided lurid copy for the newspapers. He claimed to have given a $5,000 bribe to Forbes in the bathroom of a suite at the Drake Hotel in Chicago in exchange for an assurance that Forbes would accept a bid from one of Mortimer's alleged associates on a contract for a hospital in Northampton, Massachusetts.[25] Mortimer told of drinking, gambling, carousing, a cross-country junket, and an elaborate system of secret codes that Forbes had allegedly devised to obscure bid rigging, fraud, and graft.[26] On top of Mortimer's allegations, Charles E. Sawyer, chairman of the Federal Hospitalization Board, testified about the mishandling of surplus hospital supplies at the bureau's depot in Perryville, Maryland. Sawyer claimed that Forbes had directed an effort to sell sheets, towels, and other material from the Perryville depot at a discount, defrauding the government of millions of dollars.[27]

Newspapers credulously spread the portrait of Forbes as a corrupt grifter. For his part, Forbes denied all of the charges and claimed that he was the victim of a conspiracy led by Mortimer and Sawyer. However, few believed his protestations. Eventually, Forbes would serve two years in the federal penitentiary at Leavenworth, Kansas. His conviction for bribery in federal court was based entirely on evidence presented by Mortimer and Sawyer.[28]

There were reasons, however, to discount the testimony from both of Forbes's accusers. Mortimer was a bootlegger and serial liar. He was, at the time, under multiple investigations by the FBI. Mortimer admitted that he was motivated by a desire for revenge against Forbes, whom he blamed for his own divorce.[29] Sawyer—a homeopathic physician from President Harding's hometown of Marion, Ohio—had rubbed many officials the wrong way while serving in his twin roles as Harding's personal physician and chairman of the Federal Hospitalization Board. Sawyer's position on that board made him a key bureaucratic rival to Forbes at the Veterans Bureau, and previous disputes between Forbes and Sawyer were well-known to administration insiders. Notably, in the early months of the Veteran Bureau's existence, before suspicion centered on Forbes, Sawyer had been seen by many as the main source of trouble in the bureau. In fact, Sawyer had stirred enough resistance that the 1922 American Legion Convention adopted a resolution to remove him from the Federal Hospitalization Board. That same resolution had also included a statement of confidence in Forbes.[30] Moreover, Sawyer's allegations of fraud at Perryville were contradicted by the report of the Senate committee's own investigator, who concluded that the problems at the depot were the result of "stupidity" rather than "cupidity."[31]

Harding had replaced Forbes with a new director, retired brigadier general Frank T. Hines, on March 1. In the war, Hines had been chief of the

Army Transportation Service, where he was in charge of the movement of troops between Europe and America. Later, he was chief of the Inland and Coastwise Waterways Service of the War Department. After retiring from the army in 1920, he became general manager of the Baltic Steamship Company.[32]

Upon taking charge of the Veterans Bureau, Hines immediately began cooperating with the newly inaugurated Senate investigation. Later, in testimony before Senate investigators, Hines outlined the alleged abuses under Forbes's directorship with apparent enthusiasm. Hines told the committee about "evidence of fraud" in the dental departments of veterans hospitals, where "much gold bought has not been used." He told of abuse of railroad passes. "They were issued in blank," Hines said, "and I found plenty of people who were traveling but doing very little work." And he complained about a man who was on the payroll for $4,800 a year but "had only done two hours' work."[33] In his private communications with investigators, Hines conveyed an unflinching commitment to administrative efficiency. "Wherever inefficiency is found, it will be eliminated immediately," Hines vowed to the chairman of the investigative committee, Senator David Aiken Reed, in a personal letter.[34]

The story of Forbes as a corrupt director was so sensational that observers at the time were reluctant to question it, and thus overlooked evidence that the Veterans Bureau scandal was not quite what it seemed. Correspondence between Hines and the bureau's legal office suggests that some aspects of Forbes's alleged conspiracy were in fact directed by Sawyer. For instance, in April 1923, more than a month into Hines's tenure, an employee was caught forging signatures to obtain copies of blueprints. Investigators suspected that the man was supplying information from building plans to contractors in order to rig the bidding process. The investigator reported that the suspect "told me that if I had any business to transact with him that he would meet . . . in General Sawyer's Office."[35] After being stonewalled by both the suspect and Sawyer for several days, the investigator recommended to Hines that the suspect be arrested, concluding that "there is no question of his guilt in my opinion."[36]

This file, combined with other evidence—including documents in the Veterans Bureau records showing that Sawyer had quarreled with Forbes over which of them should have the disposition of the materiel at Perryville— seems to indicate that much of the corruption that had been attributed to

Forbes in fact continued for months after Forbes's removal, at the direction of Sawyer.[37] However, Hines overruled the investigator's clear recommendation, and the file was closed on May 26, 1923, without explanation. William Wolff Smith, who had replaced Cramer as the bureau's general counsel, had recommended to Hines that the matter to be dropped, and Hines agreed—despite his assurances to congressional investigators that "Wherever dishonesty, either in methods or procedure, is found, those guilty will be promptly dismissed, and if their methods involved criminal intent, promptly acted upon."[38]

* * *

Despite the hopes of Root and Brown, Warren G. Harding did not become a martyr for the cause of executive reorganization, and the late president's legacy was very quickly overwhelmed by revelations from a series of scandals surrounding his administration.

The Veterans Bureau scandal was just one example, but it is a characteristic and instructive one. Although the scandal was viewed by many at the time as a straightforward example of graft and public corruption, a closer examination suggests that it had more to do with the politics surrounding the elite reformers' agenda than with any particular wrongdoing by officials in the bureau. The eruption of this scandal in 1923 is perhaps best understood in the context of the congressional backlash to the Harding administration's efforts to build central control and national authority in the government.[39]

It was not a coincidence that the controversy in the Veterans Bureau came at a moment when the Harding administration was scuffling with southern lawmakers over the question of whether the Tuskegee Veterans Hospital would be staffed by white or Black doctors and administrators. The first calls for an investigation of the spurious Perryville depot allegations came from southern congressmen. Also, the early stories on the scandal from February and March 1923 seem to have relied on testimony from the same Veterans Bureau official—Assistant Director George Ijams—who had worked with southern lawmakers in defiance of Harding, Forbes, and Hines in an attempt to ensure that the hospital would be under white control.[40]

The scale and scope of endeavors such as the Veterans Bureau were too big to be legible to the public. The administrative activity of an agency of this size could easily be misconstrued by observers unused to the scale of its expenditures. The scandal, then, illuminates a potential political pitfall resulting from the elite reformers' agenda. Even if they were successful in enacting a consolidation or reorganization, proponents would have to contend with unpredictable resistance once that reorganization was put into place. Even a relatively straightforward consolidation like the one involved in the creation of the Veterans Bureau resulted in the creation of a large agency that spent large amounts of money. This reality left the new agency vulnerable to congressional critique and accusations of waste and fraud. "Big government" risked allegations of big corruption.

Chapter Nine

SOUTHERN STRENGTH

1923-1924

On December 6, 1923, shortly after the conclusion of the Veterans Bureau hearings, President Calvin Coolidge delivered his first annual message to Congress. In a terse three-sentence paragraph sandwiched between extended remarks on coal and agriculture, Coolidge affirmed his commitment to enacting the reorganization plan proposed by Warren Harding and Walter Brown. "With the exception of the consolidation of the War and Navy Departments and some minor details, the plan has the general sanction of the President and the Cabinet," Coolidge told the assembled lawmakers. "It is important that reorganization be enacted into law at the present session."[1]

Coolidge's understated endorsement reflected his administration's assessment of the plan's chances for success. The Veterans Bureau scandal and the Dyer Bill fiasco had seemed to embolden congressional hostility to the elite reformers' plans in general. Although the president and his advisers might have preferred to wait for a more opportune moment to move forward, Coolidge's hand was forced early in the New Year when the Harding-Brown reorganization plan reentered public debate in an unexpected way as Congress prepared to consider a controversial proposal to create a new federal department of education. Most elite reformers opposed the creation of a stand-alone education department because it would conflict with their proposal for a department of education and welfare. Congressional debate of the various education proposals revealed white southerners' intense opposition to a major provision of the Harding-Brown plan.

1

The proposal to create a cabinet-level department of education had emerged during mobilization for World War I after army induction examinations revealed that a quarter of the American enlistees were illiterate. This discovery helped to rekindle an old debate over the proper role of the federal government in education, and it convinced many reformers that the time had come to create a national governing institution to meet what they felt to be the federal government's responsibilities toward school-aged children.

The idea of a federal department of education was promoted primarily by the National Education Association (NEA). Founded in 1857, and chartered by Congress in 1906, the NEA still retained something of an elite cast from its origins in the nineteenth-century school reform movement, and it had not yet transformed into the teachers union it would become later in the twentieth century. During World War I, the NEA moved its headquarters to Washington, D.C., and began to shift away from the reform tactics of the previous century. The association's leaders hoped to leverage their new proximity to Congress and the White House to influence education policy.

In February 1918, the NEA formed a Commission on the Emergency in Education to draft a bill that would attempt to solve the problem of illiteracy by creating a federal department of education. The proposed department would gather information, set national standards, and provide federal funds to pay teachers and support instruction. In an attempt to neutralize anticipated opposition from southern lawmakers, the NEA convinced Senator Hoke Smith, Democrat of Georgia, to introduce their bill in October 1918.[2]

Although this initial version of the bill was favored by Protestant education reformers and many business leaders, it sparked opposition from Catholic leaders, who feared that an expanded federal role in education would undermine the existing Catholic education system, and who worried that reformers' stated goal of "Americanization" would threaten the authority of church institutions and the autonomy of Catholic families.[3]

Despite the endorsement of Senator Smith—and despite support from leaders of the Ku Klux Klan, who were impressed by the bill's anti-Catholic potential—the bill was also opposed by many white southern leaders, who worried that it would undermine local control of segregated schooling in the South. With Woodrow Wilson in the White House and Democrats in control of both houses of Congress, this southern opposition posed a significant problem for reformers. Even if a bill passed Congress, there was little chance that President Wilson would sign it, given his strict constitutionalism and his well-known commitment to segregation.[4]

The leaders of the NEA were quick to realize their mistake. "Certain of these provisions were justly criticized as permitting too much Federal interference," one NEA publication explained. "These objectionable features were eliminated and the bill carefully revised."[5]

When Congress reconvened in 1921, the revised bill was introduced in the House by Representative Horace Mann Towner, Republican of Iowa, and in the Senate by South Dakota Republican Thomas Sterling.* The Towner-Sterling Bill (as it was henceforth known) would have transferred the Bureau of Education from the Department of the Interior to a new, cabinet-level department of education.

This new department would expand considerably upon the activities of the existing Education Bureau, which had focused almost exclusively on research and data collection. The bill would have appropriated $50 million to support teacher salaries and improve instruction; $7.5 million for illiteracy; $7.5 million for immigrant education; $7.5 million for "the Americanization of immigrants," which would include teaching "immigrants fourteen years of age and over to speak and read the English language and to understand and appreciate the Government of the United States and the duties of citizenship." The bill also provided $20 million for physical education, $15 million for teacher preparation, and called for the creation of a national council on education to "consult and advise" the new secretary of education. All of these appropriations were to be made on a matching basis. In order to receive the money, the states would have to first appropriate a matching amount. The only conditions on this funding would be that states institute a school term of at least twenty-four weeks, make school attendance

---

*Hoke Smith was defeated in the 1920 Democratic primary by hardline segregationist Tom Watson. The "populist" Watson had been working tirelessly against the incumbent ever since Smith had advocated clemency for Leo Frank in 1915.

compulsory for children aged seven to fourteen, and require English as the language of instruction.[6]

The elite reformers and their allies in the Harding administration opposed to the Towner-Sterling Bill for several reasons. One was that the bill seemed to constitute a call for a classic "raid" on the nation's treasury, especially given the bill's reliance on matching grants to the states. In practice, the bill would allow states to spend federal funds without any meaningful federal oversight. This of course would violate the elite reformers' principle, articulated by Harding in his April 1921 address to Congress, that "large Federal outlay demands a Federal voice in the program of expenditure."[7]

Another objection was that the bill, if it became law, would interfere with the administration's plans for executive reorganization. Harding and Brown's proposed department was supposed to unite all of the federal government's existing education and welfare functions, including the recently created Veterans Bureau. This new department would raise the head of the federal Bureau of Education to the level of cabinet assistant secretary, without expanding the bureau's activities and without increased federal funding, but also without any explicit provisions preserving local control. But elite reformers worried that passing the Towner-Sterling Bill and establishing a free-standing department of education would make it more difficult to secure support for the Harding-Brown reorganization plan.[8]

Coolidge had explained the administration's preference in his address to Congress on December 6, 1923:

> I do not favor the making of appropriations from the National Treasury to be expended directly on local education, but I do consider it a fundamental requirement of national activity which, accompanied by allied subjects of welfare, is worthy of a separate department and a place in the Cabinet. The humanitarian side of government should not be repressed, but should be cultivated.[9]

Finally, many observers were especially troubled by the Towner-Sterling Bill's likely impact on African Americans. Statistics from the Bureau of Education showed that the problem of illiteracy was largely a problem for African Americans in the South, but the alterations that the NEA had made to assuage the fears of white southerners ensured that school segregation would continue unchallenged. An NAACP memorandum charged that the bill "especially permits and encourages the states to continue any discrimination that now exists and to have no responsibility to the Nation for their expenditure of the Nation's money."[10]

W. E. B. Du Bois criticized the bill repeatedly in his monthly column in the *Crisis*.[11] In July 1922, he described the condition of the county schools in Mississippi. "There are 353 consolidated county schools for whites, but none for Negroes," he observed. "There are 125 teachers' homes for white and none for Negroes." He noted that, in 1921, $92,000 had been raised privately—$52,000 of it from Sears president Julius Rosenwald—for the construction and maintenance of schoolhouses for African American students, while the state contributed nothing. After painting this dire portrait, Du Bois argued that "the advocates of the Sterling-Towner bill are asking the nation to give Mississippi millions of dollars of federal funds" to perpetuate this state of affairs.[12]

Florence Kelley, a white member of the NAACP's board of directors and general secretary of the National Consumers League, characterized the Towner-Sterling Bill as "an attempt on a national scale to establish forever social inequality between races."[13] She argued that the unconditional appropriation of federal money for southern states amounted to federal endorsement of segregation. "If this measure becomes law in its present form, it will legalize discrimination against equal public education for Negroes in the fifteen Southern States which are the home of Negro illiteracy," she wrote. "It will back that discrimination with a federal law and one hundred million federal dollars a year."[14]

This concern was echoed in a report produced by the U.S. Chamber of Commerce recommending the rejection of the Towner-Sterling Bill. The report—apparently a rough composite of two reports that were prepared separately—alternated between criticizing the bill as a raid on the Treasury and lamenting the bill's lack of national control. The report concluded by endorsing the Republican administration's reorganization plan, saying, "if it is considered necessary to add another member to the Cabinet, it would seem on the whole preferable that it should be a department of public welfare along the lines recommended by the President."[15]

2

In January 1924, as Congress prepared to move forward with the Towner-Sterling Bill, NAACP leaders tried to convince the bill's sponsors to adopt amendments, to be inserted into each section of the bill, that would ensure "equal educational opportunity for all persons" in states that received federal funds. The amendments were never added, however. In a memorandum describing a meeting with Senator Sterling, James Weldon Johnson, the executive secretary of the NAACP, observed that the local-control provisions in the bill "were put in for the specific purpose of making the Bill palatable to the Southern States." Johnson concluded that "it is perhaps certain that if these clauses are so changed as to make the bill distasteful to the South it will not receive votes of southern members of Congress."[16]

Concern for the sensibilities of white southerners was apparent during hearings on the bill, which were held by the House Committee on Education between February 20 and May 6, 1924. Throughout the proceedings, NEA-affiliated witnesses were careful to argue that the education emergency was a *national* problem. They emphasized illiteracy among immigrants and the need for "Americanization" in the North. They very rarely mentioned African Americans and avoided even the suggestion that education in the South was a particular problem.[17]

However, despite the care taken by the bill's advocates, it became clear during the hearings that key southern legislators viewed the Towner-Sterling Bill as an intolerable threat to white supremacy. One of the most prominent of the bill's opponents was Representative Henry St. George Tucker III, Democrat of Virginia. A constitutional scholar, advocate of states' rights, and ardent segregationist, Tucker inserted into the record of the House hearings a fifty-one-page speech that he had earlier delivered on the floor of Congress. In the speech, after winding through an elaborately filigreed exegesis on the "general welfare" clause of the Constitution and its relation to the Towner-Sterling Bill, after criticizing Alexander Hamilton's attempt to establish "upon this continent a monarchy more tyrannical than that of Imperial Rome," and after quoting at length a constitutional law treatise written by his father, John Randolph Tucker, the dean of the Washington and Lee University Law School (who, like his son, was a theorist of white supremacy), the congressman concluded on a valiant note. "The fight is on," he declared. "I invoke the aid of patriotic men of every creed and party to put their armor on and resolve never to take it off until the victory is won for the integrity of our own Constitution, the only hope of this American Republic."[18]

Tucker also inserted into the hearing's record a number of letters he had received from fellow opponents of the Towner-Sterling Bill. Most of these offered thinly veiled warnings about the dangers that central control of education would pose for white supremacy. Faculty in the Department of Romance Languages at Washington and Lee University, for instance, shared with Tucker their conviction that

> the matter of education is a question to be settled by those who are locally personally interested and informed, and a Federal officer in Washington can not be thus informed and interested as to the educational needs and the social and intellectual conditions in the several States of this wide-spread Union, nor in the local conditions within the various sections of the several States.[19]

Another letter, from a faculty member at the (Southern Presbyterian) Union Theological Seminary in Richmond, Virginia, referred more explicitly to white supremacy:

> There are local conditions, too, which would make national control of our schools simply intolerable. We have a race problem in the South. It should be left to the section to settle. There is as much conscience of duty here as in the other sections of these United States. And our own people understand the terms of the problem better than peoples living at a distance. Understanding the terms, they are the people to solve the problem. We want a pure Caucasian people preserved in the South. We look with horror on a leveling down into a negroid population.[20]

Moreover, the hearings showed that southern Democrats feared *any* change in federal responsibility for education. It eventually became clear that they viewed the Harding-Brown plan for a department of education and welfare as even more of a threat to white supremacy than the Towner-Sterling Bill. Southern congressmen and their allies were even less comfortable with comprehensive executive reorganization—with its potential to concentrate administrative responsibility in Washington—than they were with block grants distributed by an independent department of education.

Hoping to sidestep this resistance, education reformers offered several alternatives to the Towner-Sterling Bill and to the Harding-Brown plan's proposed department of education and welfare. However, none of these were acceptable to the South.

One option was to simply expand the research functions of the Education Bureau without removing it from its current position in the Department of the Interior, and without creating a new funding scheme. Just before the House committee hearings in 1924, a bill embodying this plan was introduced by the chairman of that committee, Representative Frederick Dallinger, Republican of Massachusetts. In their House testimony, both Nicholas Murray Butler, who was president of Columbia University, and Charles W. Eliot, the president of Harvard College, favored this plan. However, although Dallinger's bill won backing from the National Catholic Welfare Council as an acceptable alternative to a new department, southern proponents of local control opposed this bill just as fervently as they had opposed Towner-Sterling.[21]

The record of the debate on this idea helps to unmask the casual racism that pervaded the hearings, and it helps illustrate how much southern segregationists feared even the most modest expansion of central power in national education policy. After one witness testified in favor of the Dallinger Bill and argued that the current Bureau of Education produced excellent research but would perform even better if it were to receive more funding, Bill G. Lowrey, Democrat of Mississippi, interrupted the proceedings with a joke that turned on the ancestry of the African American abolitionist and author Frederick Douglass. The stenographer recorded that the joke was greeted with "laughter." Lowrey said:

> Apropos of the doctor's statement that the bureau has done such wonderful work with its limited opportunity, I am going to ask the committee's indulgence to permit me to tell a story. A white fellow down South was listening to a speech made by Fred Douglass, and he turned to a negro and said, "John, the man that made that speech was a half n——." And the negro said, "My Lord, boss, what would he have done if he had been a whole n——."[22]

Another option was to create a new department of education, but with no new federal expenditures, no expansion of federal activity, no assurance of local control, and no connection to any broader reorganization plan.[23]

This was the rationale behind the bill introduced in the Senate by Charles Curtis, Republican of Kansas, and in the House by David Alden Reed, Republican of New York. The goal was simply to enable more efficient execution of the existing educational functions of the federal government. While this new proposal addressed the qualms of budget hawks and elite reformers over the Towner-Sterling Bill, and while it satisfied the desire of school reformers for a cabinet-level department, it was still unacceptable to Catholic activists. And while some southerners had been willing to support the Towner-Sterling Bill, they were solidly against the new Curtis-Reed Bill, which accentuated what they felt were the administrative dangers of the previous without the benefits of increased federal funding that could be distributed by local politicians without national oversight.

* * *

Debates about education reform illustrate how the prerogatives of white southerners constrained the possibilities for government reformers after the Dyer Bill's defeat, even though Democrats remained in the minority in Congress. In the post-Dyer era, any adjustment to government institutions was now off-limits unless it accommodated the preferences of white southerners. Although the elite reformers were pleased in general by the defeat of the Towner-Sterling Bill, they now had extra reason for concern. In the process of that defeat, southern Democrats had demonstrated that they were firmly opposed to one of the major provisions of the Harding-Brown reorganization plan.

The white southerners who opposed all of these proposals recognized that even a modest increase in federal responsibility would undermine local control. They realized that such benign-seeming provisions as standard setting and data collection would ultimately pose a threat to white supremacy and segregation. It was, after all, data collected by the Bureau of Education in the first place that had revealed wartime illiteracy to be a problem that was most severe among African Americans in the South. This reality was highlighted in the U.S. Chamber of Commerce report on the various proposals on offer in 1924, which noted that, "When the Federal Government begins by setting up standards, no matter how good or necessary they may be, and in giving some one the power to withhold appropriations, Federal control has begun."[24]

Chapter Ten

CONGRESSIONAL COUNTEROFFENSIVE
Spring 1924

The historian Frederick Jackson Turner spent much of 1924 poring over maps and voting tables. Using the latest technology, Turner directed a photographic assistant to superimpose maps of county-level vote tallies atop maps of farm productivity. In an article describing his progress, Turner mused about the connection between politics and geography in American history. "Habit rather than reasoning," he observed, "is the fundamental factor in determining political affiliation of the mass of voters, and there is a geography, a habitat, of political habit."[1]

The administration of Calvin Coolidge was also preoccupied with political geography in early 1924. The opposition from western senators that had bedeviled the Harding administration had only strengthened in the months since "Silent Cal" had taken office. And, since Coolidge had not been elected to the presidency, western Republicans seemed to view his nomination at Republican National Convention in 1924 as an open question.

The president's most serious threat came from William Borah. The "Lion of Idaho" had built a reputation as a progressive on economic policy, but he had emerged as a leading opponent to the bulk of the elite reformers' agenda. Borah had backed the Wilson-friendly McCormick Bill in the budget debates, and he had proved himself an ally to white southerners by helping them scuttle the Dyer Bill in 1922. In the realm of foreign affairs,

Borah was a staunch unilateralist—an "Irreconcilable" on the question of U.S. membership in the League of Nations and a leading opponent of U.S. membership in the World Court.

Another potential challenger was Senator Hiram Johnson of California. Johnson had been a leading candidate in 1920 and was Theodore Roosevelt's Progressive Party running mate in 1912. Since then, he had remained a leader of the Farm Bloc promoting policies that favored agricultural interests. He and Borah had supported the restriction of immigration from Japan.

However, both men held back from declaring their own candidacies during the early months of 1924, preferring to use the threat to run as leverage in policy debates against the Coolidge administration. In contrast, Wisconsin progressive Robert La Follette made it known that he was determined to contest the nomination and was prepared to launch a third-party bid in the general election if he failed at the Republican convention. "Fighting Bob" was reliably radical when it came to economic policy. In contrast to Johnson and Borah, he carefully avoided making commitments on civil rights and immigration.

Throughout the early months of 1924, these three senators and their allies used the threat of a convention challenge as political leverage. Coolidge therefore faced a delicate task. He had committed to continuing Harding's administrative reform efforts, but he could not effectively defend those efforts without antagonizing the western wing of his party. To make matters worse, western Republicans in Congress were in perhaps the strongest position they had ever enjoyed, and they were as determined as ever to assert control over the White House. Lacking Warren G. Harding's popular appeal, Coolidge was forced to accommodate rather than challenge this faction. The strength of the westerners was illustrated in May 1924 by the passage of the Bonus Act and the Immigration Act and by the defeat of the Harding-Brown executive reorganization plan in June. Just weeks before the Republican National Convention, these events illustrated the new limits placed on the elite reformers in the post-Dyer era.

1

Agitation in favor of "adjusted compensation" for World War I veterans began soon after the armistice. Advocates argued that inflation had diminished the value of salaries calculated during wartime, an injustice that was compounded when those salaries were compared to the profits made by those who had stayed home during the war. A "Bonus" payment was necessary, they said, to balance the scales.

Woodrow Wilson had opposed calls for a Bonus, and he was initially joined in this position by the leadership of the American Legion. However, as the 1920 election season got underway, the Bonus movement intensified. In March of that year, in response to mounting pressure, the leadership of the American Legion changed course and announced that they would support the enactment of a cash payment for all veterans of the war.[2]

Henry Stimson's Committee for Aid to Disabled Veterans, formed to promote improvement of the veterans hospital system, took the lead in the fight against the Bonus. When Stimson announced the formation of the committee in 1920, he argued that, in an era when policy makers were increasingly intent on fiscal retrenchment, agitation for a Bonus could distract lawmakers from the task of helping disabled veterans. "The chief concern of every sound ex-service man is to see that the wounded and disabled and the dependents of those who were killed in the war get a square deal," Stimson said. "The last thing he wants to do is to stand in the way of their getting it." Stimson warned that, if the Bonus were enacted, it would be "with the inevitable result that the wounded and disabled and dependent of the war will be made to suffer for the benefit of those who came through unscratched."[3]

The first Bonus bill passed the House in July 1921, about a month after the passage of the Budget and Accounting Act and a month before passage of the Sweet Act that created the U.S. Veterans Bureau. In response, Harding made an unexpected personal appearance in the Senate chamber. In what most observers either hailed or criticized—depending on their point of view—as a bold assertion of executive prerogative, Harding urged senators to postpone further action. Noting that the economy was in the midst of an "industrial depression," Harding argued that the bill would bring "disaster to the nation's finances." Senate leaders deferred to Harding and let the Bonus bill die.[4]

However, Harding's handling of the issue provided early fodder for Democratic critics such as Mississippi senator Pat Harrison. When Congress reconvened in September, Harrison rebuked those who had acquiesced to Harding's demand, comparing the Republican senators to slave dealers.

"Oh, yes; you promised adjusted compensation to the soldiers," Harrison said, "and you gave them the auction block!"[5]

When the Bonus bill was resurrected in 1922, Harding opposed it again. The elite reformers viewed the bill as a direct threat to good government. They agreed with the editors of the *Nation*, who in March 1922 described the Bonus as

> the merest raid upon the Treasury, a sordid demand for a cash payment which will bear no relation to any financial losses any given soldier may have sustained by his service and in many cases will be of no genuine benefit, an entering wedge toward repetition of the shameful history of the Grand Army's pension-grabbing.[6]

Elite reformers also viewed congressional clamor for a Bonus as evidence of the need for increased federal power and central executive control. Budget director Dawes made this connection explicit in a July 26, 1922, memo to Harding: "The plea constantly made for uncoordinated expenditures for veteran relief is indicative of that pressure which exists for the ruinous decentralization in government business which resulted in such general waste and inefficiency in the past."[7]

However, the Harding administration's public anti-Bonus rhetoric tended to focus solely on cost and left Dawes's concerns about "ruinous decentralization in government business" unmentioned. For instance, after the Bonus bill passed both the House and the Senate in the summer of 1922, Harding vetoed the bill on Tuesday, September 19—just two days before Republicans would introduce the Dyer Anti-Lynching Bill in the Senate. In his veto message, Harding complained that "the bill has been enacted without even a suggested means of meeting the cost." One day later, on September 20—the day before Republicans introduced the Dyer Bill in the Senate—the House overrode Harding's veto, but the Senate tally came four votes short of the required two-thirds majority.[8]

Most observers agreed that the Bonus issue would be dead for the remainder of Harding's term, but after the president's death in August 1923, both sides of the Bonus battle began to prepare for a new round of conflict. A November 1923 article in the *American Legion Weekly* revealed the tenor of this new effort. Titled "Big Business Trains Its Guns on Adjusted Compensations," the article denounced Stimson's committee—which had been renamed the "Ex-Service Men's Anti-Bonus League" after passage of the Sweet Act—as a corrupt effort by Wall Street elites to cheat veterans out of their deserved compensation.* The story presented the issue in starkly populist terms, emphasizing the prominent role played by men such as Stimson and the group's ties to Wall Street. The members of the league's advisory board, the *Weekly* pointed out, were "all wealthy and all identified with big business." The league, the *Weekly* author charged, was working in concert with other business groups such as the U.S. Chamber of Commerce and was engaged in a "big game," using "trickery" and a "slush fund" "to fog up the issue."[9]

However, belying the fears of conspiracy theorists, there was little that Stimson's group or the Coolidge administration could do to stop the Bonus bill. Despite firm opposition from elite reformers, the Bonus had grown steadily in popularity since Harding's veto. Congressional support increased still further in early 1924 after the introduction of a new version of the Bonus bill that was designed to allay the concerns of budget hawks. Instead of granting an immediate Bonus payment, the new bill called for providing veterans of World War I with an interest-bearing certificate that would mature in twenty years. This would entitle them to receive $1.25 for every day of overseas wartime service and $1 for every day of domestic wartime service, plus 4 percent interest. Veterans could expect to receive a Bonus certificate worth up to $625, depending upon the length of their service, that could be redeemed at face value in 1945.[10] In 1924, $625 amounted to about half of the average production worker's annual wages.[11]

This new Bonus bill passed by wide margins in both houses. Following Warren Harding's example, and proving his loyalty to the ideals of the elite reformers, Coolidge vetoed the bill on May 15, 1924, even though the vote to override on May 19 was a foregone conclusion.

2

On the same day that Coolidge vetoed the Bonus, the House and Senate passed a bill imposing new restrictions on immigration. The Immigration

---

*The author of this article, Marquis James, won the 1938 Pulitzer Prize for Biography for his two-volume life of Andrew Jackson: *Andrew Jackson, the Border Captain*, and *Andrew Jackson, Portrait of a President* (Indianapolis: Bobbs-Merrill Company, 1933 and 1937, respectively).

Act of 1924 built upon a series of earlier laws that had already placed tight limits on immigration. The Immigration Act of 1917 imposed literacy requirements and created an "Asiatic Barred Zone" that applied to all of Asia except for the Philippines and Japan. The Emergency Immigration Act of 1921 imposed quotas on European immigrants, limiting the annual number of immigrants from each nation to 3 percent of the total population of that nationality among the foreign-born residents recorded in the 1910 census. The 1924 Immigration Act carried the anti-immigration cause even further. It expanded the Asiatic Barred Zone to include Japan, and it further tightened quotas so that new immigrants would be limited to 2 percent of the total population of that nationality among the foreign-born residents recorded in the 1890 census.[12]

The 1924 bill was sponsored by Representative Albert Johnson, Republican of Washington, who had also sponsored the 1921 act. Johnson represented a district in the southwest corner of Washington State that was a regional stronghold for the Ku Klux Klan and included a large number of white loggers, mill workers, and cannery workers. Johnson himself was an outspoken proponent of white nationalism. Cosponsoring the bill in the Senate was David Aiken Reed, the Pittsburgh Republican who during the previous year had led the Senate committee charged with investigating the U.S. Veterans Bureau.[13]

As the immigration bill advanced through Congress in early 1924, officials in the Coolidge administration became concerned. Although Harding had encouraged passage of the 1921 act, the 1924 bill's inclusion of Japan in the Asiatic Barred Zone threatened to undermine the Four-Power Treaty between the United States, the United Kingdom, France, and Japan, which had been negotiated by the Harding administration at the Washington Naval Conference in 1921. That treaty was viewed as a major triumph by elite reformers. It had been the culmination of careful diplomacy begun by Elihu Root during the Roosevelt administration and secured by Harding's secretary of state, Charles Evans Hughes. Their efforts reflected the admiration they felt toward the nation of Japan as well as their sense that a constructive relationship with Japan was essential to the national security of the United States. Thus, the new immigration bill threatened to undo two decades of careful effort and spark antagonism with a potentially dangerous rival.[14]

Secretary of State Hughes worked for several months to try to convince congressional leaders to abandon the provisions in the bill that would ban immigration from Japan. When those efforts failed, Hughes encouraged his counterparts in the Japanese government to register their disapproval of the bill. Taking Hughes's advice, Japanese ambassador Masanao Hanihara—an experienced diplomat and an old friend of Elihu Root's—sent a public letter of protest to Hughes in which he warned of "grave consequences" to "the otherwise happy and mutually advantageous relations between our two countries." However, rather than causing opponents to reconsider, the letter was viewed by western congressmen as a threat of military retaliation, leading them to redouble their support for the bill.[15]

After the bill passed on May 15, 1924, Hughes urged Coolidge to keep his veto pen at the ready. However, given the political realities of 1924, the president and his advisers were reluctant to challenge the populist western Republicans who led the anti-immigrant movement. Although Coolidge briefly considered following Hughes's advice, the vote margins of 319–72 in the House and 72–11 in the Senate made it clear that a veto would certainly be overridden. With the Republican National Convention less than a month away, Coolidge and his advisers did not relish the prospect of a second overridden veto so soon after the Bonus disaster.[16]

In signing the bill, Coolidge's instincts on this occasion matched those of Commerce Secretary Herbert Hoover. Despite his general reputation as an internationalist and his membership in the Council on Foreign Relations, on this issue Hoover sided with those expressing racist animosity toward Asian immigrants. This was perhaps not surprising given that Hoover had spent much of his youth in the agricultural Far West, where such attitudes tended to predominate. As cabinet members debated the bill, Hoover opined that there were "biological and cultural grounds why there should be no mixture of Oriental and Caucasian blood."[17]

One puzzling aspect of the roll call vote on the Immigration Act of 1924 was the large numbers of southern Democrats who joined their western colleagues from across the aisle in voting "Yea." Especially in a presidential election year, a vote in favor of the Immigration Act was in clear conflict with the interests of the national Democratic Party. Immigrants were a key constituency for Democrats in the industrialized North, and party leaders had opposed earlier restrictive legislation. For instance, Woodrow Wilson had vetoed the 1917 act, and he tried to kill the 1921 act with a "pocket veto."[18]

For observers who had followed the antilynching debate, however, the rekindled alliance between southern Democrats and western

Republicans—an alliance first forged during the debate over the Federal Elections Bill of 1890—made a certain amount of sense. It also seemed to explain the some of the more mystifying aspects of the Dyer Bill's defeat in 1922. It seemed significant, for instance, that one of the leading voices in favor of the immigration bill in 1924 was Senator Samuel Shortridge, Republican of California. It had been Shortridge's seemingly naive blunder in managing the bill's introduction that allowed southern Democrats to launch their initial impromptu filibuster and delay debate until after the midterm elections in 1922. Among those who drew a connection between the filibuster of the Dyer Bill in 1922 and the passage of the Immigration Act in 1924 was W. E. B. Du Bois, who later explained that he had not fully understood "what killed the anti-lynching bill" until after the Immigration Act of 1924. "It was a bargain between the South and the West," Du Bois wrote. "By this bargain, lynching was let to go on uncurbed by Federal law, on condition that the Japanese be excluded from the United States."[19]

3

After these two setbacks, the elite reformers' third major defeat in 1924 came on June 3, when the Joint Committee on Reorganization issued its report, presented by Reed Smoot, the Republican senator from Utah. The reorganization plan outlined in the committee's report essentially matched the Harding plan, and it was principally an executive-centered proposal. The main difference between the final plan of the joint committee and Harding's plan was the absence of a proposed department of defense. The joint committee's plan retained a "department of education and relief," which would have been formed by the merger of "the scattered agencies which now perform work in the field of public health, public education, and the care of veterans." It also retained Harding's proposal to transfer the Bureau of the Budget from the Treasury Department to the office of the president.[20]

The elite reformers were pleased with the plan. What had begun, from their point of view, as an unpromising exercise in Congress-centered executive reorganization—an attempt to assert legislative dominance over the executive branch—had, through the initiative of Warren G. Harding and Walter F. Brown, produced a plan that would have dramatically increased central power in the national government.[21]

However, the plan was so focused on empowering the president and the executive branch that it did not offer wavering congressmen any explicit promise of budgetary savings. Coming so soon after congressional victories on the Bonus and immigration—and given the impact of the antilynching debate—passage of the bold, executive-centered plan was out of the question for congressional leaders, and Coolidge was not in a position to force the issue.

The intent of the committee's congressional leaders to scuttle Brown's plan was evident even in the format of the committee's published report. Brown's recommendations were undercut by a ten-page preface outlining the history—stretching back to the 1850s—of Congress-centered executive reorganization and highlighting the budgetary savings that had been achieved in the process. The published report also contained a brief minority report coauthored by Pat Harrison, chief critic of the Republican administrations and leader of the Dyer Bill filibuster, and Virginia Democratic representative R. Walton Moore. Harrison and Moore emphasized the Harding plan's failure to promote budgetary savings. "It has become evident that the expectation of reaching results which would bring about any considerable economies will not be realized," Harrison and Moore wrote. The tenor of the report made it clear that the bill stood little chance of passage. Given the mismatch between the goals outlined in Harding's plan and the preferences of the western and southern legislators who controlled the plan's fate in Congress, it is not surprising that it was smothered in Congress without ever coming to a vote.[22]

4

Four days after the joint committee's report, the passage of the World War Veterans Act on June 7 provided the lone bright spot for the Coolidge administration and the elite reformers as they prepared for the Republican National Convention. This law comprised the legislative response to the previous year's investigation of corruption at the U.S. Veterans Bureau. Remarkably, the Coolidge administration had managed to shape the investigation—which had begun as an attempt to hobble the Harding administration's agenda—so that it provided a rationale for *enhancing* central control and national authority within the Veterans Bureau.

The Senate Select Committee had issued a report on the findings of its investigation in February 1924. That report struck a careful balance between supplying lurid details of Forbes's alleged misdeeds, on the one hand, and offering organizational and administrative recommendations, on the other. These recommendations conformed to the preferences of the elite reformers. The first section of the report was devoted to "organization of the bureau."[23] In a list of twenty-two reforms proposed by the chairmen of the committee, the first was a call to ensure that "full authority is given to the director to put in force a complete administrative reorganization."[24] The report suggested that any changes "be limited to structural provisions, leaving reasonable latitude to the director to modify the details of the organization as experience and necessity from time to time may indicate to be desirable." The text continued in this vein, explaining that "the existing law is liberal in vesting great authority and power in the director of the bureau. I do not believe this power should be curtailed because it has been abused in the past. The remedy is not to handicap an efficient director but to insure efficiency in the directorate."[25]

Most of the report's recommendations were enacted in the World War Veterans Act. Commentary in the press framed the object of the specific reforms instituted by this act as "decentralization," but the investigation report noted that "views differ widely as to the meaning of the term."[26] It is clear, however, that by "decentralization," the committee meant something akin to the business reorganization then underway at firms such as DuPont and General Motors, where certain functions were moved from headquarters to the department level. Such changes, however, did not represent a loss of authority or power for upper management. In fact, those changes were made so that the corporation would be better able to carry out the strategy devised by upper management.[27] Similarly, the reforms in the Veterans Bureau were not intended to create a dispersal of authority, but rather to make central authority more effective by specifying which decisions could best be made at the division level and which were best left with headquarters in Washington. "Decentralization" in this sense referred to the creation of orderly lines of administrative authority and the functional delegation of discretion to allow for the better enactment of executive authority.

As if to emphasize that the Veterans Bureau scandal had not shaken some policy makers' faith in the need for concentrated administrative authority in that organization, then, the policy solutions enacted in response to abuses of power by the old director (Charles R. Forbes) granted increased administrative power to the new director (Frank T. Hines). The problem of corrupt administrators abusing power and authority for personal gain was redefined as a lack of "efficiency in the directorate," meaning that the solution of choice would be to grant current administrators increased power and authority.[28]

* * *

By the time the Republican National Convention convened in Cleveland, Ohio, on June 10, 1924, Calvin Coolidge had managed to consolidate his position as party leader. In the convention hall, the president secured the nomination easily, receiving 1,065 out of 1,109 votes on the first ballot. The only dissenters were 24 delegates from Wisconsin who voted for Robert La Follette, 10 delegates from North Dakota who also voted for La Follette, and 10 from South Dakota who voted for Hiram Johnson. While La Follette and Johnson had sought to lead the party back to a 1912-style progressivism, the realities of the post-Dyer era had foreclosed any possibility of resurrecting the 1912 Progressive coalition of western insurgents and northeastern social and economic progressives. It was no longer possible to paper over the differences on civil rights within that coalition. After a worrisome moment during the convention when it seemed that William Borah might be selected as the vice-presidential nominee, the elite reformers were pleased when the nomination finally went to former budget director Charles Dawes.[29]

The intraparty squabbles on display in Cleveland quickly faded from public memory as the Democratic Party held its own fractious convention at Madison Square Garden in New York City. Stretching for fifteen long days, from Tuesday, June 24, to Wednesday, July 9, 1924, the Democratic National Convention revealed intense divisions between the party's various regional wings. For nearly 100 ballots, the delegates were deadlocked between New York governor Alfred E. Smith and California senator William G. McAdoo. Smith had the support of northern progressives; McAdoo, the son-in-law of Woodrow Wilson, the support of white southerners. An embarrassing dispute over an anti–Ku Klux Klan resolution helped sink McAdoo's chances, but anti-Catholic southern and western delegates were reluctant to support Smith. On the 103rd ballot, the delegates selected a compromise nominee, Wall Street lawyer John W. Davis.[30]

Davis's nomination created a brief crisis for Coolidge. Many elite reformers in the Republican Party considered supporting Davis, whose bona fides as a statesman and as a leader of the New York Bar meant that many of them held him in higher esteem than they did the president. However, as the Democrat nominee, Davis was obliged to promote the party platform rather than the elite reformers' preferences.[31]

Coolidge won easily in November. Key to his victory was the effort to evade the stain of scandal that had seemed to sully the legacy of the Harding administration. In addition to the Veterans Bureau scandal—which had been kept alive as Charles Forbes prepared to face bribery charges in federal court—investigations and charges of corruption had also touched the secretary of the interior with the Teapot Dome scandal, the Office of Alien Property Custodian, and the Office of the Attorney General. The Republicans' general strategy in dealing with these scandals was to cast Warren G. Harding as a bumbling naïf who allowed corruption under his watch thanks to his inability to police his "friends"—and to contrast this with the current administration's efforts to clean up the corruption that had supposedly flourished under Coolidge's hapless predecessor.

In the case of the Veterans Bureau scandal, the Republicans were aided by journalists' credulous coverage of Forbes. Few were curious about the fact that the bribe allegedly received by Forbes was tied to the construction of a veterans hospital in Northampton, Massachusetts, where Coolidge had made his career and had served as mayor. In all cases, Coolidge was able to claim to have turned the page on the scandals simply by replacing Harding's nominees with his own. This strategy was aided in the case of the Teapot Dome scandal by the fact that the Democratic front-runner, William McAdoo, had also been implicated in the affair. However, from the point of view of the elite reformers, the downside of this effort was that Coolidge and his allies began to shift back to the earlier model of good government advocacy that emphasized anticorruption over administrative reform.

Chapter Eleven

LOW EXPECTATIONS
1924–1927

The price of Coolidge's victory was the solidification of new limitations on the elite reformers' agenda after 1924. However, even in this new era of limitations, it was possible to achieve limited, qualified victories. The passage of the World War Veterans Act in 1924 had cast a small ray of hope; with enough care, perhaps the elite reformers could leverage public preoccupation with scandal and corruption to expand federal power by making incremental improvements in national administration. Debates over Prohibition enforcement seemed to provide an opportunity for one such victory. Carrying this logic further, Secretary of Commerce Herbert Hoover sought to use the nonpartisan National Civil Service Reform League to promote executive reorganization. Perhaps, Hoover and his allies reasoned, reformers could circumvent legislative opposition to administrative reform by appealing directly to enlightened public opinion.

1

National alcohol Prohibition had been enacted largely through the efforts of the Anti-Saloon League (ASL). Founded in 1893 in Oberlin, Ohio, the ASL pioneered modern issue-advocacy politics in the United States, dramatically expanding the impact of the nineteenth-century temperance movement and broadening its traditional base of support. While the earlier temperance crusade was dominated by northern Methodists and Congregationalists, the ASL's membership was geographically diverse and drawn from Protestant churchgoers of various denominations, with Southern Baptists and Presbyterians particularly well represented. The ASL used its broad bipartisan membership to put pressure on vulnerable politicians. In contrast to earlier temperance organizations, it was self-consciously pragmatic rather than idealistic or moralistic. It would support any politician—regardless of party affiliation, whether personally "wet" or "dry"—as long as they toed the ASL line on policy. The ASL's efforts to ensure that officeholders followed its directions were made even more effective by its use of modern bureaucratic techniques pioneered in big business. This gave the league administrative capacity to mobilize quickly at the local, state, and national levels.[1]

While temperance laws were generally a state-level phenomenon, national involvement in alcohol regulation had a long history. The federal government had briefly collected taxes on whiskey during the presidential administrations of George Washington and John Adams. Permanent national taxes on liquor had been in place since the Civil War. During World War I, acting under the authority of the Food and Fuel Control Act of 1917, President Wilson issued a series of executive orders placing the Bureau of Internal Revenue in control of the wartime production of "distilled spirits for beverage purposes." The terms of the Food and Fuel Control Act were limited to the duration of the war, but ten days after the armistice, under pressure from the ASL, Congress passed the incongruously named Wartime Prohibition Act. This law forbade the sale of alcoholic beverages during the period beginning June 30, 1919, and lasting "until the termination of demobilization"—an end date that was open to interpretation.[2]

Wartime Prohibition was enacted against a backdrop of intense agitation by the ASL for constitutional Prohibition. Congress had approved the league's proposed constitutional amendment on December 18, 1917. Even the most optimistic activists within the ASL had expected ratification in the states to take many years, so opponents and proponents alike were caught off guard on January 16, 1919, when—less than two months after the passage of the Wartime Prohibition Act and six months before that act's provisions were scheduled to take effect—the Eighteenth Amendment was ratified.[3]

The amendment specified that national Prohibition would take effect one year after ratification. In the early months of 1919, Wayne B. Wheeler, leader of the ASL, drafted a bill that would enact the provisions of the amendment. His draft was then revised, over the course of several more months, by Representative Andrew Volstead, Republican of Minnesota, in consultation with other Democratic lawmakers. Once introduced in the House by Volstead, the bill passed easily. It also passed easily in the Senate, although with slight amendments. After the final bill emerged from conference committee, it was sent to President Woodrow Wilson on October 10, 1919.[4]

Wilson vetoed the bill on October 27. The Volstead Bill framed postwar Prohibition as a continuation of wartime efforts at combating alcohol consumption, and this commingling of temporary, wartime functions with constitutional questions was an offense to Wilson's scruples, as he noted in his veto message. It also set a dangerous precedent that might embolden reformers who wanted to extended other wartime laws, such as the Overman Act. While it took Wilson seventeen days to issue his veto, the House took only a few hours to respond, voting 210–73 to override the veto later that same day. One day later, the Senate overrode the veto by a vote of 69–20. The act was set to take effect at the first moment allowed by the Eighteenth Amendment: midnight on January 17, 1920.[5]

The Volstead Act retained the structure of the Wartime Prohibition Act by making the commissioner of internal revenue responsible for enforcing Prohibition, but the permanent, constitutional character of the new law—and the need to enforce it in peacetime, which deprived Prohibition of the cloak of wartime patriotism—meant a significant increase in responsibility for the commissioner. The law created a federal "Prohibition director" for each state, and it exempted these officers, as well as their subordinates, from civil service rules. The law did not specify the enforcement organization to be put in place within the Bureau of Internal Revenue, so there was no statutory mechanism for the commissioner to supervise the forty-eight Prohibition directors. To carry out enforcement, Treasury Secretary Carter Glass—during his last days in the cabinet—created an ad hoc "Prohibition Unit," led by an unofficial "Prohibition commissioner" working informally under the commissioner of internal revenue.[6]

The loose-knit federal enforcement organization created by the Volstead Act had been crafted to satisfy the dry coalition assembled by the ASL, which included many groups that would not have supported a bill creating anything resembling a centralized national police force. Perhaps the most notable of these groups was the recently reconstituted Ku Klux Klan. The Klan's commitment to local control of law enforcement, racial purity, and Protestantism made it naturally supportive of the system of Prohibition enforcement created by the Volstead Act. The role that alcohol and saloons seemed to play in encouraging racial mixing and miscegenation led the group's members to view freely available alcohol as a prime threat to white supremacy. Klan fears of politically organized Jews and Catholics meant that it shared enemies in common with the ASL since both religious groups tended to be on the "wet" side of the question of Prohibition. In some locales, ASL leaders went so far as to enlist Klan vigilantes to help enforce the law.[7]

2

When the elite reformers looked at the federal Prohibition-enforcement effort in the mid-1920s, the system's informal structure, dispersed authority, evasion of civil service rules, and location within the disorderly Treasury Department seemed designed for inefficiency and prone to scandal. The reformers were particularly offended by the Volstead Act's exemption of state Prohibition directors and their subordinates from civil service requirements, which was a boon for party leaders. The ASL's official rationale for keeping these positions outside of the merit system was that civil service exams did not distinguish between "wet" and "dry" applicants. In practice, as civil service reformers routinely complained, this provision opened up a whole new field of opportunity to the "Spoilsmen." Party leaders at all levels of government were now able to dispense positions in Prohibition-enforcement offices in addition to traditional plums such as postmasterships. One result was that some opportunistic leaders supported the Volstead Act's enforcement system even if the law conflicted with the preferences of their "wet" constituencies.

Most elite reformers had argued against Prohibition before enactment. They tended to be sympathetic to the temperance cause, but in an era marked by intense political conflict between "wet" and "dry," most elite reformers were best classified as "semi-dry." They favored self-discipline for all and especially hoped to curb excessive drinking by workers and the poor. However, they felt that moral causes were best addressed through moral movements, not through constitutional amendments and coercive laws.

Elihu Root spelled out this point of view in a letter written December 20, 1919, less than a month before Prohibition was scheduled to take effect:

> I have always been of the opinion that external compulsion is the poorest way to reform character, and that if you wish a temperate people the best way is to bring such influences to bear that people will themselves prefer to be temperate. It has seemed that the steady decrease of intemperance among the American people for more than fifty years past has indicated that our people have been acquiring satisfactory standards of conduct in this respect, and have been in the course of establishing real temperance upon the permanent basis of their own free will, and it has seemed to me a great mistake upon purely temperance grounds to interrupt that process by compulsion of law.[8]

Many of Root's peers expressed similar reservations in the period before Prohibition took effect. For instance, William Howard Taft and Herbert Hoover both personally favored temperance, and they both opposed ratification of the constitutional amendment. However, after the Supreme Court rejected Root's arguments against Prohibition in March 1920, most of the elite reformers came to view Prohibition as settled law. Henceforth, Root, Taft, Hoover, and other elite reformers would argue that the law ought to be enforced effectively and efficiently.[9] Resistance to settled law, they pointed out, struck at the very basis of good government. Harvard Law professor Felix Frankfurter—a protégé of Root's protégé Henry Stimson—laid out the elite reformers' reasoning in 1923. Noting the effective nullification of the Reconstruction Amendments in the South, Frankfurter asked, "How many provisions of the Constitution can be flouted with impunity, without undue stress and strain on popular confidence in the Constitution, upon which the present social structure finally rests?" Frankfurter concluded that "the only way out, then, is honest and effective enforcement."[10]

However, the lack of an effective national enforcement organization presented an obstacle to "honest and effective enforcement." The most obvious solution was to transfer the Prohibition Unit from the Treasury to the Department of Justice. The National Budget Committee had made this recommendation as part of its executive reorganization plan in 1921. "The enforcement of the Prohibition Act is a matter which is in no sense germane to the proper functions of the Treasury," the committee insisted.[11] William F. Willoughby, the director of the Institute for Government Research, made the same recommendation in 1923. "Both from [the] standpoint of relieving the overburdened Bureau of Internal Revenue of a task not properly belonging to it and from that of vesting responsibility where it belongs," Willoughby wrote, "this service should be transferred to the Department of Justice."[12]

This idea gained little traction during the early 1920s, even though it had the support of Treasury Secretary Andrew Mellon and other leaders in the Harding and Coolidge administrations.[13] Unable to make headway in their attempt to transfer Prohibition enforcement from the Treasury to Justice, reformers set their sights on what seemed to be a more achievable goal. Starting in 1923, they made several attempts to pass bills creating a formal bureau of Prohibition within the Treasury. One such bill, which also included a provision for bringing employees under civil service rules, passed the House in 1924. However, it never came to a vote in the Senate.[14]

Reformers did not expect that these proposals would win support from party leaders or groups like the ASL or the Ku Klux Klan, but—as an IGR report noted—reformers were surprised when proposals to create a separate bureau subject to civil service laws "encountered vigorous opposition from an unexpected quarter, namely, the legitimate users of industrial alcohol and the manufacturers of pharmaceuticals, extracts, and toilet preparations in which alcohol is used as a necessary solvent."[15]

Among the leaders of this opposition were executives at the DuPont Company. Charles Lee Reese, chemical director at DuPont, explained his firm's position in a November 1924 letter. Reese pointed out that, under the original structure created by the Volstead Act, although the Prohibition commissioner had sometimes made "rulings which are extremely deleterious to the handling of the legitimate alcohol business," industrial users could appeal to the commissioner of internal revenue. As Reese explained, industrial users were comfortable with that arrangement because the commissioner was "thoroughly familiar with the details of this work." Leaders at DuPont and at other businesses that relied on a supply of alcohol for industrial use feared that any enforcement structure that bypassed the Bureau of Internal Revenue would put their fate in the hands of anti-alcohol activists affiliated with the ASL. "If these duties are put into the hands of the Prohibition Unit," Reese warned, "a lot of inexperienced fanatics will be put in charge of this industry which will undoubtedly cause a great deal of trouble."[16]

On April 1, 1925, Treasury Secretary Andrew Mellon took matters into his own hands and issued an order creating a new assistant secretary in charge of customs, the Coast Guard, and Prohibition. Other functions in the Bureau of Internal Revenue were placed under a new assistant secretary in charge of internal revenue and miscellaneous. Two months later, Mellon announced that this new assistant secretary in charge of Prohibition enforcement, Brigadier General Lincoln C. Andrews, would reorganize the Prohibition Unit. Over the course of several months, Andrews revamped the field service, replacing the forty-eight field directors—one for each state—with twenty-four "Prohibition administrators" in charge of districts that shared boundaries with federal judicial districts. Andrews also refined the division of labor between his staff in Washington and the administrators in their districts. District administrators were given authority to issue permits and perform other functions related to the physical control of alcohol. Andrews and his headquarters staff in Washington made it their priority, as the commissioner of internal revenue explained in his 1925 annual report, "secure uniformity of procedure, standardization, coördination, etc."[17]

In a manner similar to the reforms enacted through the World War Veterans Act the year before, Mellon framed this shuffling of functions and responsibilities as "decentralization." In his own annual report in 1926, Mellon put an antistatist gloss on these changes, asserting that "the Treasury felt with respect to local law enforcement that too much responsibility had been placed upon the Federal Government." Yet, as a seasoned corporate executive and a shrewd government administrator, Mellon surely recognized that, by refining the assignment of functions and responsibilities within the organization, and by providing the means for headquarters staff to set a strategy that the district administrators would implement, the Prohibition Unit's new "decentralized" structure in fact served to expand federal power in the effort to enforce Prohibition.[18]

Although Mellon's reorganization brought more "business efficiency" to national Prohibition enforcement, in some ways it actually exacerbated the Prohibition Unit's organizational problems. One of the unit's most offensive attributes—for organization-minded observers at least—was that it did not actually exist under the law. The Prohibition Unit remained an unofficial group formed to carry out the functions statutorily entrusted to the commissioner of internal revenue by the Volstead Act. As an IGR report noted, by dividing the functions of the Bureau of Internal Revenue and creating two new assistant secretaries without congressional authorization, Mellon had created a situation in which legal authority and de facto authority were vested in different officers.[19]

Reformers used this mismatch to put new pressure on Congress to act. On March 3, 1927, the last day of the Sixty-Seventh Congress, President Coolidge signed a law creating the Bureau of Prohibition, which was to be housed within the Treasury. The new bureau was led by an official commissioner of Prohibition, who was assisted by several other headquarters staff positions, all of which were to be appointed by the secretary of the Treasury. The act gave the Treasury secretary discretion to define the specific duties of the Prohibition commissioner, who was given power to appoint employees in the administrative districts. Although the elite reformers still hoped to eventually move the Bureau of Prohibition to the Department of Justice as part of a comprehensive executive reorganization plan, they were pleased with this clear, albeit small, victory.[20]

3

By 1925, executive reorganization had assumed a position in the minds of the elite reformers alongside civil service reform and the national budget system as the unfinished third pillar in a sort of holy trinity of good government. This was the theme struck by Secretary of Commerce Herbert Hoover when he addressed the annual meeting of the U.S. Chamber of Commerce on May 21, 1925. The speech was widely quoted in newspapers, distributed as a self-published booklet, and published in the June 5, 1925, edition of the chamber's magazine, *Nation's Business*, under the title "200 Bureaus, Boards and Commissions! The Administrative Branch of the Government Needs Complete Overhauling. As Important as Civil Service Reform and the Budget."[21]

> Over many years our people have been striving to better the federal administration. We have succeeded in two major steps; we still have a third equally important and perhaps more difficult one to accomplish. The first was the establishment of government employment based upon merit. The second was

the establishment of adequate control of appropriations through the budget system. There still remains the third and even greater but more obscure waste—that of faulty organization of administrative functions. And the two first steps will never reach the full realization without the third.[22]

In the speech, Hoover decried the divided responsibility created by the scattering of similar administrative functions and services in the government's hodgepodge arrangement of bureaus and agencies. "There is not a single successful business organization in the country that confuses such functions the way we do in government," Hoover said, using the business-government analogy long favored by the elite reformers. He also made clear his preference for executive-centered rather than Congress-centered reorganization. His goal was not merely budget reduction or "economy," he explained, but to increase functional efficiency in order to expand federal power and enable national policy making. "The divided responsibility, with the absence of centralized authority, prevents the constructive and consistent development of broad national policies."[23]

The day after this speech, Hoover's secretary, Harold Phelps Stokes, received a letter from Harry W. Marsh, secretary of the National Civil Service Reform League. "I have just read the report of Hoover's speech before the Chamber of Commerce and am very much impressed by it," Marsh wrote. "It strikes me that we have in this speech the very thing, put in concrete form, that we have been looking for as a subject for new and increased activities of the League."[24]

Many prominent citizens—including presidents, cabinet members, business leaders, and jurists—appeared on the NCSRL's letterhead over the years. By the 1920s, however, the league was losing funds and membership, and struggling to attract a new generation of supporters. Largely thanks to its efforts, the merit system had expanded gradually during the Progressive Era. In 1923, nearly 80 percent of federal positions were classified under civil service rules.[25] Ironically, this long-term success gave observers the impression that the work of civil service reform had already been done. At the same time, the NCSRL faced a challenge from a new generation of academic scholars who viewed the genteel league as a throwback to a bygone era. In a letter to members in 1923, the NCSRL's president, William Dudley Foulke, issued a desperate plea:

We who now form the Council and Executive Committee and manage the League are nearly all old and in a few years there will be no one to carry on the work... We must, moreover, have a number of young men in the League for active work. I confess I know hardly any... You must know some young men who will undertake it and your interest in the reform prompts me to believe that you will induce them to do so. Please give me the names, addresses and qualifications of those whom you would consider available and who would be willing to undertake the task.[26]

By Spring 1925, the NCSRL had formed a three-person "committee of young men" to explore possibilities for expanding the league's activities.[27] This committee held a series of meetings in June and July "to ask for suggestions as to the most fruitful lines of activity for the League to pursue" from prominent policy makers and policy advocates in New York and Washington. Their schedule included a meeting with Herbert Hoover on June 4, a week and a half after the secretary's Chamber of Commerce speech on reorganization.[28] During that meeting—and following up on the suggestion already made by the league's secretary to Hoover's secretary—Hoover suggested to the young men that, if the league was considering expanding its activities, it ought to join the effort to bring about executive reorganization. The committee embraced the idea, and within a week the NCSRL's secretary reported back to Hoover's secretary that the council of the NCSRL agreed.[29]

The league was slow to make progress, however, and it ultimately took more than a year to move beyond initial discussions. In October 1925, Secretary Marsh of the NCSRL secured a brief meeting with Hoover in Washington. Hoover described what he viewed as the real problem: despite broad elite support for executive reorganization in these years, the subject of executive reorganization seemed to inspire general indifference among voters. The solution, he argued, was to build public opinion that could put pressure on Congress. Accordingly, NCSRL leaders decided to mount a public-relations campaign in favor of reorganization. However, they did not produce a manifesto for this campaign until May 1926. Although it had taken time to produce, the statement was a forceful call for executive-centered reorganization that focused on the need for central authority in the national government:

> The National Civil Service Reform League has determined to extend its activities by promoting the simplification of the administrative branch of the federal government. At the present time, no matter how able an administration is in office, there is unavoidable waste, duplication of effort and lost motion. The machinery of government is too complicated and there is a lack of centralized responsibility, which makes it impossible to have the proper cooperation between branches of the government engaged in similar work.[30]

In consultation with Hoover's office, the league's council decided that the best course of action would be to form a special reorganization committee comprised of prominent citizens who had shown an interest in the problem of executive reorganization. Despite his own role in persuading the NCSRL to take up the cause of reorganization, Hoover was careful to avoid leaving his own fingerprints on the project. Back in 1922 and 1923, during discussions of the Harding reorganization plan, Hoover had aroused the ire of other cabinet members who felt that the secretary of commerce was using reorganization to feather his own nest. In a letter to the NCSRL conveying Hoover's recommendations for committee members, Hoover's secretary cautioned the NCSRL's secretary that "Mr. Hoover will much appreciate your consulting him in the matter but would naturally not want to be put in a position of dictating any committee make-up, or having invitations sent as in any way coming from him."[31]

By the time that the NCSRL issued its reorganization manifesto, the league had already assembled the four men who were meant to serve as the core members of the committee. The first two men to join were Charles Evans Hughes and Henry Stimson.[32] A year earlier, they had been cochairs of a commission to reorganize the government of New York State, and they were eager to apply their ideas at the national level.[33] Having secured these two prominent Republican corporate lawyers and statesmen, the NCSRL planning committee next approached the two leading Democratic lawyers on Wall Street: John W. Davis and Frank L. Polk, partners in the firm of Davis, Polk and Wardwell. Polk was undersecretary of state in the Wilson administration and had led the American Commission to Negotiate Peace in 1919 in addition to managing Davis's presidential campaign in 1924.[34]

The committee would not be filled until another round of invitations was sent out at the end of October 1926. Hoover himself was also invited to serve but did not join officially until December 1926. That invitation was sent on behalf of the NCSRL by Hoover's former personal secretary, Harold Phelps Stokes, who had left Commerce during the previous year for a position on the editorial board of the *New York Times*; he had also been a long-standing member of the NCSRL. As Hoover's new secretary explained to Stokes, the secretary of commerce still wished to avoid any appearance that the NCSRL's reorganization committee was *his* committee.[35]

Nearly two years after Hoover's speech, the league was finally ready, on May 12, 1927, to publicly announce the formation of its seventeen-man reorganization committee. The committee's lineup, as it was announced in 1927, provides some insight into the political coalitions and alliances that supported national administrative reform in the mid-1920s. Notably, there were no academic scholars of public administration. The only professor on the list was Edwin Gay, dean of Harvard Business School, who had led the Central Bureau of Planning and Statistics during the war. In fact, the committee was comprised overwhelmingly of men with significant experience in the business world.[36] In addition to the four Wall Street lawyers, four members had general experience as business executives and another four had been executives in the publishing industry.[37]

Hoover was joined on the committee by another future president: Franklin D. Roosevelt. In these years, FDR was widely known as a business-friendly supporter of the elite reformers' agenda. As assistant secretary of the navy during the debate on budget reform in 1919, he had been the only member of the Wilson administration to support the NBC's proposal to place a new budget bureau in the office of the president rather than in the Treasury, and he regularly spoke in support of executive reorganization. In a February 1920 speech at the Harvard Union, Roosevelt argued that the United States should "make our government as efficient as we would conduct our own private individual business." In March 1920, the *New York Times* printed his letter to Representative R. Walton Moore, Democrat of Virginia (who would be named to the Joint Committee on Reorganization at the end of the year). In the letter—several typescript copies of which are preserved in the NCSRL reorganization committee files—FDR proclaimed his support of executive reorganization in a formulation that nicely encapsulates the agenda of business-minded administrative reformers of this era. "I believe America stands, as a whole, for business efficiency in the conduct of its affairs," he wrote. "In this respect," FDR asserted, "the Congress of the United States and the executive departments of the Government need

Americanizing more than any of our other institutions." Roosevelt also served on the advisory board of the IGR's Bureau of Public Personnel Administration, an organization devoted to sharing administrative expertise between leaders in business and government. In 1925, when the NCSRL's committee of young men held its meetings with selected policy makers and policy advocates to consult about the league's future plans, one of their first meetings—before Herbert Hoover—was with FDR.[38]

4

However, despite broad, bipartisan support, despite the list of eminent public men who made up the committee, and despite Hoover's high hopes for his joint venture with the NCSRL, the league's reorganization campaign never got off the ground. A publicity campaign of the scale that Hoover and NCSRL leaders envisioned would be expensive, and the most obvious stumbling block was the difficulty of raising funds toward the committee's proposed annual budget of $25,000.[39] In January 1929, when the NCSRL made a final funding request to John D. Rockefeller Jr.'s office, Rockefeller's secretary, Thomas Appleget, "observed that" achieving executive reorganization "was a problem of considerable magnitude and wondered how the League could do much toward that end."[40]

Although NCSRL leaders were mystified by this demurral, Rockefeller and his advisers had decided against funding the reorganization committee after the league's initial pitch in 1926.[41] The lack of enthusiasm from Rockefeller and his associates for the NCSRL and its reorganization campaign stemmed from their awareness of the political obstacles that would confront any attempt at national administrative reform. Ever since the mid-1910s, when farm-state congressmen had interpreted a Rockefeller-funded farm-improvement project as an attempt by Rockefeller Jr. to control the federal government, Rockefeller had been wary of stirring up southern and western opposition to his activities.[42] Applying the lessons from that debacle, whenever Rockefeller-affiliated organizations ventured into national administrative reform, they made sure to limit their efforts to "scientific" inquiry and to avoid seeming to advocate specific governmental reforms.[43]

This also led Rockefeller and his advisers to adopt a policy by which it hoped to avoid contributing to organizations whose work might conflict or

LOW EXPECTATIONS

overlap with other Rockefeller-funded enterprises. An internal report—drafted in response to the NCSRL's preliminary request in 1926—concluded that the league lacked capacity for the project and, further, "that it would be advisable to combine this League with the Bureau of Public Personnel Administration making one the publishing and aggressive body and the other the research and fact finding body."[44] At the time, Rockefeller was giving $25,000 a year to the Bureau of Public Personnel Administration (BPPA), which had been formed as a subsidiary of the IGR in 1922 to conduct "scientific research" into public personnel administration methods and to serve as a clearinghouse of information and advice to personnel managers in government and business.[45]

Rockefeller's insistence on well-coordinated support for the scientific study of public administration eventually caused the BPPA itself—after a brief period of operating at the University of Chicago—to be shut down in order to provide a broader field for the Public Administration Clearing House, a research organization that was underwritten by the Rockefeller-connected Spelman Fund of New York and directed by Louis Brownlow, a pioneer in the academic study of public administration.[46]

Part of the problem for the NCSRL was poor timing. Its attempt to form a reorganization committee coincided with the emergence of a new ecosystem of foundation-funded social science inquiry and public administration professionalization. The Public Administration Clearing House (organized in 1930) was just one of the many social science research organizations formed in the years following World War I. The list of new institutions formed in the 1920s includes the National Bureau of Economic Research (1920), the National Institute of Public Administration (reconstituted from the Bureau of Municipal Research in 1921), the Social Science Research Council (1923), and the Brookings Institution (formed by merging the IGR with the Institute of Economics in 1927). This proliferation of research organizations was fueled by an increase in funding from philanthropic foundations. The largest part of this funding came from the various foundations funded by the Rockefeller family (which underwent their own comprehensive reorganization in 1928), including the Rockefeller Foundation and the Spelman Fund. Other important donors included the Russell Sage Foundation, the Carnegie Corporation, the Rosenberg Fund, Edward Filene's Twentieth Century Fund (now the Century Foundation), and the Maurice and Laura Falk Foundation.[47]

In this setting, the NCSRL and its committee of "eminent men" seemed a hopeless anachronism. In the early 1920s, citizens' committees staffed by the "best men" could still garner some respect among the populace. But by the late 1920s, groups like the NCSRL seemed to lack legitimacy when compared to the Social Science Research Council and other modern research organizations. This was illustrated starkly in 1932 when, in response to the league's appeal for an increased contribution to its general operating budget, Rockefeller's secretary went as far as to suggest that the NCSRL be replaced entirely and that "merging the activity of the National Institute of Public Administration and the American Political Science Association" would "more adequately" cover "the ground now covered by the National Civil Service Reform League."[48]

* * *

The Prohibition Enforcement Act of 1927 provided a welcome victory for advocates of national administrative reform. Like the World War Veterans Act of 1924, it showed that small improvements in the federal administration were possible. Apart from this small victory, the late 1920s were a time of disappointment and frustration for advocates of national administrative reform. The passage of the Budget and Accounting Act of 1921 remained their biggest achievement, and their attempts to build upon that success had met mostly with failure. However, even though they were boxed in by a coalition of southern racists and western white nationalists, the elite reformers remained committed to building central control and national authority. Although the NCSRL's committee had failed to make any progress toward the of goal executive reorganization, some reformers were optimistic that the emerging ecosystem of philanthropically funded social science might hold the possibility of long-term success.

Chapter Twelve

THE GREAT ENGINEER
1929–1931

The election of 1928 seemed to provide new hope for advocates of good government. The Republican majorities in both chambers of Congress expanded considerably and, after Inauguration Day 1929, the White House would be occupied by a long-time champion of executive reorganization. Herbert Hoover drew a sharp contrast with his fellow alliterative commander in chief Calvin Coolidge. "Silent Cal" had been almost a caricature of the provincial New England Yankee, and many elite reformers wondered whether he could effectively advance their agenda. These worries were reflected in a 1925 letter in which leaders of the National Civil Service Reform League gossiped about Coolidge's apparent shortcomings in a way that illustrated their own priorities:

> He attaches a ridiculous importance to New England birth and education. He can't see anything in bulk or mass, but has to see it in terms of a New England personality. If . . . a fine Vermont boy is being kept out of the air service by [Postmaster General] New, that is a good argument. The opinion of . . . any well known [New England] Republican is another, but any argument about law enforcement or good in bulk is lost on him. He never looks below the surface and demands nothing but optimistic reports.

His whole idea of government is to lop off expenses without discrimination; it is useless to put up to him broad arguments[. T]he way to stop him is to say that if he should lop this particular branch[,] a deserving Republican a graduate of a New England college or a resident of N. E. will lose his job. That holds him.

He doesn't understand civil service or any other question and never will.[1]

1

For his part, Hoover had transcended his roots in the rural Far West and cultivated a reputation as a cosmopolitan man of action. As secretary of commerce under Harding and Coolidge, "the Great Engineer" had proven himself to be one of the most effective policy advocates among the elite reformers. Surrounded by a cadre of young aides who were slavishly loyal to the man they insisted on calling "the Chief," Hoover was widely admired not only within the northeastern business community, but also among many self-styled progressives who agreed with the assessment of the aged welfare pioneer Louisa Lee Schuyler. In a 1923 letter to Franklin Delano Roosevelt, Schuyler urged the young man to recruit the secretary of commerce to run for the Democratic Party's presidential nomination, writing: "There is no man in our country, holding an official position, for whom I have a greater admiration and esteem than for Mr. Hoover, both for his great mental capacity and his integrity of character."[2]

After his inauguration, the vigor that Hoover promised to bring to the White House was perhaps best symbolized by the president's daily 7:00 a.m. game of "Hooverball." Each morning, before assembling for work, the Chief, his staff, and several cabinet members would gather on the White House lawn to play a cross between tennis and volleyball using a six-pound medicine ball.[3]

However, belying his reputation for vitality and dynamism, once in the White House Hoover took a decidedly cautious approach when it came to advancing the elite reformers' agenda. Rather than charge ahead, as the Harding administration had done in its first months, Hoover spent the first year of his presidency working carefully to build support for his agenda for administrative reform before taking any definite steps.

This approach reflected Hoover's view of political realities and the lessons of the previous decades. The Republican victory in November 1928 had been decisive, but not decisive enough to overcome the forces arrayed against the elite reformers. The party's majorities in Congress were larger than those of the Coolidge era, but smaller than those of Harding's first two years. Southern Democrats remained resolutely opposed to central control and national authority, and they had proven their willingness to use the obstructive tools of the Senate to block any policy at odds with their preferences. At the same time, the divisions between northeastern and western Republicans were more fraught than ever. The "Farm Bloc" of western Republicans and southern and western Democrats held potential majorities in both chambers of Congress, and western leaders such as William Borah and Reed Smoot were skeptical of the president's plans and ready to join the southern Democrats when it suited them.

However, Hoover believed it was possible to pursue his agenda while sidestepping the opposition that had hamstrung the efforts of the previous decades. To avoid sparking southern opposition, Hoover was careful to steer clear of any suggestion that he sought to interfere with Jim Crow. His strongest signal in this direction had come before the Republican National Convention in 1928. In a throwback to Theodore Roosevelt's strategy in 1912, Hoover had struck agreements with several "Lily-White" delegations from southern states. During the general election campaign, although the 1928 Republican platform included an antilynching plank resembling the one inserted in 1920, Hoover was careful to maintain an accommodationist tone.[4]

In November, Hoover had scored Electoral College wins in Tennessee, Virginia, North Carolina, Florida, Oklahoma, and Texas. This had given him some optimism that he might be able to win over white southerners. However, while Hoover might have taken this as vindication of his southern strategy, these victories likely had more to do with the nomination of the Catholic New York governor Alfred E. Smith on the Democratic ticket.

For his part, Smith had gone to great lengths to mollify southern leaders during the campaign. For instance, in September 1928, when Smith was accused of employing an African American woman as his private stenographer, his campaign issued an earnest denial: "Governor Smith does not have, and never has had, a Negro stenographer, and in the employment of Negroes by the State of New York under his administration this has been done only to fill such jobs as they are given in the South, to wit: porters, janitors, char-women, etc."[5]

Writing in the *Nation*, W. E. B. Du Bois excoriated Smith's record on race. "The interesting thing about this statement is that it is perfectly true," Du Bois wrote. "In all Governor Smith's long career, he has sedulously avoided recognizing Negroes in any way or manner." However, Du Bois lamented that Hoover was hardly better, writing that "Hoover's silence ... has been nearly as great as Smith's. He has said not a single public word against lynching or disfranchisement or for Negro education and uplift."[6]

At the same time that Hoover sought to distance himself from civil rights advocacy, he also sought to align himself more closely with the new social science research organizations and philanthropic foundations that funded them. Perhaps, Hoover reasoned, his proposals could fare better in Congress if they had the imprimatur of the experts at the Brookings Institution, the Public Administration Clearing House, or the Social Science Research Council. If Hoover's plans could be framed as the product of politically neutral social scientists rather than the councils of eminent public men on Wall Street, it might be possible to avoid some of the opposition that had frustrated the elite reformers' earlier efforts.

So, rather than emulating Harding's strategy of lining up eminent public men as supporters of his policies and charging ahead with legislation, Hoover began his administration by launching a series of social-scientific studies conducted by leading academic investigators. If controversial action was required, Hoover could cite "science" as the rationale. As Hoover's first year progressed, his eyes were fixed on large, long-term goals rather than on quick policy victories.

2

The first of Hoover's major studies focused on the problem of education. The election of 1928 had followed a decade of failure in the effort to reform the organization of federal education activities. Most elite reformers still viewed national standards in education as a necessary component of the country's success, but political resistance remained firmly in place.

In his inaugural address on March 4, 1929, Hoover's statement on education was sufficiently vague that it could be read either as a call to arms or an admission of defeat:

> Although education is primarily a responsibility of the States and local communities, and rightly so, yet the Nation as a whole is vitally concerned in its development everywhere to the highest standards and to complete universality. Self-government can succeed only through an instructed electorate. Our objective is not simply to overcome illiteracy. The Nation has marched far beyond that. The more complex the problems of the Nation become, the greater is the need for more and more advanced instruction.[7]

In May 1929, Hoover selected Secretary of the Interior Ray Lyman Wilbur to organize a fifty-two-member National Advisory Committee on Education. Wilbur and Hoover had been close friends since the early 1890s, when they were both students at Stanford University. While Hoover pursued a career as a mining engineer, Wilbur became a medical doctor, eventually joining the faculty at his alma mater. Rising in the university administration, in 1916 he became president of Stanford.[8]

In announcing the committee, Hoover referred to the controversy that had surrounded previous attempts to reform federal education activities. "In view of the considerable difference of opinion as to policies which should be pursued by the Federal Government with respect to education," he explained, "I have appointed a committee representative of the important educational associations and others to investigate and present recommendations."[9]

Given the proximity of education policy to problems of civil rights and racism, the members of Wilbur's education committee faced a difficult political situation. If they were to strongly endorse federal assurance of equal educational opportunities for African Americans, they would further rile white southern opposition. But if they ignored the problem of racism altogether, they would offend African Americans, further alienating a key group of Republican voters—one that was already frustrated with Hoover's embrace of Lily-Whiteism at the Republican National Convention in 1928.[10]

Wilbur's education committee included representatives from various constituencies. Notably, it included Catholic educators—a strategic choice since the National Catholic Welfare Council had led the opposition to the

Towner-Sterling Bill and other education-reform proposals during the Harding-Coolidge years.[11]

However, the initial roster did not include any African American educators. In response to criticism on this score, Wilbur eventually added three African American college presidents to the committee: John W. Davis, of the West Virginia Collegiate Institute (no known relation to his namesake and fellow West Virginian, the Democratic presidential nominee of 1924); Mordecai Johnson, of Howard University; and Robert Russa Moton, of the Tuskegee Institute.[12]

When Wilbur's committee published its findings in October 1931, its majority report acknowledged that the education of African Americans was "one of the most perplexing problems" that it had faced in its work. Yet the overarching tone of the statements on racism in the report was one of accommodation. The report stated that "Negroes are American citizens and as such are entitled to such schooling as will give each his utmost chance." And it applauded "the impressive advance made by the colored people, largely by their own efforts, in their steady progress up from slavery, their steadily increasing attendance at high school and college, and their steadily rising standards of living."[13]

However, these statements were prelude to an argument *against* federal aid directed at bringing further improvements to African American education. Echoing some of Hoover's arguments in other realms of policy making, the majority report advanced the argument that voluntaristic contributions were preferable to government-directed aid. Carrying this logic further, they averred that the social progress made by African Americans could ultimately be attributed to the efforts of accommodationist philanthropic organizations. "This advance, stimulated by generous gifts of private funds and directed by patriotic leaders of both races," the majority asserted, "has accomplished in a generation vastly more than could have been achieved by any special grant of federal funds, however great." The report did not offer any supporting evidence for the majority's counterfactual assertion about the limits of what "could have been achieved by any special grant of federal funds."[14]

This was a strange rhetorical shift. In earlier years, reformers had often proposed educational initiatives as a more palatable alternative to direct agitation for civil rights. But the Wilbur committee's majority report inverted this logic, making the reverse argument that education reform was ill-advised because of problems arising out of racism and segregation. "It seems clear that the actual limitations which still operate to handicap Negroes are primarily due to imperfections in the political, economic, physical and social conditions often surrounding them." Since these problems did not stem from problems in educational policy, the committee argued, education reform was neither wise nor necessary.[15]

The majority report went further than merely obfuscating the problem. Elsewhere in the text, the authors struck a brazen compromise with advocates of local control and recommended that federal aid be given "generally" to the states, with no matching requirements or restrictions on use. At the same time, they recommended the creation of a federal department of education. "To realize the policies presented in this report," the committee explained, "there must be in the Government, close to its head coordinator, the Chief Executive, a spokesman for the American spirit and method in education, who may on all occasions express that enlightened public opinion upon educational matters which is our surest guide in formulating public policy." In short, the majority created a near replica of the Towner-Sterling Bill, preserving the aspects of the bill that civil rights advocates in the early 1920s had criticized for essentially giving federal backing to segregated education.[16]

The committee's majority concluded its discussion of education for African Americans by firmly endorsing local control and asserting that its recommendations would be sufficient to solve the problem:

> Policies regarding dependence on local autonomy, and regarding federal grants for education in general to be administered by the States, as outlined in this report, when applied to the Negroes, will in the end result in more lasting benefit to them than would federal action directed toward supplying quickly any special educational facilities for the Negro under federal supervision or administration.[17]

The members of the committee voted 43–8 in favor of the majority report. A separate vote was held on the committee's recommendation for a department of education. The results of that vote were 38–11 in favor, with two members abstaining.[18]

The three African American members of the committee voted against the report and produced their own minority report.[19] As their selection by

Hoover and Wilbur for this committee attests, John W. Davis, Mordecai Johnson, and R. R. Moton were not known as radical activists. All three had been longtime supporters of Hoover and all three were seen as firmly inhabiting the moderate or accommodationist tradition of Booker T. Washington. Thus, their dissenting minority report was devastating for the majority's claim to have thoroughly considered the issue of race, especially since the majority had cited the success of "private" efforts as a reason to avoid government involvement. These three men were in fact leaders in those private efforts to aid education, and they knew much better than the white members of the committee the nature of the problems facing African Americans under southern segregation. In their report, Davis, Johnson, and Moton affirmed their basic agreement with "the principles of local autonomy with decentralized control, and of general grants." However, they argued that this policy on its own would be "inadequate to define the line of action which the Federal Government should pursue in discharging its obligation to those States which are struggling with the problem of Negro education."[20]

Davis, Johnson, and Moton argued boldly that it was in fact the responsibility of the federal government to solve the problems faced by African American students. "A firm grappling with this problem will lead the Government inevitably in the direction of some form of special grant for at least a limited number of years."[21] They argued that the "heavy educational disadvantages" facing African Americans in states where schooling was segregated by race were "descended from historical situations which all of the States cooperated to maintain." Therefore, they wrote, "it is the deep rooted historic duty of all the States expressing their will through the Federal Government, to help in overcoming these conditions."[22]

Echoing earlier criticism of the Towner-Sterling Bill, Davis, Johnson, and Moton argued that the majority report's plan for "general grants" would not improve the situation in the southern states, because the problems in those states derived not merely from lack of school funding, but from disfranchisement—or, as they put it more delicately, "the abnormal relationship which prevails between the people of the disadvantaged racial minority and the public life."[23] To help overcome the problems created by general grants, they advocated "special Federal grants." These special grants should be "conditioned upon some definite increase in the per capita amounts and in the percentages of State support made available for Negro education." To ensure that the grants were used for their intended purpose, they suggested that they "should require simple reports and audits, for it will be sufficient for the Federal Government to know that the monies did go into Negro education and that they did go into the definitely agreed upon relationship to increased State funds." The three Black educators concluded with an understated challenge. "No State will resent such helpfulness," they wrote, "except it be the deliberate purpose of such a State to maintain its Negro citizens in a permanent state of educational disadvantage."[24]

A separate minority report was written by the committee's two Catholic educators, the Reverends Edward A. Pace and George Johnson, who laid out objections to the majority report that likely had more sympathy in Congress than did the objections of Davis, Johnson, and Moton. After voicing approval for what they viewed as the committee's "fundamental principle"—"that there should be no centralized federal control of education and that the autonomy of the States in regard to the purposes and processes of public education should be preserved"—Pace and Johnson argued that the proposal for a federal department of education was in opposition to that principle. Further, they wrote that it was "obvious" that the proposed department would "inevitably bring about centralization and federal control of education."[25]

Despite Hoover's hopes, Wilbur's committee had simply recreated and rehashed the debates around the Towner-Sterling Bill, and no action was taken on the recommendations contained in either the majority or the minority report. Yet Hoover was still interested in trying to solve the education problem. When Wilbur's committee published its report in October 1931, Hoover already had another education study under way.

3

This new education study was conducted as part of Hoover's ambitious President's Research Committee on Social Trends. Formed in December 1929, the committee included the nation's leading social scientists and relied on institutional support from the Social Science Research Council. The Committee on Social Trends was charged with conducting a survey of American society in all its aspects. Research teams were to conduct multiyear projects that would result in the production of data and the publication of monographs on such topics as (to quote the titles of several representative chapters) "The Population of the Nation," "Rural Life," and "Labor Groups in the Social Structure." In order to ensure that this project could avoid the fate of the Taft Commission, which was killed when Congress stopped its appropriation, Hoover secured funding from the Rockefeller Foundation.[26]

Throughout the life of the committee, Hoover repeatedly emphasized that the various studies produced by the project would be the sole product of the experts employed to conduct the research, and that he had no role in shaping the outcome of its investigations. As he put it in his introduction to the committee's summary report, "The survey is entirely the work of the committee and its experts, as it was my desire to have a complete, impartial examination of the facts."[27] Nevertheless—and not surprisingly, since Hoover and his advisers had directed the selection of researchers and research topics—the researchers' inquiry remained firmly within the bounds established by the Chief. For instance, the project investigating "Races and Ethnic Groups in American Life" did not threaten Hoover's efforts to make his agenda palatable to southerners. The study focused solely on demographic and "biological" questions and avoided any serious discussion of racism or racist violence.[28]

The leader of the Committee on Social Trend's study on education was Charles H. Judd, of the University of Chicago. During the early postwar years, Judd had been a leading critic of racial segregation in education and a bold voice in favor of a department of education. A decade earlier, Judd had spoken in favor of national control in education in 1920. However, as a member of Secretary Wilbur's National Advisory Committee on Education in 1931, he voted in favor of the committee's majority report.[29]

In his report for the Committee on Social Trends, Judd was even more careful than the majority of the Wilbur committee had been, avoiding the subjects of race and sectionalism altogether. One of the only points in Judd's study to contain even a hint of an acknowledgment of sectional problems was a discussion about the evolution of secondary school curricula. Summarizing a table showing the "five states which in 1928 [had] the highest percentages of enrollment in the traditional subjects of Latin and algebra," Judd acknowledged that "the readjustments in the curricula of American secondary schools have not been made uniformly in the various states" and that "the southeastern states are more conservative than are the northern and western states in adopting a curriculum suited to the varying needs of young people of different social groups."[30]

Turning to the question of federal organization, Judd resigned himself to simply listing the various options that had been considered over the years. It was an open question, he observed, whether national education policy should be coordinated through "the organization of a new federal department," or through "the creation of a council," or by "some other device." However, Judd did not end up endorsing any of these plans. "There are many divergent opinions," he wrote, before concluding on a downcast note: "The one principal on which there seems to be general agreement is that no federal agency should be endowed with power to control the educational systems of the states."[31]

4

The most contentious political question during Hoover's term in the White House was Prohibition. The president and his allies shared the elite reformers' conviction that law—especially a law enshrined in the Constitution—ought to be enforced. However, on the eve of the election in 1928, agitation in favor of repealing the amendment had suddenly increased.

Since 1919, the Association Against the Prohibition Amendment (AAPA) had been the most prominent organization in opposition to Prohibition. The association's bylaws forbade the filling of any leadership role, or the acceptance of any funding from, persons involved in the liquor business. However, at the end of 1927, the leadership of the AAPA was taken over by a group of men with ties to the DuPont Company—the same group that had earlier led the opposition to establishing an independent Prohibition bureau. The new head of the association was Pierre S. DuPont, chairman of General Motors and DuPont. Also involved in the new leadership group were Pierre's brothers, Irénée and Lamont, as well as John Raskob, an executive at GM and DuPont.[32]

With this change of leadership, the AAPA adopted a new, more aggressive stance against Prohibition and for repeal of the Eighteenth Amendment. This was made possible by the financial resources of the new leadership group. Emulating the strategies pursued in their business affairs, the leaders of the new, post-1927 AAPA invested in innovation by creating a research department, headed by John C. Gebhart, who had been an investigator for a study of Prohibition conducted by the Social Science Research Council in 1926.[33] For most of the decade, the Anti-Saloon League had been able to flood the nation with promotional material extolling the benefits of Prohibition. But starting in 1928, with its increased funding and its research department, the AAPA quickly began to out-pamphlet the ASL, alerting the public to the various evils wrought by Prohibition.[34]

The AAPA also began to develop close ties with the Democratic Party. After pro-repeal New York governor Al Smith won the party's presidential nomination in 1928, Smith invited AAPA board member John Raskob to serve as chairman of the Democratic National Committee. Hoping to turn the election of 1928 into a national referendum on Prohibition, the AAPA succeeded in inserting pro-repeal planks into the Democratic Party platform and placed its considerable resources behind Smith's candidacy.[35]

However, the 1928 election did not turn out the way the AAPA had hoped. Despite the best efforts of organized wets, Hoover won convincingly. And, his personal skepticism about the wisdom of constitutional Prohibition notwithstanding, Hoover remained committed to the elite reformers' view that the law should be enforced as effectively and efficiently as possible. In February 1928, early in his campaign for the Republican nomination, Hoover had affirmed this commitment in a public letter to Senator William Borah in which he characterized Prohibition as "a great social and economic experiment, noble in motive and far-reaching in purpose."[36]

Once in the White House, one of Hoover's priorities was to build upon the creation of the Bureau of Prohibition in 1927 by enacting the organizational reform that had first been suggested by the National Budget Committee in 1921. In his March 4, 1929, inaugural address, Hoover asserted that "it is essential that a large part of the enforcement activities be transferred from the Treasury Department to the Department of Justice as a beginning of more effective organization." Hoover also called for the formation of an expert national crime commission to survey the problem of Prohibition enforcement in the context of "a searching investigation of the whole structure of our Federal system of jurisprudence." That same day, Congress approved funding for such a commission in the amount of $250,000.[37]

Hoover selected George Wickersham to serve as chairman. A prominent corporation lawyer and a committed civil service reformer, Wickersham had developed among his peers a reputation for sound judgment, integrity, and pragmatism. During the Taft administration, he served as attorney general. After Taft's defeat in 1912, Wickersham earned admiration even from his political opponents by following through on his promise to refuse Washington retainers for two years. Throughout his career, Wickersham maintained a close friendship with Taft. On the subject of Prohibition, Wickersham—like Taft, Stimson, and Hoover—was committed to enforcing the law.[38]

In addition to its namesake chairman, the Wickersham Commission included ten other commissioners: the Democratic wartime secretary of war Newton D. Baker; three federal judges, William S. Kenyon, Paul J. McCormick, and William I. Grubb; former Washington State Supreme Court chief justice Kenneth Mackintosh; Dean Roscoe Pound of Harvard Law; Ada Comstock, president of Radcliffe College; and three private attorneys from outside of New York City, Henry W. Anderson of Richmond, Virginia, Monte M. Lemann of New Orleans, and Frank J. Loesch of Chicago. Ada Comstock—the sole woman on the roster—was the only commissioner who was not a lawyer by training.[39]

Early in its work, on November 21, 1929, the Wickersham Commission delivered its preliminary report to the president. Similar to the way that the Dawes Commission in 1921 settled organizational questions before any actual study of veterans health care had been done, the Wickersham Commission's first order of business was to propose the transfer of the Bureau of Prohibition Enforcement from the Treasury to the Department of Justice. The commissioners cited what they saw as the basic problem with the current arrangement: "It is an anomaly that the cases are investigated and prepared by agencies entirely disconnected with and not answerable to those which are to prosecute them." Explaining the rationale for shifting the bureau from Treasury to Justice, they summarized the basic idea that had animated the elite reformers from the beginning: "All experience of administration shows the importance of concentration rather than diffusion of responsibility."[40] In a letter transmitting the committee's preliminary report to Congress, Hoover affirmed his own faith in the power of administrative organization, writing, "I believe the administrative changes mentioned above will contribute to cure many abuses."[41] The commission's recommendation was clearly a reflection of Hoover's own feeling, as he had put it at the outset of the commission's work in June 1929, that "the reorganization and concentration of responsibility in administration of the federal bureaus connected with prohibition enforcement" was "greatly needed to improve their effectiveness."[42]

The commission's investigations into Prohibition enforcement did not in fact get underway until the beginning of December. An October 25, 1929, progress report, written by the Wickersham Commission's secretary, Max Lowenthal, stated that the commission had at that point not yet secured investigators to conduct the survey. When the preliminary report was drafted, the commission had only made an initial "compilation of all available facts on, or relating to," a number of questions, including "various kinds of possible transfers from Treasury to Justice," but Lowenthal described this as "pending the selection of the right man to direct this work." [43]

The commission did not secure researchers for its Prohibition investigation until December 3, 1929, and it did not formally approve a plan for that investigation until January 8, 1930. However, an initial draft of a bill for transferring the Bureau of Prohibition Enforcement to the Department of Justice was already in circulation by October 23, 1929. By mid-November, the commission had already started working with attorneys in the Prohibition Bureau to produce a final draft of the bill.[44]

Among those who declined Wickersham's offer to lead the Prohibition investigation was Robert A. Taft, the ex-president's son and future senator from Ohio. In a letter to Wickersham, the younger Taft outlined his own view of the problem at hand and voiced his approval for expanded federal power in law enforcement. "While of course the local police cannot be subjected to a national police," Taft averred, "it does seem to me that a national police organization ought to be set up, interested not only in the enforcement of national laws, but also in the co-ordination of the activities of all local police."[45]

On January 14, 1930, the day after Hoover transmitted the commission's preliminary report to Congress, representative William Williamson, Republican of South Dakota, introduced the Hoover administration's bill "to transfer that portion of the Bureau of Prohibition now engaged in the enforcement of Prohibition from the Treasury Department to the Department of Justice."[46] Williamson was chairman of the House Committee on Expenditures in the Executive Departments and known as a supporter of the elite reformers' agenda. His status as a representative from the rural West made him an ideal choice, in the reformers' view, to sponsor the legislation—Representative James Good of Iowa had filled much the same role with the budget bill at the beginning of the decade. In his report on the Prohibition transfer bill, Williamson provided a clear explanation of the reformers' agenda in Prohibition enforcement:

> Division of authority, duties, and responsibilities is not conducive to the best results where a specific end is sought. This is especially true where the object in view is law enforcement. Simplicity of procedure, unity of direction, and definite responsibility for results are greatly in the interest of efficiency and certainty. Not until authority and responsibility for the enforcement of prohibition are centered in one head can there be a real test of the mooted question, "Can prohibition be enforced?"[47]

Benefiting from the large Republican majorities of the Seventy-First Congress, as well as from support provided by the Wickersham Commission's endorsement, the bill proceeded through Congress without significant opposition. The transfer, which created a new Bureau of Prohibition within the Department of Justice, was enacted July 1, 1930.[48]

* * *

The transfer of the Bureau of Prohibition was the first major administrative reform to be accomplished during Hoover's presidency. That it took nearly sixteen months to achieve this advance—despite Hoover's career-long preoccupation with administrative reform—helps to underscore the pitfalls inherent in his strategy of obtaining a social-scientific stamp of approval before attempting to enact his policy proposals. Hoover's approach was characteristically self-contradictory—simultaneously overambitious and overcautious. It also reflected his supreme self-confidence. He and his advisers seemed to assume that he would be reelected in 1932, that they would have a full eight years to leisurely advance their agenda, that his approach would be suitable to any problem that might arise, and that the public would remain supportive of his leadership—come what may.

Chapter Thirteen

DASHED HOPES
1930–1933

By 1930, as the nation slid deeper into the Great Depression, the mandate and momentum provided by Herbert Hoover's landslide victory in 1928 had been squandered. Nevertheless, he remained committed to his plans for administrative reform, and to his strategy of taking time for social-scientific investigation before taking action. As ever, executive reorganization was his top priority. The success of the Prohibition Bureau transfer seemed to provide a path forward. When congressional leaders began to push for budget cuts in response to Depression-induced budget deficits, Hoover tried to leverage these calls for "economy" into a rationale for his own vision of comprehensive executive reorganization. Hoover viewed reorganization as the best way to achieve both budgetary savings and increased administrative effectiveness—economy *and* efficiency, in the old formulation. To prepare the ground for comprehensive reorganization, Hoover successfully pushed for reorganization of the federal veterans agencies. While he hoped that this might provide a springboard for further success, the political dynamics of recent years were still firmly in place, and Hoover was unable to translate these small advances into a larger victory.

1

While the World War Veterans Act of 1924 had helped to improve the administrative structure of the federal veterans relief system, at the beginning of Herbert Hoover's presidency, one aspect of what Charles Dawes had viewed in 1921 as "ruinous decentralization" in that system remained unreformed. The government was still running parallel pension and hospital programs. Veterans of the world war were served by the U.S. Veterans Bureau while those of earlier wars were served by the Pension Bureau of the Department of the Interior and the independent National Home for Disabled Volunteer Soldiers. The Harding-Brown reorganization plan had envisioned a merger of the U.S. Veterans Bureau and the Bureau of Pensions into a division within a new federal department of education and welfare. However, enacting that plan was for the moment out of the question. The solution proposed by Hoover and his allies was to combine the Veterans Bureau with the two older veterans agencies to create a single new independent agency.

The idea to merge the Veterans Bureau with the two Civil War–era veterans agencies had been in circulation even before the formation of the Veterans Bureau. In 1920, the National Budget Committee had advocated merging the Bureau of War Risk Insurance and the Federal Board for Vocational Education with the Bureau of Pensions.[1] The idea had gained in popularity since then. In February 1927, a conference of the heads of the independent veterans associations—including the American Legion and the Veterans of Foreign Wars—released a joint statement calling for the placement "under one head [of] the veterans' bureau, the pension bureau and soldiers' homes."[2] Veterans Bureau director Frank T. Hines outlined his own support for the plan in his 1928 annual report:

> The director of the bureau has given considerable study to the subject of veterans' relief, and has publicly proposed that there be established a separate department to handle all matters affecting the extension of direct benefits to veterans and to the dependents of veterans; and will vigorously support any legislation that has for its object this unified plan of control. In the opinion of the director, the main advantage of such a consolidation would be in bringing together in one definite agency under the President matters which are so closely related at this time as to make it essential for those charged with the administrative duties to be familiar with all phases of the problem.[3]

By the time of Hoover's inauguration, this plan enjoyed broad support. However, it was firmly opposed by the heads of the Bureau of Pensions and the National Home for Disabled Soldiers, who feared that the new arrangement would render their organizations subservient to the Veterans Bureau. It was also opposed by the American Medical Association, whose leaders feared the impact of a larger and stronger government-run veterans hospital system.[4]

Hoping to find a way to overcome this opposition, Hoover, characteristically, formed a Committee to Coordinate Veterans' Activities to study the problem in May 1929. The committee included Hines, as well as Ray Lyman Wilbur (secretary of the interior), George H. Wood (the head of the National Home for Disabled Soldiers), and Walter H. Newton (the president's secretary). However, after several meetings, the committee members were unable to agree on a plan—perhaps not surprising, given their competing bureaucratic interests.[5]

Ignoring this deadlock, Hoover went ahead with his own plan. In the House, William Williamson, Republican of South Dakota—the same representative who had sponsored the bill transferring the Prohibition Enforcement Bureau to the Department of Justice—introduced a bill that would consolidate the Pension Bureau and soldiers' homes with the Veterans Bureau to form a new institution, the U.S. Veterans Administration. The House Committee on Expenditures in the Executive Departments, where Representative Williamson served as chairman, began hearings on the bill on January 8, 1930.[6]

At the hearings, the members of Hoover's veterans committee rehashed the arguments they had made months earlier. Veterans Bureau director Hines, who supported the plan, was the first witness to testify.[7] Three days later, Secretary of the Interior Wilbur argued in his testimony for "coordination" of the three agencies rather than "consolidation."[8] Wilbur averred that the bill was "bound to invite some very severe opposition" and that consolidation would be "going too far—going too fast."[9] The next week, Colonel Earl D. Church, commissioner of pensions in the Department of the Interior, protested to the committee that the consolidation bill was "an intensified form of bureaucracy and not in accord with the fundamental principles of the Government which have obtained from its very inception."[10] Church complained that consolidation would "simply mean absorption in the Veterans' Bureau," and he proposed an alternative bill that would "coordinate" the three agencies under the Department of the Interior.[11]

On January 23, Wood, head of the National Home for Disabled Soldiers, also argued in favor of coordination rather than consolidation, saying he preferred "placing the three eggs under one hen" rather than "scrambling them."[12] Wood argued that transferring the soldiers' homes to the Veterans Bureau would result in inefficiency, pointing out that the per-day, per-patient cost in the Veterans Bureau was $4, while the cost in the soldiers' homes was only $2.39. Wood argued that the transfer of soldiers' home patients to the Veterans Bureau would cost the government an extra $3 million per year.[13]

In response to these arguments, Williamson, the committee's chairman, reasserted that consolidation made "good common sense," and invited Hines to testify a second time to rebut his rivals' testimony.[14] Hines was the only witness given this opportunity. Recapping his earlier testimony, Hines echoed the old business analogy long favored by the elite reformers. "I come before you simply as a manager of one of your subsidiary companies would come before a board of directors," Hines said. "And I look upon the Members of Congress as the board of directors of this great business of the United States Government."[15]

To rebut Wood's claims about the Veterans Bureau's inefficiency, Hines questioned whether Wood's comparison was appropriate. "There is a considerable difference in the type of service rendered in the bureau hospitals and in the soldiers' homes hospitals." He compared the cost of care in Veterans Bureau hospitals with care provided in army, navy, and private hospitals, before dismissing the soldiers' homes as "old institutions that were established many years ago and have been in operation for a considerable length of time. The administration of these institutions has therefore been stabilized. This, to an extent, tends to more economical administration." Finally, raising a point sure to appeal to advocates of good government, he pointed out that "the administration of the national soldiers' homes is not under United States civil service regulations, nor is it under the supervision of the classification law."[16]

Despite opposition from Wilbur—a cabinet official and a lifelong friend of President Hoover—Hines's arguments prevailed, and Congress passed the Williamson Bill on July 3, 1930.[17] The law authorized Hoover to create the United States Veterans Administration by executive order. When he signed the order on July 8, 1930, naming Hines as administrator of the new agency, Hoover noted that "The consolidated budget of these services for the present fiscal year amounts to approximately $800,000,000, so that the new establishment becomes one of the most important functions in the government." Hoover's assessment was echoed by the historian Charles A. Beard in his 1930 survey of the federal government, in which he expressed his hope that the consolidation of these agencies in the Veterans Administration would "contribute materially to the efficiency of administration."[18]

2

The law that created a new Bureau of Prohibition within the Department of Justice included a generous concession to the industrial users who had stalled the reorganization in 1927 and who were now represented by the Association Against the Prohibition Amendment. While Prohibition would be enforced by the Department of Justice, the function of granting permits to industrial users would remain within the Treasury.[19]

Despite this accommodation, the AAPA continued to ramp up its push for repeal, and the group's rhetoric focused even more on the alleged dangers of central administrative power in national Prohibition enforcement, citing the power of the new bureau as a key rationale for repealing the Eighteenth Amendment. At the same time, the AAPA aligned itself even more closely with the Democratic Party, and it became a reliable source of criticism toward Herbert Hoover, even though some key AAPA leaders, such as Pierre DuPont and James M. Beck, had long been active in the Republican Party.[20]

In this atmosphere of increasing agitation for repeal, the Wickersham Commission conducted its investigation and issued its final report at the beginning of 1931. The report, which included a confusing series of conclusions and recommendations that were supplemented by individual statements from each of the commissioners, prevaricated on the question of repeal. However, amid the chorus of criticism that greeted the report, very few contemporary observers noticed the commission's statements on the question of central administrative power in national enforcement. The majority of the commissioners affirmed that the 1927 and 1930 reorganization acts had improved the efficiency of national enforcement.[21] Ironically, this was one source for the commission's equivocation on the question of repeal. The majority believed that these organizational advances justified a further trial for Prohibition. The commission's investigation suggested that the new organization seemed to be working, and the majority of commissioners felt that the noble experiment needed more time.[22]

The only commissioner to call unambiguously for repeal was former secretary of war Newton D. Baker, who favored state-level regulation of alcohol. Born in West Virginia and reared in Virginia, Baker graduated from Johns Hopkins University in Baltimore in 1892, and earned a law degree at Washington and Lee University Law School in 1894. Baker then moved to Cleveland, Ohio, where he pursued a successful career in law and Democratic politics. Baker had been a student of Woodrow Wilson's at Johns Hopkins and remained one of his protégés. Baker's advocacy of national repeal and state-level regulation reflected his own preference—shared in common with his mentor Wilson—for local control of public administration. It was also a wise political move considering his status as a leading contender for the Democratic presidential nomination in 1932.[23]

Apart from Baker, however, the committee was unanimous. Even those who favored *eventual* repeal agreed that, in the meantime, as long as the Eighteenth Amendment remained in effect, the government should continue to try to make enforcement more effective and efficient. Some pro-repeal observers viewed this unanimity as evidence of a dry conspiracy on the committee that allowed the anti-repeal forces to win by technicality. In fact, it simply reflected the commissioners' adherence to the elite reformers' viewpoint.[24]

For instance, this viewpoint is clear in the individual statement of commissioner Monte M. Lemann, who was cited as one of the pro-repeal commissioners by contemporary commentators. Although Lemann was a New Orleans lawyer and leader of the Louisiana Bar, he was also a graduate of Harvard (1903) and Harvard Law (1906) and a longtime advocate of civil service reform. Lemann's roommate at Harvard Law was Felix Frankfurter, who called Lemann "about the best lawyer south of the Mason and Dixon line."[25] In his individual statement, Lemann explained that he favored eventual repeal but that he supported the commission's recommendations for "a reasonable extension of federal efforts at enforcement which it is the duty of Congress to make so long as the Eighteenth Amendment remains in the Constitution." This was essentially in line with the argument that Frankfurter had made in 1923.[26]

George Wickersham, in his own individual statement in the commission's final report, argued that reforms implemented in 1927 and 1930 were crucial. "Not until after the act of 1927 had extended the Civil Service law over the enforcement agents," he wrote, "were there the beginnings of such an organization as might have been expected to command the respect of other services, the courts and the public, and thus secure reasonable observance of the law and enforcement of its provisions."[27] He elaborated on this point in a letter to Philadelphia attorney and AAPA-affiliated Republican congressman James M. Beck, who had been U.S. solicitor general under Harding and Coolidge. Beck had kept his anti-Prohibition views to himself during his time in that office, but by 1930 he was a leading voice against Prohibition and a leading critic of the Wickersham Commission. Responding to a critique from Beck, Wickersham emphasized the importance of the organizational transfer brought about by the 1927 and 1930 reorganizations:

> It was obvious to me, when I got into a study of the situation, that the administration of the law had been a ghastly failure, and it was because I and several others of the Commission recognized how bad the administration of the law had been under the Treasury Department, and how Prohibition had never had "a Chinaman's chance" of actual enforcement, until after 1927, that we were unwilling to say that the law could not be enforced.[28]

While the work of the Wickersham Commission illustrated the elite reformers' commitment to law enforcement and their belief in the importance of organizational efficiency, the commission's investigation also illustrated the extent to which the Republican Party in the Hoover years had become intent on avoiding any engagement in questions involving civil rights and racism. This was in stark contrast to Wickersham's interest in the antilynching cause a decade earlier during consideration of the Dyer Bill. In 1922, Wickersham had been one of the first of the elite reformers to decide that the Dyer Bill was in fact constitutional. And yet, despite the Wickersham Commission's focus on lawlessness and its investigation of police brutality, it avoided the topics of racism and lynching entirely.

Amid criticism and coordinated pressure from civil rights advocates, the commission eventually decided to conduct a study of crime among African Americans, titled *The Negroes' Relation to Law Observance*. But that report focused only on crime among African Americans; it did not examine crime against African Americans or consider the impact of racism in law enforcement. When Congressman Leonidas Dyer himself appeared before the Wickersham Commission, the entirety of his recorded remarks were devoted to discussion of the question of what percentage of alcohol causes intoxication.[29]

3

Emboldened by the transfer of national Prohibition enforcement to the Department of Justice and the formation of the U.S. Veterans Administration, in 1931 Hoover sought to advance a comprehensive executive reorganization plan along the lines suggested in 1923 by Warren G. Harding and Walter F. Brown, who was now serving as Hoover's postmaster general.[30]

However, the political setting for the second half of Hoover's term was significantly worse than that of his first two years. The 1930 election brought the House under control of the Democrats and reduced the margin of the Republican majority in the Senate to a single vote. This meant that the Farm Bloc—composed of southern Democrats with western Republicans and Democrats—had solidified their effective control of the legislative branch.[31]

Near the end of 1931, congressional leaders began to attack the Hoover administration for ballooning deficits and began to talk about imposing rigid fiscal restraints on the executive branch. The worsening Depression had led to renewed concerns about the national debt and, with fiscal restraint reborn as a potent issue, Congress-centered executive reorganization reemerged as a viable policy proposal. After several legislators proposed reorganization plans focused on the reduction of executive expenditures, Hoover—reluctant to cede authority on a topic that had preoccupied him for his entire public career—directed his staff to compile lists of his previous statements on executive reorganization and distribute them to influential journalists as he refined his own proposal.[32]

Hoover had often touted the budgetary savings that would accrue from increased managerial efficiency in the national government. In the second half of the 1920s, however, he shifted his rhetorical strategy and began to actively emphasize "economy" and downplay "efficiency." One reason for this shift can be found in the responses to Hoover's Chamber of Commerce speech on reorganization in 1925. In that speech, he had emphasized functional efficiency and central administrative responsibility as a means toward effective national policy making, and he framed budgetary savings as a secondary by-product of reorganization. In the weeks after the speech and its publication in the *Nation's Business*, however, Hoover received hundreds of responses from Chamber of Commerce members in all sections of the country—all in praise of the speech. In all of those letters, however, only a few had engaged Hoover in discussion of the managerial benefits of reorganization. These were written by leading elite reformers such as Samuel McCune Lindsay and Robert S. Brookings. Aside from that handful, however, the rest invariably focused on the budgetary aspects of reorganization.[33]

This had confirmed Hoover's belief that reorganization's popular appeal lay in its potential for budgetary savings, and Hoover accordingly began to shift his argument for reorganization. In a December 7, 1926, speech before the American Mining Congress, for instance, Hoover experimented with an antigovernment argument to justify reorganization. "If we had the courage to combine all the activities of these agencies working toward the same end," he said, "we would limit the expansion of government in business and would curtail the number of points of contact between business and government."[34]

Hoover provided the initial outlines of his plan for comprehensive reorganization at a press conference on December 29, 1931. The centerpiece of his pitch was the $10 to $15 million that Veterans Administration director Frank T. Hines claimed had been saved by consolidation of the veterans agencies. After noting that "the question of economy in government is prominently before the country," Hoover asserted that "the most constructive direction for economy in Federal expenditure beyond a rigid reduction of appropriations and the resolute opposition to any new legislation, lies in the consolidation of Government bureaus and the general reorganization of the Federal Government." The implication of this statement was that "a rigid reduction of appropriations and the resolute opposition to any new legislation" was a bad thing and something Hoover wished to avoid.[35]

After noting his long-standing commitment to executive reorganization, Hoover first mentioned his proposal to consolidate "the construction activities of the Government" under an "Administrator of Public Works" who would report directly to the president:

> There are very large economies to be made there by a thorough reorganization of all construction activities. We have, I should think, 10 different

agencies of the Government engaged in construction at the present time; each one of them with its separate organization spread over the entire country; every one of them with a separate organization in Washington, with duplication of engineers and architects and activities, and competition in the purchase of supplies; no one of which can be properly eliminated unless we can bring all those activities under one head.[36]

Despite Hoover's opportunistic emphasis on the possible budgetary savings that would result from the reorganization, his message to Congress and his press statements revealed that he retained his old commitment to the elite reformers' ideal of achieving functional efficiency in the national government. Although Hoover was careful not to mention it, in practice his proposed public works administration would give the president considerable leverage in moderating the business cycle through the timing of the government's extensive construction activities. Elsewhere in his announcement, he cited the importance of "having single-headed direction under which policies can be formulated and where they will be much more under public inspection." And he added that his plan "would enable policies in connection with different Government activities to be better developed and better directed." These points echoed statements made a dozen years earlier by Henry Stimson, who was now serving as Hoover's secretary of state.[37]

The editors of the *New York Times* applauded Hoover's announcement—not surprisingly, perhaps, since Hoover's former chief assistant, Harold Phelps Stokes, himself a longtime champion of executive reorganization, had become a member of the paper's editorial board after leaving Hoover's employ. "Sisyphus, the chap who kept rolling his rock up a hill only to see it roll down again, was the direct progenitor of the American Presidents who have sought to reorganize the Federal Government," the *Times* editors—or, most likely, Stokes himself—wrote. "So far they have all failed. Here and there a bureau has been shifted or a batch of services consolidated, like those which now comprise the Veterans Administration, but the rest remain." Endorsing Hoover's plan, and noting the government's desperate financial situation, the editors echoed the president's own strategic vision when they observed that "It would be a fine thing if adversity could accomplish in this respect what prosperity brought to nothing."[38]

4

A month and a half later, in a special message to Congress on February 17, 1932, Hoover offered more details for his plan. He began by asserting that "the amount of saving in public funds to be effected by a thoroughgoing reorganization, while difficult to estimate accurately, will be material, amounting to many millions of dollars annually." Hoover then recommended that Congress grant the president "authority under proper safeguards" to transfer and consolidate agencies by executive order. Essentially, this would have provided the president permanent reorganization authority for which the Taft Commission had advocated twenty years earlier and which had been envisioned by those who wished to extend the Overman Act after World War I. Mindful of congressional prerogatives, however, Hoover attempted to counterbalance this enhancement of executive prerogative by proposing that, once the president submitted these orders, Congress would have sixty days to "request suspension of action."[39]

House Democrats responded to Hoover's proposal with "open hostility," according to *New York Times* Washington correspondent Arthur Krock. John Nance Garner, of Texas, the new Democratic House Speaker, called Hoover's plan "idiotic and astounding." Krock reported that Democrats in the Senate "feared greater centralization of power in Executive hands if the President should be given carte blanche, such as he asks." Hoover's message was timed to preempt a resolution—offered the day before by Speaker Garner and Appropriations Committee chairman Joseph Byrns, of Tennessee—that proposed a special House "Economy Committee" to identify ways that the executive branch might cut expenditures. When the House approved that resolution five days later, on February 23, Garner declared that the House leadership was opposed to Hoover's "suggestion that Congress abdicate its prerogatives and give the President blanket power."[40]

This scuffle inaugurated a year of conflict on these matters between Hoover and House leaders. The next month, when Hoover announced potential budget cuts identified by his administration, Congressman Byrns replied that the president's proposal "seems to be an effort to assume credit in advance for any economies that the committee may be able to bring about as a result of the investigations it is now making." Illinois Democrat Henry T. Rainey blamed Hoover personally for the budget deficit. "No living man is more responsible than the President for this increase in the Federal budget,"

Rainey proclaimed, referring to expenses incurred during Hoover's tenure as secretary of commerce. "One of the great increases in government expenses is the Department of Commerce Building containing fifty-two acres of floor space, an ante-room 250 feet long and a private dining room for the Secretary, which are reached by a private elevator, with two operators." Rainey, who himself would assume the speakership a year later—after Garner became vice president—and preside over the House during the first months of the New Deal, continued: "This building, probably erected by the President for himself, is as magnificent as any royal palace in Europe."[41]

The result of this back-and-forth between Hoover and the House Democrats was the Economy Act, which became law on June 30, 1932. The act gave Hoover the power to reorganize the executive branch through executive orders, as he had suggested in February; but it gave either house of Congress the power to veto Hoover's orders within sixty days. With the presidential election campaign underway, Hoover decided to bide his time in hopes that he might be in a stronger position after November. However, Hoover's overwhelming defeat at the hands of Franklin D. Roosevelt placed the outgoing president in the weakened position of a lame duck.[42]

Hoover finally submitted his reorganization orders on December 9, 1932. The plan largely resembled proposals offered earlier in the 1920s by the National Budget Committee, the Institute for Government Research, and Warren G. Harding and Walter F. Brown. Hoover's plan, which touched fifty-eight agencies, would have created two new divisions in the Department of Interior, each under new assistant secretaries: one for public works and another for education, health, and recreation. The public works division would have also included the nonmilitary construction activities of the War Department—thus going further even than Hoover's earlier proposals, which had left army construction units untouched.

Taking advantage of the provisions of the Economy Act, the Democrats in the House vetoed Hoover's proposals on January 19, 1933. In the debates leading up to the veto, Democrats argued that Hoover's plan didn't go far enough to eliminate expenditures, and that the reorganization of the government ought to be left to the incoming Democratic administration.[43]

* * *

On January 2, 1933, while House Democrats prepared to reject Hoover's reorganization plan, the reports produced by the researchers on Hoover's

Committee on Social Trends project were finally published. In his essay on "Public Administration," University of Chicago political scientist Leonard D. White assessed the developments of the first third of the twentieth century. "That we are living in a period of substantial change in the character of our governmental institutions is plain," he wrote.[44] White's remarks on the national executive pointed to one major achievement. "In the federal government," he wrote, "the passage of the Budget and Accounting Act in 1921 was the signal for a general tightening up of all administrative operations." Acknowledging the resistance that had blocked executive reorganization, White seemed to anticipate the defeat of Hoover's plan. "No effective steps have yet been taken to reorganize the federal departments to create unifunctional agencies in place of the present illogical distribution of services, although the matter is under consideration at the time of writing (1932)."[45]

White also included a hopeful note about the rise of social science research and the formalization of the study of public administration. "During the last thirty years very remarkable progress in research has been made, so that today there exist scores of centers whose prime business is improvement in administrative method on the basis of scientific unemotional inquiry," White wrote. "We have passed, in short, from an era of crusade to an era of technique."[46]

The Committee on Social Trends was meant to be the exemplar of this new "scientific unemotional inquiry." President Hoover, in his forward to the project's summary reports, dated October 11, 1932, expressed his hope that the results "should serve to help all of us to see where social stresses are occurring and where major efforts should be undertaken to deal with them constructively."[47] However, as it turned out, the project instead seemed to symbolize the squandered promise of Hoover's presidency. And the report's close identification with Hoover himself meant that leaders in the incoming administration of Franklin Roosevelt were reluctant to embrace the report's findings and recommendations.[48]

Although advocates of administrative reform could blame the congressional leaders—particularly those from the South and West—who remained wary of any effort to expand federal power, in the end many felt that Hoover's own obstinance and arrogance were to blame. His failure to enact much of substance, combined with his failure to respond effectively to the Depression, gave many elite reformers the sense that, after all, Hoover may not have been the man for the job. His inclination to rely upon experts seemed, ironically, to mask a large and inflexible ego. Many agreed with the assessment made by Frederic Delano, who had come into regular contact with Hoover while working as chairman of the National Capital Park and Planning Commission. In early 1932, in a letter to his nephew, New York governor Franklin Delano Roosevelt, Delano offered some underlined advice. "In whatever you do, *my advice is to take enough time for thought*," he wrote. "Don't be stampeded as the President is. He is unfortunately a man who acts a good deal without thinking."[49]

CONCLUSION

The elite reformers' quest to expand federal power was thwarted by a political coalition that sought to maintain local control over public administration. During the 1910s, the elite reformers' proposal for a national budget system was blocked by the presidential administration of Woodrow Wilson, who preferred a system that would preserve a role for Congress and limit the ability of the Budget Bureau to serve as a presidential staff agency. However, after Warren Harding moved into the White House, the Budget and Accounting Act was quickly passed. During the Harding administration, as the elite reformers began to make progress toward their goal of executive reorganization, they applied their centralizing and nationalizing logic to the problem of meeting the nation's obligations to veterans of the world war, creating the U.S. Veterans Bureau. But this progress came to a swift and sudden halt when they attempted to tackle the problem of lynching. After the filibuster of the antilynching bill in late 1922, the elite reformers would find their every effort met with overwhelming resistance by a coalition of southern and western congressmen. The success of Harding's early months was followed by a decade of stalemate and defeat. While the elite reformers and their allies won a few small victories between 1923 and 1933, in most cases the southern Democrats and their allies came out on top.

CONCLUSION

As a result, when the New Deal began in 1933, the elite reformers' quest to expand federal power remained incomplete and the national government remained weak. Administrative reformers in later years would be forced to build atop a shaky foundation.

1

The election of 1932 helped to set in motion a general reshuffling of political coalitions in domestic policy debates. Henceforth, Republican leaders would be more likely to fight against central control and national authority than in favor of administrative reform or civil rights. As the Grand Old Party shifted into an opposition role during the New Deal, and as western leaders in Congress gripped the reins of party leadership even more firmly, the influence of Republican elite reformers waned. Frozen out of domestic policy debates, many followed the lead of Elihu Root and Henry Stimson and began to focus their efforts on foreign affairs. Working through the Council on Foreign Relations and other institutions, Root and Stimson helped build the advocacy coalition that would eventually become known as the "foreign policy establishment" after World War II. With the Republican Party no longer a viable vehicle for efforts to expand federal power, much of the agenda pursued by the elite reformers in the 1920s was taken up in the 1930s by Franklin Delano Roosevelt and the New Dealers.[1]

Early in his presidency, FDR faced concerted opposition from the same group that had helped to lead attacks against Herbert Hoover. The movement to repeal Prohibition had contributed substantially to Roosevelt's election in 1932, but ratification of the Twenty-First Amendment in 1933, while it left the Association Against the Prohibition Amendment with a strong organization, ample funding, and a large membership, it left the AAPA without an obvious villain. For the previous four years, the DuPont and General Motors executives and Democratic Party leaders at the helm of the AAPA had directed their attacks against the growth of federal power in the form of national Prohibition enforcement. In 1934, the leaders of the AAPA decided to form a new organization, the American Liberty League, and direct their well-funded firepower at FDR and the New Deal.[2]

For a time, the American Liberty League drew some support from among the Wall Street–allied businessmen who had supported the National

CONCLUSION

Budget Committee back in 1920. Many business-minded reformers worried that the New Deal might provide the means for a dangerous "raid" on the Treasury. However, the league's antidemocratic aspirations ultimately led stalwart elite reformers such as Henry Stimson to decline membership in the organization. Characteristically, Herbert Hoover, for his part, refused to join the Liberty League, not because of his commitment to democracy, but because he held a personal grudge against its leaders, whom he blamed for his defeat in 1932.[3]

The Liberty League ceased its anti–New Deal publicity campaigns shortly after FDR's landslide reelection in 1936 and it folded altogether in 1940. However, even though the league's lifespan was short, it had a profound impact on American politics, serving as the vanguard for a rising "conservative coalition" of southern segregationists and western white nationalists in Congress that would continue to fight against federal power.[4]

Franklin D. Roosevelt had been a longtime proponent of executive reorganization and the elite reformers' agenda. In 1919 and 1920, he had been one of the only officials in the Wilson administration to support the proposals of the NBC. In the mid-1920s he had joined the National Civil Service Reform League's executive reorganization committee. As president, he retained his interest in administrative reform, but he was forced to wait several years before he could move forward.[5]

During his first term, FDR generally accommodated the demands of the white southern leaders who controlled the Democratic Party in Congress. Most of the agencies created to carry out the policies of the New Deal, from the Agricultural Adjustment Administration (1933), to the Civilian Conservation Corps (1933), to the Social Security Administration (1935), had been crafted so that they would not jeopardize local control of public administration. The effective veto wielded by southern Democrats in Congress, which ensured that no policy could be enacted if it might threaten Jim Crow, remained firmly in place.[6]

However, during his second term, FDR began to push back against the constraints imposed by white southerners in his party. After the power of southern Democrats was diluted by the electoral gains of northern Democrats in 1934 and 1936, Roosevelt attempted to enact a comprehensive executive reorganization plan.* In 1937, he proposed a plan based on the

---

* This was also the background for Franklin D. Roosevelt's "court packing" plan in 1937.

CONCLUSION

recommendations of a committee of academic experts that he had appointed during the previous year.[7]

The President's Committee on Administrative Management was led by three prominent social scientists, Louis Brownlow, Luther Gulick, and Charles Merriam. The leaders of the Brownlow Committee, as it came to be known, had also led the effort to professionalize public administration as an academic discipline during the previous decades. Brownlow ran the Public Administration Clearing House. Gulick led the Institute of Public Administration. Both organizations had been created when the Rockefeller Foundation reorganized the Bureau of Municipal Research in the early 1920s. Merriam, a professor at the University of Chicago, was a founder of both the Social Science Research Council and the PACH and directed Hoover's Committee on Social Trends study on the subject of "government and society."

Although the initial recommendations of the Brownlow Committee were pared down by southern Democrats in Congress, they eventually became law through the Reorganization Act of 1939. FDR succeeded in achieving one of the long-standing goals of the elite reformers by transferring the Bureau of the Budget from the Treasury to the newly formed Executive Office of the President, for the first time providing the executive branch with a real presidential staff agency. The 1939 act also created the Federal Works Agency, which coordinated the construction activities of several agencies—a small step toward the public works administration that Hoover had envisaged in the 1920s. And it made progress toward fulfilling the elite reformers' goals for education reform, transferring the Office of Education from the Department of the Interior to the newly created Federal Security Agency.[8]

The ambitions of the elite reformers in the 1910s and 1920s finally came closest to fulfillment in the years after World War II. The National Security Act of 1947 consolidated the army and navy under the newly created Department of Defense—a proposal that had been stripped from the Harding-Brown plan in 1923 at the urging of congressional leaders. Also in 1947, President Harry Truman formed the Commission on Organization of the Executive Branch of the Government and chose former president Herbert Hoover to lead it.[9]

The "Hoover Commission" submitted recommendations in 1949, most of which were enacted by Truman and his successor, Dwight Eisenhower, between 1949 and 1953, when Congress approved a second Hoover Commission that produced further recommendations. The reforms that emerged from these projects dramatically strengthened the Executive Office of the President, and even managed to achieve one of the more controversial goals of the Harding-Brown plan by creating the Department of Health, Education, and Welfare in 1953. Yet, there were still political limits on administrative reform. For instance, Hoover was ultimately forced to abandon his pet project, the creation of a public works administration. However, two decades after the ignominious end of his presidency, Hoover had overseen a thoroughgoing reorganization of the federal executive branch with the creation of a relatively robust presidential staff office and the establishment a truly modern managerial structure.[10]

2

While the 1930s, 1940s, and 1950s brought gradual progress on the old administrative reform agenda of the elite reformers, those decades produced very little action on civil rights. Northern Democrats attempted on several occasions to pass antilynching bills, but those attempts each met the same fate as the Dyer Bill in 1922. However, with support from several philanthropic foundations, the NAACP had continued the strategy of supporting legal challenges to segregation that had begun with *Moore v. Dempsey*. That strategy finally paid off in 1954 with the Supreme Court's decision in *Brown v. Board of Education*, which ruled against racial segregation in public schools. However, it would take another decade of protest and civil disobedience by civil rights activists before Congress was moved to pass the Civil Rights Act of 1964 and the Voting Rights Act of 1965. Two months after signing the Voting Rights Act, President Lyndon B. Johnson signed the Immigration and Nationality Act of 1965, which eliminated the race and nationality restrictions that had been in place since 1924.[11]

During the middle third of the twentieth century, both parties remained internally divided over questions of national public administration and civil rights. The Democratic Party was split between its southern wing and a growing contingent of northern Democrats who favored central control, national authority, and equal protection under the law for African Americans and other racialized minorities. The Republican Party was split between an ever-shrinking remnant of the elite reformers, primarily in the

CONCLUSION

Northeast, and increasingly powerful contingent of antigovernment white nationalists in the West. These internal divisions are apparent in the roll call votes for the Civil Rights Act of 1964, the Voting Rights Act of 1965, and the Immigration Act of 1965. Each of these laws was passed by bipartisan majorities that included northern Democrats and northeastern Republicans. However, the rolls of "nays" for these votes were weighted with southern Democrats. The votes against the Civil Rights Act and Immigration Act also included a significant number of western Republicans. The enactment of these laws sparked an antigovernment backlash that would transform American politics in the half century that followed. Eventually, the alliance of southern racists and western white nationalists—first forged in response to the Federal Elections Bill of 1890, and strengthened in opposition to the Dyer Bill in 1922 and in support of the Immigration Act of 1924—would become institutionalized within the Republican Party, creating the pattern of "red states" familiar to viewers of Election Night TV coverage in the twenty-first century.[12]

The mid-twentieth-century expansion of federal power in the United States emerged from a particular line of argument about the connection between administration and democracy. Managerial control over the executive branch was necessary to increase the administrative capacity of the national government. Increased administrative capacity would make it possible for the national government to carry out national policies. The ability to carry out national policies would, in turn, make American democracy more effective. Elections would be decided by policy debates, not by patronage or pork barrel politics. When the leaders of the Brownlow Committee argued during the New Deal that managerial control was necessary for the proper functioning of American democracy, they believed they were sustaining a tradition founded by Woodrow Wilson and other academic experts before the turn of the twentieth century.[13]

However, as this book shows, during the two decades that preceded the New Deal, it was the elite reformers and their allies who were the most persistent and prominent promoters of this argument. While many academic experts advocated varieties of budget reform and executive reorganization, it was elite reformers with experience in big business who viewed an executive budget system as the keystone for effective policy making. It was elite reformers with experience in big business who recognized the potential of a budget bureau directly under the president to serve as a presidential staff agency. It was elite reformers with experience in big business who sought to use executive reorganization to increase the president's managerial control over the federal executive branch rather than as a method of cutting costs.

Woodrow Wilson and his allies did not make these arguments in the 1910s and 1920s. Often, they made the opposite argument.

Thus, by focusing on debates over budget reform, executive reorganization, and antilynching—that is, on debates that pertain directly to the administrative strength of the national government—in the 1910s and 1920s, this book reveals the elite reformers as forgotten founders of the modern American administrative state.

This book also suggests revisions to several early twentieth-century concatenations that have become standard touchstones for partisan mythologizers and survey-course lecturers alike. For instance, this book shows that the abandonment of wartime experimentation actually came during the last years of the Wilson administration, and not with a "return to normalcy" during the Harding administration. The story told here also raises the possibility that Harding's reputation as a uniquely corrupt president may have as much to do with his administration's civil rights activism as with the prevalence of corruption during his presidency. It reveals that the Republican Party's abandonment of Black voters by 1932 had its origins not in a post–World War I turn to conservatism or reaction, but rather in the efforts of Calvin Coolidge and Herbert Hoover to evade the post–Dyer Bill backlash led by southern Democrats and western Republicans.[14] It suggests, in turn, that the fabled "party switch" on civil rights advocacy was actually even more dramatic than commonly acknowledged—and also that this role reversal was accompanied by an equally dramatic transposition on questions of central control and national authority in public administration.

The social democracies and welfare states of post–World War II Europe emerged in most cases after an earlier period during which political and economic elites built a national administrative apparatus that could facilitate their own participation in global capitalism. It was only after this foundation had been constructed that left-leaning reformers were able to turn the preexisting array of modern governing institutions toward providing social benefits for all citizens. Leading reformers such as William Howard Taft, Elihu Root, and Henry Stimson were acutely aware that the

CONCLUSION

United States lagged behind the nations of Europe when it came to administrative organization, and they were explicit in their desire to follow the example of other industrial nations in facilitating access for American business to expanding markets at home and abroad. The elite reformers' attempt in the 1910s and 1920s to reinforce the weak foundations of the American state were, in this regard, a belated attempt to rectify one key aspect of American exceptionalism.[15]

What if the elite reformers had succeeded in the 1920s? What if reformers in later eras had been able to build atop a stronger foundation? What might American reformers have been able to achieve in the post–World War II era? Could the legal recognition of civil rights for African Americans and other racialized groups have happened sooner than it did? Could that legal recognition be better enforced today? Would the American state have more capacity to solve national problems in the twenty-first century?

Alas, to even consider such counterfactuals requires a suspension of disbelief that is hard to maintain in the United States in the 2020s. The history recounted in this book affirms that racism has been a persistent and omnipresent force in American history, a force that has shaped every aspect of public life—even those, like budgeting and administrative organization, that scholars have traditionally viewed as insulated from questions of civil rights. If we wish to understand the historical development of the modern American state, we must study debates on topics such as budget reform and executive reorganization alongside and in context with the history of racism in America. Studied in isolation, it might appear that this or that debate was shaped solely by internal technicalities—or by preternatural national traditions, or dimly perceived shifts in an imagined national mood. However, as this book makes clear, the history of administrative reform and the history of racism are intertwined.

To identify racism as the ultimate cause of the elite reformers' failure is not to damn every opponent of executive reorganization or even antilynching as personally bigoted. Nor is it to bless every proponent of these policies as racially enlightened. The details recounted here show that the development of the American state in these years was shaped by a wide array of forces, in pursuit of varied purposes. However, each of these forces were arranged amid a sort of tug-of-war between two dominant forces, both with the power to pull the other contestants into a two-dimensional struggle. The story here is not a simple tale of Left versus Right, Republican versus Democrat, or even liberal versus conservative. Nor is it the story of a clash between economic interests. The contest over federal power in the 1910s and 1920s was anchored on one side by corporate elites who sought to build democratic governing institutions that could embody their vision of the national interest—however imperfect or self-serving that vision might have been. It was anchored on the other side by those who were bent on preserving the arbitrary power to enforce racism. Uncovering the story of the elite reformers' quest to expand federal power helps to reveal the political forces that shaped the development of the American state in their time—forces that continue to limit the possibilities of American politics a century later.[16]

ACKNOWLEDGMENTS

Completing this book in isolation during a historic pandemic has amplified my already acute awareness of the various debts that I owe, both personal and institutional.

This book draws on extensive and wide-ranging archival research in dozens of manuscript collections, conducted over the course of the past decade. That research was made possible by financial assistance from many organizations, including the American Council of Learned Societies; the American Heritage Center at the University of Wyoming in Laramie; the Department of History, the History Associates, and the Baker-Nord Center for the Humanities at Case Western Reserve University in Cleveland, Ohio; the Hagley Library in Wilmington, Delaware; the Herbert Hoover Presidential Library Association in West Branch, Iowa; the Friends of the Princeton University Library; the Joint Center for History and Economics at Harvard University and the University of Cambridge, supported by the Institute for New Economic Thinking; the Rockefeller Archive Center in Sleepy Hollow, New York; and the Roosevelt Institute in Hyde Park, New York.

Portions of chapters 2, 3, and 4 make use, in substantially revised form, of material published in "Corporate Lessons for Public Governance: The Origin and Activities of the National Budget Committee, 1919–1923," *Seattle University Law Review* 42, no. 2 (January 2019). Portions of chapters 11, 12, and 13 make use, also in substantially revised form, of material published

ACKNOWLEDGMENTS

in "The Quest to Bring 'Business Efficiency' to the Federal Executive: Herbert Hoover, Franklin Roosevelt, and the Civil Service Reformers in the Late 1920s," *Journal of Policy History* 31, no. 4 (October 2019). I thank the editors of those journals.

In various venues, many colleagues have improved my arguments and conclusions by offering comments, questions, suggestions, complaints, protests, and encouragement in formal and informal settings. I am particularly thankful to Edward Balleisen, Edward Berkowitz, Elliot Brownlee, Christy Chapin, Daniel Ernst, David Farber, Louis Galambos, Shane Hamilton, Roger Horowitz, Richard John, Jeffrey Kahana, Pamela Laird, Naomi Lamoreaux, Ken Lipartito, Ashton Merck, Todd Michney, Shaun Nichols, William J. Novak, Scott Randolph, David Reinecke, Laura Phillips Sawyer, David Sicilia, Elizabeth Tandy Shermer, David Stebenne, Sean Vanatta, Benjamin Waterhouse, and Mary Yeager.

Several colleagues generously read some version of the entire manuscript. Their feedback improved the book and saved me from many pitfalls and pratfalls. This group includes Devin Fergus, John Flores, Louis Hyman, Bethany Moreton, Julia Ott, Robert Post, Noah Rosenblum, Peter Shulman, Joseph White, and Christopher Wilson. David Hammack, Thomas Pegram, and Mark Wilson deserve special thanks for reading multiple drafts and responding to repeated queries. I am also grateful to two anonymous reviewers at Columbia University Press who offered extremely generous and useful advice. However, none of these readers was able to save me from myself, and I take responsibility for any and all errors, inconsistencies, oversights, oversimplifications, or forceful overstatements that appear in these pages.

Three years of teaching at Loyola University Maryland shaped my development as a historian in profound ways. I was particularly lucky to work in close proximity to Tom Pegram. In addition to being a reliable source of knowledge and insight about the period covered by this book, Tom provided a welcome source of wise counsel and wry humor.

As a graduate student at Case Western Reserve University, I learned from many distinguished scholars. Jonathan Sadowsky gave me the opportunity to teach a small class on American history in the period covered by this book—a fruitful experience. Peter Shulman provided thoughtful instruction and careful encouragement with characteristic good humor. Dan Cohen provided invaluable support as coordinator of graduate

ACKNOWLEDGMENTS

studies; as a teacher, he provided the benefit of his deep knowledge of historical scholarship, and the shining example of his own scholarly rigor and discipline. Ted Steinberg's generosity is unmatched—I will be forever grateful for his support. Finally, David Hammack, my doctoral adviser, remains an ideal mentor. His insight, skill, and sagacity have been invaluable. Although he encouraged me to boldly follow my own inclinations throughout my work on this project, readers who are familiar with David's work will see evidence of his influence on every page of this book.

I came to graduate school after a brief period working as a journalist. Any special sense or touch that I might possess as a writer must owe something to my time with Mike Henderson at the University of Washington, John de Leon at the *Seattle Times*, and Bruce Shapiro at the Dart Center for Journalism and Trauma.

At Columbia University Press, I had the good fortune to work with two very talented editors while writing this book. Bridget Flannery-McCoy recognized the potential of this project at an early stage and offered insightful suggestions for rearranging the manuscript. With a sharp eye and sure hand, she helped me to see possibilities that I had not considered. Stephen Wesley took over while there was still much work to be done. With a discerning ear and critical eye, he wielded the red pen with wit and wisdom, guiding the book to completion with admirable equanimity during the chaos of the pandemic. After the final draft was complete, Ryan Perks improved the book considerably with his thoughtful copyediting.

I am grateful for my friends and extended family. In lieu of another long list here, I will simply express the hope that I will be able to thank each of them in person before too long. I also wish to say "yakoke" to the Choctaw Nation of Oklahoma for its continued support for my family.

It is largely thanks to the interest and attention I received from my great-grandmother (my mother's mother's mother) Mikki Guilliaume, and from her daughter (my mother's mother) Karen Platt, that I became a historian and ever thought about writing a book in the first place. If they were still living, I know they both would be happy to see this book published. My mother Debra Hunt is—and has always been—a source of unconditional encouragement.

Finally, my greatest debt is owed to three particularly remarkable women. In addition to offering occasional unpaid research support and proofreading—and reliable responses to my always excellent jokes—my daughters Vivian and Elenora have helped me in ways that are beyond my capacity to describe. My wife Jamie Rue has remained relentlessly supportive despite being busy changing the world with her own important work. She provides the sustaining force in my life.

ABBREVIATIONS

ORGANIZATIONS AND AGENCIES

AAPA	Association Against the Prohibition Amendment
COH	Consultants on Hospitalization
HCE	House Committee on Education
HCEED	House Committee on Expenditures in the Executive Departments
HCIFC	House Committee on Interstate and Foreign Commerce
HSCB	House Select Committee on the Budget
IGR	Institute for Government Research
JCR	Joint Committee on the Reorganization of Government Departments
NAACP	National Association for the Advancement of Colored People
NACE	National Advisory Committee on Education
NBC	National Budget Committee
NCLOE	National Law Observance and Enforcement Commission
NCSRL	National Civil Service Reform League
NEA	National Education Association
PRCST	President's Research Committee on Social Trends
SCCNB	Senate Committee on Consideration of a National Budget

ABBREVIATIONS

SCIUSVB   Senate Select Committee on Investigation of the United States Veterans Bureau
USCC   United States Chamber of Commerce

ARCHIVAL REPOSITORIES

CUL   Columbia University, Rare Book & Manuscript Library, New York, N.Y.
FDRPL   Franklin D. Roosevelt Presidential Library, Hyde Park, N.Y.
LOC   Library of Congress, Manuscript Division, Washington, D.C.
HHPL   Herbert Hoover Presidential Library, West Branch, Iowa.
NA1   National Archives I, Washington, D.C.
NA2   National Archives II, College Park, Md.
PUL   Seeley G. Mudd Manuscript Library, Princeton University, Princeton, N.J.
RAC   Rockefeller Archive Center, Sleepy Hollow, N.Y.
YALE   Sterling Memorial Library, Yale University, New Haven, Conn.

MANUSCRIPT COLLECTIONS

BSP   Benjamin Strong Jr. Papers, Federal Reserve Bank of New York. https://fraser.stlouisfed.org/archival-collection/papers-benjamin-strong-jr-1160
CGDP   Charles G. Dawes Papers, Northwestern University Library, Evanston, Ill.
GMCAP   George McAneny Papers, PUL.
HH-CP   Herbert Hoover, Papers as Secretary of Commerce, HHPL.
HH-PP   Herbert Hoover, Papers as President, HHPL.
HLSP   Henry L. Stimson Papers, YALE, microfilm edition.
JDRP   Office of the Messrs. Rockefeller records, FA313, Civic Interests, Series D, RAC.
NAACPP   NAACP Papers, LoC.
NCLOEP   National Commission on Law Observance and Enforcement, Record Group 10, NA2.
NCSRLP-C NCSRL Papers, Cornell University Library, Ithaca, N.Y.
NCSRLP-W NCSRL Papers, American Heritage Center, University of Wyoming, Laramie, Wyo.

ABBREVIATIONS

RFR   Rockefeller Foundation Records, RG 1.1, ser. 200, RAC.
USVB-DF   Director's File, Veterans Administration Records, Record Group 51, NA1.
WFBP   Walter F. Brown Papers, Ohio Historical Society, Columbus, Ohio.

PUBLISHED PRIMARY SOURCES

POWW   Arthur S. Link, ed., *The Papers of Woodrow Wilson*. 69 vols. Princeton, N.J.: Princeton University Press, 1967–1994.

NOTES

INTRODUCTION

1. The literature on civil service reform is vast. See especially Leonard D. White, *The Republican Era, 1869–1901: A Study in Administrative History* (New York: Macmillan, 1958); Stephen Skowronek, *Building a New American State: The Expansion of National Administrative Capacities, 1877–1920* (New York: Cambridge University Press, 1982), 47–84, 177–211; Paul P. Van Riper, *History of the United States Civil Service* (Evanston, Ill.: Row, Peterson and Company, 1958); Ari Hoogenboom, *Outlawing the Spoils: A History of the Civil Service Reform Movement, 1865–1883* (Urbana: University of Illinois Press, 1961); William Dudley Foulke, *Fighting the Spoilsmen* (New York: G. P. Putnam's Sons, 1919). Viewing "good government" as an effort to undercut more radical movements is common, especially in accounts of nineteenth-century politics. See, for instance, Sven Beckert, *The Monied Metropolis: New York City and the Consolidation of the American Bourgeoisie, 1850–1896* (New York: Cambridge University Press, 2001), 189–190, 318–319.
2. Although scholars have tended to eschew the term "big government," its popular use has continued unabated. My engagement with the term is influenced in part by Steven Conn, ed., *To Promote the General Welfare: The Case for Big Government* (New York: Oxford University Press, 2012).
3. A similar time comparison is made by Leonard D. White at the opening of *The Republican Era*. Statistics here are drawn from U.S. Bureau of the Census, *Historical Statistics of the United States, 1789–1945* (Washington, D.C.: U.S. Government Printing Office, 1949), 294, 296–297, 299–300.
4. Stephen Skowronek in *Building a New American State* used the phrase "state of courts and parties" to describe the weakness of the national government in the nineteenth century. Since then, however, historians of nineteenth-century politics

INTRODUCTION

and policy have identified many examples of sometimes robust state activity at the national level. For a critique of "courts and parties," see Richard R. John, "Rethinking the Early American State," *Polity* 40, no. 3 (July 2008): 333–339. For further scholarship in this vein, see, for instance, Brian Balogh, *A Government Out of Sight: The Mystery of National Authority in Nineteenth-Century America* (New York: Cambridge University Press, 2009); Richard R. John, *Spreading the News: The American Postal System from Franklin to Morse* (Cambridge, Mass.: Harvard University Press, 1995); and Gautham Rao, *National Duties: Custom Houses and the Making of the American State* (Chicago: University of Chicago Press, 2016). Based on the accumulation of such studies, and following the argument made by William J. Novak, "The Myth of the Weak American State," *American Historical Review* 113, no. 3 (June 2008): 752–772, some have argued that the American state was not in fact weak. However, here I am suggesting a distinction between government activity (the reach and touch of the state) and governing capacity (the strength of the state). Consider an example discussed later in this book: the Bonus Act of 1924 certainly represents a significant expansion of state action—new types of government assistance to a new group of recipients—but it did almost nothing to enhance the strength of the government.

5. Many of the elite reformers should be familiar to careful readers of Stephen Skowronek's *Building a New American State* as leaders of an "executive-professional reform coalition" (see 172–174, 254). Some of them also play a prominent role in Daniel R. Ernst, *Tocqueville's Nightmare: The Administrative State Emerges in America, 1900–1940* (New York: Oxford University Press, 2016). Finally, several also appear as villains in books by New Left scholars, such as (for example) in Gabriel Kolko, *The Triumph of Conservatism: A Reinterpretation of American History, 1900–1916* (New York: Free Press, 1963).

6. The key text remains Alfred D. Chandler Jr., *The Visible Hand: The Managerial Revolution in American Business* (Cambridge, Mass.: Harvard University Press, 1977). Although many scholars have argued that the managerial revolution was neither as thoroughgoing nor as widespread as Chandler and his followers seemed to suggest, contemporary observers on Wall Street in the 1910s and 1920s certainly believed that something like what Chandler described had taken place. Several of Chandler's contemporaries emphasized how the movement toward managerial efficiency in business in the early twentieth century was paralleled in other aspects of American life, including government. See especially Robert H. Wiebe, *The Search for Order, 1877–1920* (New York: Hill and Wang, 1967), and the various studies cited in Louis Galambos, "The Emerging Organizational Synthesis in Modern American History," *Business History Review* 44, no. 3 (Autumn 1970): 279–290.

7. Henry L. Stimson, "A National Budget System," *World's Work*, August 1919, 372.

8. The connection between Root and Stimson is well-known. Frankfurter's relationship with Stimson is less well-known, but it is evident in their correspondence, and it is noted in Ernst, *Tocqueville's Nightmare*, 18. On Frankfurter's reputation, see Fred Rodell, "Felix Frankfurter, Conservative," *Harper's Magazine*, October 1941. The contradictions and nuances of political identification in this era have been analyzed by numerous scholars over the past century. In the hurly-burly detail of political history, distinguishing progressives from conservatives, reactionaries, radicals, and liberals can sometimes be difficult. The outlines of the problem can

INTRODUCTION

be traced in the following: Robert H. Wiebe, *Businessmen and Reform: A Study of the Progressive Movement* (Cambridge, Mass.: Harvard University Press, 1962); Otis L. Graham, *An Encore for Reform: The Old Progressives and the New Deal* (New York: Oxford University Press, 1967); Gabriel Kolko, *Main Currents in Modern American History* (New York: Pantheon, 1976); and Daniel T. Rodgers, "In Search of Progressivism," *Reviews in American History* 10, no. 4 (December 1982): 113–132. Perhaps erring on the side of expediency, my solution here has been to generally eschew such labels, as they seem to obscure more than they reveal in the debates described in this book.

9. Historical interpretations of governmental change tend to fall within two closely related general theories. In one, federal power expands when progressive presidents are able to overcome the power of business interests. This "Progressive synthesis" was forged during the period covered by this book by historians such as Charles A. Beard and Frederick J. Turner, and held aloft by popular mid-century historians such as Arthur M. Schlesinger Jr. For a still-valuable guide, see Richard Hofstadter, *The Progressive Historians: Turner, Beard, Parrington* (New York: Knopf, 1968). For an incisive critique of the continued power of the Progressive synthesis, see Brian Balogh, *The Associational State: American Governance in the Twentieth Century* (Philadelphia: University of Pennsylvania Press, 2015), 1–22. In the second general theory, reform efforts succeed when moderate or conservative policy makers pursue government cooperation with (or co-optation by) business. This interpretation has been advanced in studies of the "associative state" and "corporate liberalism." The term "associative state" was coined by Ellis W. Hawley in "Herbert Hoover, the Commerce Secretariat, and the Vision of an 'Associative State,' 1921–1928," *Journal of American History* 61, no. 1 (June 1974): 116–140. Also see Hawley's *The Great War and the Search for a Modern Order: A History of the American People and their Institutions, 1917–1933* (New York: St. Martin's Press, 1979). To gauge the interpretive spectrum of work that falls within the "corporate liberalism" school, see Kolko, *Main Currents in Modern American History*, and James Weinstein, *The Corporate Ideal in the Liberal State, 1900–1918* (Boston: Beacon, 1968). The affinities between the associative and corporate traditions are noted somewhat ruefully in a retrospective historiographic essay in Ellis W. Hawley, *The New Deal and the Problem of Monopoly: A Study in Economic Ambivalence*, rev. ed. (New York: Fordham University Press, 1995).

10. This book is a work of political history, influenced and informed by various approaches toward making sense of the past and present. A cursory scan of the notes in these pages will show that it draws especially on interpretations from the political science subfield of American political development, as well as from business history, public administration studies, and legal history. In many ways, my approach here fits within the tradition sometimes called "the new institutionalism"— although my conception of what counts as an "institution" is perhaps broader than that of other scholars. In additional to tracing the evolution of commonly recognized institutions—government bureaus, agencies, and offices; law; political parties, voluntary associations, and advocacy organizations; business and administrative practices—this book also treats cultural traditions such as racism and antigovernment politics as institutions that can act as agents of change. In the course of tracing the development of these institutions, I engage, while drawing on

various disciplinary approaches, the historian's prerogative of methodological flexibility. By tracing the interactions of a wide array of institutions in contests over central control and national authority during a relatively brief period in the early twentieth century, this book aims to suggest the outlines of a new answer to its central question: What forces have shaped the development of the American state?

11. Few general studies of the period before 1933 depart significantly from the arguments made by Arthur M. Schlesinger Jr., for whom the 1920s constituted the original *cycle of reaction* that gave meaning to the *cycles of reform* that framed it. See Arthur M. Schlesinger Jr., *The Age of Roosevelt: The Crisis of the Old Order, 1919– 1933* (Boston: Houghton Mifflin, 1957), and *The Cycles of American History* (Boston: Houghton Mifflin, 1986). Notable exceptions include Ernst, *Tocqueville's Nightmare*; Gerald Berk, *Louis D. Brandeis and the Making of Regulated Competition, 1900– 1932* (New York: Cambridge University Press, 2009); and Laura Phillips Sawyer, *American Fair Trade: Proprietary Capitalism, Corporatism, and the "New Competition," 1890–1940* (New York: Cambridge University Press, 2017). For a pioneering study of city-level reform in this period, see Daniel Amsterdam, *Roaring Metropolis: Businessmen's Campaign for a Civic Welfare State* (Philadelphia: University of Pennsylvania Press, 2016). The ubiquitous appeals to "business efficiency" in these years have largely escaped the attention of historians. A notable exception is Rosemary A. Stevens, *A Time of Scandal: Charles R. Forbes, Warren G. Harding and the Making of the Veterans Bureau* (Baltimore: Johns Hopkins University Press, 2016), and "The Invention, Stumbling, and Reinvention of the Modern U.S. Veterans Health Care System, 1918–1924," in *Veterans' Policies, Veterans' Politics: New Perspectives on Veterans in the Modern United States*, ed. Stephen R. Ortiz (Gainesville: University Press of Florida, 2012), 38–62.

12. Although the creation of the Budget Bureau has been repeatedly analyzed by specialists, the subject has held little interest for most historians. My focus here on budget reform is inspired in part by the idea that what Alfred D. Chandler Jr. and Fritz Redlich said in 1961 about the importance of a budget in business firms might also be true about a budget in government: "As a matter of fact, the first appearance of a budget in business enterprise cannot be overestimated in its historical importance. It is an indicator of emerging bureaucratization of business, the correlative to modern large-scale enterprise." See Chandler and Redlich, "Recent Developments in American Business Administration and Their Conceptualization," *Business History Review* 35, no. 3 (Spring 1961): 26. Two particularly useful overviews from the perspective of public administration studies can be found in Roy T. Meyers and Irene S. Rubin, "The Executive Budget in the Federal Government: The First Century and Beyond," *Public Administration Review* 71, no. 3 (2011): 334–344, and Naomi Caiden, "Paradox, Ambiguity and Enigma: The Strange Case of the Executive Budget and the United States Constitution," *Public Administration Review* 47, no. 1 (1987): 84–92. The budget debate plays a pivotal role in Skowronek's subfield-founding *Building a New American State*. Skowronek called the Budget and Accounting Act "a watershed in the creation of a new American state and the establishment of a new bureaucratic politics" (207), but few of his many followers have carried forward his interest in budgetary reform, or in the details of public administration generally. A recent noteworthy exception is John A. Dearborn, "The 'Proper Organs' for Presidential Representation: A Fresh

INTRODUCTION

Look at the Budget and Accounting Act of 1921," *Journal of Policy History* 31, no. 1 (January 2019): 1–41, and John A. Dearborn, *Power Shifts: Congress and Presidential Representation* (Chicago: Chicago University Press, forthcoming). See also Jesse Tarbert, "Corporate Lessons for Public Governance: The Origin and Activities of the National Budget Committee, 1919–1923," *Seattle University Law Review* 42, no. 2 (January 2019): 565–589.
13. The best overview of the long history of executive reorganization is Peri Arnold, *Making the Managerial Presidency: Comprehensive Reorganization Planning, 1905–1996*, 2nd ed. (Lawrence: University Press of Kansas, 1998). Also essential for its analysis of the post–World War II reorganizations is Joanna L. Grisinger, *The Unwieldy American State: Administrative Politics Since the New Deal* (New York: Cambridge University Press, 2014). A useful overview is Ronald C. Moe, *Administrative Renewal: Reorganization Commissions in the 20th Century* (Lanham, Md.: University Press of America, 2003). The classic monographs on executive reorganization during the New Deal are Barry D. Karl, *Executive Reorganization and Reform in the New Deal* (Cambridge, Mass.: Harvard University Press, 1963), and Richard Polenberg, *Reorganizing Roosevelt's Government* (Cambridge, Mass.: Harvard University Press, 1966).
14. For most of the twentieth century, historians arguing within the Progressive, associative state, and corporate liberalism traditions tended to overlook racism as a political force. In recent years, however, a number of political scientists have worked to bring racism and racist violence into the history of the American state. For work in this vein, see Paul Frymer, *Uneasy Alliances: Race and Party Competition in America* (Princeton, N.J.: Princeton University Press, 1999); Jeffery A. Jenkins, Justin Peck, and Vesla M. Weaver, "Between Reconstructions: Congressional Action on Civil Rights, 1891–1940," *Studies in American Political Development* 24, no. 1 (April 2010): 57–89; Kimberley Johnson, *Reforming Jim Crow: Southern Politics and State in the Age Before Brown* (New York: Oxford University Press, 2010); Ira Katznelson, *Fear Itself: The New Deal and the Origins of Our Time* (New York: Norton, 2013); Megan Ming Francis, *Civil Rights and the Making of the Modern American State* (New York: Cambridge University Press, 2014); Robert Mickey, *Paths Out of Dixie: The Democratization of Authoritarian Enclaves in America's Deep South, 1944–1972* (Princeton, N.J.: Princeton University Press, 2015); Eric Schickler, *Racial Realignment: The Transformation of American Liberalism, 1932–1965* (Princeton, N.J.: Princeton University Press, 2016); David A. Bateman, Ira Katznelson, and John S. Lapinski, *Southern Nation: Congress and White Supremacy After Reconstruction* (Princeton, N.J.: Princeton University Press, 2018); and Boris Heersink and Jeffrey A. Jenkins, *Republican Party Politics and the American South, 1865–1968* (New York: Cambridge University Press, 2020). For a stimulating reassessment of Woodrow Wilson's political thought with implications for American political development, see Stephen Skowronek, "The Reassociation of Ideas and Purposes: Racism, Liberalism, and the American Political Tradition," *American Political Science Review* 100, no. 3 (August 2006): 385–401.
15. My argument here draws upon Gary Gerstle's analysis of the conflict between "racial nationalism" and "civic nationalism" in *American Crucible: Race and Nation in the Twentieth Century* (Princeton, N.J.: Princeton University Press, 2001), and Rogers Smith's argument about the importance of the "ascriptive

INTRODUCTION

tradition" in American politics in "Beyond Tocqueville, Myrdal, and Hartz: The Multiple Traditions in America," *American Political Science Review* 87, no. 3 (September 1993): 549–566.

1. ADMINISTRATION AND ACCOMMODATION: BEFORE 1913

1. On the creation of the spoils system and its impact on the federal administration, see Richard John, "Affairs of Office: The Executive Departments, the Election of 1828, and the Making of the Democratic Party," in *The Democratic Experiment: New Directions in American Political History*, ed. Meg Jacobs, William Novak, and Julian Zelizer (Princeton, N.J.: Princeton University Press, 2003), 50–84. On the operation of the spoils system in the late 1800s, see Ari Hoogenboom, *Outlawing the Spoils: A History of the Civil Service Reform Movement, 1865–1883* (Urbana: University of Illinois Press, 1961); William Dudley Foulke, *Fighting the Spoilsmen* (New York: G. P. Putnam's Sons, 1919); and Leonard D. White, with the assistance of Jean Schneider, *The Republican Era, 1869–1901: A Study in Administrative History* (New York: Macmillan, 1958).
2. On Roosevelt's career, see Doris Kearns Goodwin, *The Bully Pulpit: Theodore Roosevelt, William Howard Taft, and the Golden Age of Journalism* (New York: Simon and Schuster, 2013), 130–143, 259–264; Richard D. White Jr., "Theodore Roosevelt as Civil Service Commissioner: Linking the Influence and Development of a Modern Administrative President," *Administrative Theory & Praxis* 22, no. 4 (December 2000): 696–713; and Jacob A. Riis, "The Making of an American: An Autobiography. Chapter XIII," *Outlook*, September 7, 1901, 35–50.
3. The totals were 13,780 out of 131,208 positions in 1884, 106,205 out of 256,000 in 1901. See U.S. Bureau of the Census, *Historical Statistics of the United States, 1789–1945* (Washington, D.C.: U.S. Government Printing Office, 1949), 294.
4. See Goodwin, *Bully Pulpit*, 219–220, 502.
5. Quoted in Goodwin, 390.
6. Goodwin provides a serviceable collection of the high points of Taft's biography. For an incisive analysis of Taft's political and legal thought, see Robert Post, *The Ambivalent Construction of Modernity, 1921–1930*, vol. 10 of *The Oliver Wendell Holmes Devise History of the Supreme Court of the United States* (New York: Cambridge University Press, forthcoming).
7. "Taft the Busiest Man of a Busy Government," *New York Times*, December 4, 1905. The first American appearance of the Root telegram anecdote seems to be Bernard Moses, "Stories of Governor Taft in the Philippines," *World's Work*, December 1903, 4231. This joke was also repeated in Walter Wellman, "Taft, Trained to be President," *American Review of Reviews* 37 (June 1908): 679.
8. Wellman, "Taft," 679.
9. William H. Taft, "Draft of Inaugural Address, ca. March 4, 1909," typescript with Taft's emendations, March 4, 1909," William H. Taft Papers, LoC, https://www.loc.gov/item/pin3601/.
10. The work and significance of the commission are described in Peri Arnold, *Making the Managerial Presidency: Comprehensive Reorganization Planning, 1905–1996* (Lawrence: University Press of Kansas, 1998), 26–51, and in Stephen Skowronek,

1. ADMINISTRATION AND ACCOMMODATION: BEFORE 1913

Building a New American State: The Expansion of National Administrative Capacities, 1877–1920 (New York: Cambridge University Press, 1982), 186–194. Other useful accounts include Ronald C. Moe, *Administrative Renewal: Reorganization Commissions in the 20th Century* (Lanham, Md.: University Press of America, 2003); Bess Glenn, "The Taft Commission and the Government's Record Practices," *American Archivist* 21, no. 3 (July 1958): 277–303.

11. *Purposes and Methods of the Bureau of Municipal Research* (New York: Bureau of Municipal Research, 1907), and Henry Bruere, "The Bureau of Municipal Research," *Proceedings of the American Political Science Association* 5 (1908): 111–121. For analysis of the motivations and importance of the municipal research movement, see Ariane Liazos, *Reforming the City: The Contested Origins of Urban Government, 1890–1930* (New York: Columbia University Press, 2019), and David C. Hammack, *Power and Society: Greater New York at the Turn of the Century* (New York: Russell Sage Foundation, 1982), 110–157, 185–203.

12. On Norton, see "Charles D. Norton, Banker, Dies at 53," *New York Times*, March 7, 1923, and David C. Hammack, "The Regional Plan of New York and Environs: A Plan and a Planning Service," in *Social Science in the Making: Essays on the Russell Sage Foundation, 1907–1972*, ed. David C. Hammack and Stanton Wheeler (New York: Russell Sage Foundation, 1995), 59–80.

13. Arnold, *Making the Managerial Presidency*, 14–15; Skowronek, *Building a New American State*, 187. My emphasis on Frederick Cleveland's business experience fits with Peri Arnold's observation that Cleveland's "major scholarly work in public administration began after his work for Taft." See Arnold, *Making the Managerial Presidency*, 33. Taft said of Cleveland that "for years he had been conducting work in reorganization and revision of methods and procedure in large corporations, both public and private." See William H. Taft, "Economy and Efficiency in the Federal Government: II," *Saturday Evening Post*, February 13, 1915, 14. For Cleveland's own summary of his career, which began, as he put it, with "a practice of law on the west coast, where there were a great many financial wrecks of the corporation kind and where we had a good deal of that practice," see HSCB, *National Budget System*, 66th Cong., 1st sess. (1919), 514–515.

14. Arnold, *Making the Managerial Presidency*, 33. For a careful argument that the work of the commission reflected Taft's views rather than Cleveland's, see Irene Rubin, "Early Budget Reformers," *American Review of Public Administration* 24, no. 3 (1994): 244–245.

15. Arnold, *Making the Managerial Presidency*, 22–51.

16. Arnold, 47–48.

17. Skowronek, *Building a New American State*, 192–193; Glenn, "The Taft Commission," 285–286.

18. On the Lodge Bill, see Richard M. Vallely, "Partisan Entrepreneurship and Policy Windows: George Frisbee Hoar and the 1890 Federal Elections Bill," in *Formative Acts: American Politics in the Making*, ed. Stephen Skowronek and Matthew Glassman (Philadelphia: Pennsylvania University Press, 2007), 126–152, and Charles W. Calhoun, *Conceiving a New Republic: The Republican Party and the Southern Question, 1869–1900* (Lawrence: University Press of Kansas, 2006).

19. For a brief but incisive recent analysis, see Jamelle Bouie, "If It's Not Jim Crow, What Is It?," *New York Times*, April 6, 2021. The literature on Jim Crow is

1. ADMINISTRATION AND ACCOMMODATION: BEFORE 1913

voluminous. See, for instance, Henry Louis Gates Jr., *Stony the Road: Reconstruction, White Supremacy and the Rise of Jim Crow* (New York: Penguin, 2019); Nell Irvin Painter, *Creating Black Americas: African-American History and its Meanings* (New York: Oxford University Press, 2006), 129–172; Glenda Gilmore, *Gender and Jim Crow: Women and the Politics of White Supremacy in North Carolina, 1896–1920* (Chapel Hill: University of North Carolina Press, 1996); Leon Litwack, *Trouble in Mind: Black Southerners in the Age of Jim Crow* (New York: Vintage Books, 1998). Still valuable is C. Vann Woodward, *The Strange Career of Jim Crow* (New York: Oxford University Press, 1955).
20. The lynching literature is also voluminous. See, for instance, Alfreda M. Duster, ed., *Crusade for Justice: The Autobiography of Ida B. Wells*, 2nd ed. (Chicago: University of Chicago Press, 2020); Crystal N. Feimster, *Southern Horrors: Women and the Politics of Rape and Lynching* (Cambridge, Mass.: Harvard University Press, 2011); Stewart E. Tolnay and E. M. Beck, *A Festival of Violence: An Analysis of Southern Lynchings, 1882–1930* (Urbana: University of Illinois Press, 1995).
21. Louis Harlan, *Booker T. Washington: The Making of a Black Leader, 1856–1901* (New York: Oxford University Press, 1972).
22. The expletive appears unredacted in Tillman's statement. Deborah Davis, *Guest of Honor: Booker T. Washington, Theodore Roosevelt, and the White House Dinner that Shocked a Nation* (New York: Simon and Schuster, 2012), 227; Harlan, *Booker T. Washington*, 305–324.
23. Edward P. Kohn, "Teddy Roosevelt's Confederate Uncles," *New York Times*, June 25, 2014, https://opinionator.blogs.nytimes.com/2014/06/25/teddy-roosevelts-confederate-uncles/; Goodwin, *Bully Pulpit*, 35–36. However, white southerners did not view Roosevelt as one of their own. See, for instance, Henry F. Pringle, "Theodore Roosevelt and the South," *Virginia Quarterly Review* 9, no. 1 (Winter 1933): 14–25. For analysis of Roosevelt's views and actions regarding civil rights and racism, see Gary Gerstle, "Theodore Roosevelt and the Divided Character of American Nationalism," *Journal of American History* 86, no. 3 (December 1999): 1280–1307, and Sidney M. Milkis and Daniel J. Tichenor, *Rivalry and Reform: Presidents, Social Movements, and the Transformation of American Politics* (Chicago: University of Chicago Press, 2019), 83–96.
24. *Address of President Roosevelt at the Lincoln Dinner of the Republican Club of the City of New York, Waldorf-Astoria Hotel, February 13, 1905* (Washington, D.C.: U.S. Government Printing Office, 1905), 8–9, 16–17, 21–22.
25. *Address of President Roosevelt at the Lincoln Dinner*, 25–27.
26. Goodwin, *Bully Pulpit*, 511–515; John D. Weaver, *The Brownsville Raid* (New York: Norton, 1970).
27. Goodwin, *Bully Pulpit*, 511–515.
28. Goodwin, 511–515.
29. Washington to McAneny, February 6, 1908; McAneny to Taft, February 26, 1908; and Taft to McAneny, February 27, 1908, box 107, folder "Jeanes Foundation 1907–1921," GMcAP.
30. William H. Taft, "Draft of Inaugural Address, ca. March 4, typescript with Taft's emendations, March 4, 1909," William H. Taft Papers, LoC, https://www.loc.gov/item/pin3601/.

2. THE ELITE REFORMERS IN EXILE: 1913-1918

31. For Du Bois's assessment of the reach of the "Tuskegee Machine," see W. E. B. Du Bois, *The Autobiography of W. E. B. Du Bois: A Soliloquy on Viewing My Life from the Last Decade of Its First Century* (New York: Oxford University Press, 1968), 152.
32. On the founding of the NAACP, see Megan Ming Francis, *Civil Rights and the Making of the Modern American State* (New York: Cambridge University Press, 2014), 29–58.
33. *PoWW*, 25:449.
34. "The Last Word in Politics," editorial, *Crisis* 5, no. 1 (November 1912): 29. On the NAACP's choice in 1912, see Milkis and Tichenor, *Rivalry and Reform*, 92–99.
35. Skowronek, *Building a New American State*, 192–193; Glenn, "The Taft Commission," 285–286.

2. THE ELITE REFORMERS IN EXILE: 1913-1918

1. Megan Ming Francis, *Civil Rights and the Making of the Modern American State* (New York: Cambridge University Press, 2014), 64–68; Sidney M. Milkis and Daniel J. Tichenor, *Rivalry and Reform: Presidents, Social Movements, and the Transformation of American Politics* (Chicago: University of Chicago Press, 2019), 99–106.
2. Francis, *Civil Rights and the Making of the Modern American State*, 67. Wilson to Villard, July 23, 1913, in *PoWW*, 28:65.
3. Francis, *Civil Rights and the Making of the Modern American State*, 68. Dixon to Wilson, July 27, 1913; Wilson to Dixon, July 29, 1913, in *PoWW*, 28:88–89, 94.
4. Saladin Ambar, "Woodrow Wilson: Life Before the Presidency," Miller Center, University of Virginia, accessed June 10, 2021, https://millercenter.org/president/wilson/life-before-the-presidency; "Woodrow Wilson Boyhood Home," National Park Service, U.S. Department of the Interior, accessed June 10, 2021, https://www.nps.gov/nr/travel/augusta/wilsonhouse.html.
5. See Stephen Skowronek, "The Reassociation of Ideas and Purposes: Racism, Liberalism, and the American Political Tradition," *American Political Science Review* 100, no. 3 (August 2006): 385–401. Woodrow Wilson, *Congressional Government: A Study in American Politics* (Boston: Houghton Mifflin, 1885), 40.
6. Woodrow Wilson, *A History of the American People* (New York: Harper and Brothers, 1902), 5:59, 62; Skowronek, "Reassociation of Ideas and Purposes," 391.
7. See Mark E. Benbow, "Birth of a Quotation: Woodrow Wilson and 'Like Writing History with Lightning,'" *Journal of the Gilded Age and Progressive Era* 9, no. 4 (October 2010): 509–533.
8. The delegation included Henry Bruere, one of the bureau's directors; John Purroy Mitchel, a progressive Democrat; and Louis D. Brandeis. See Peri Arnold, *Making the Managerial Presidency: Comprehensive Reorganization Planning, 1905-1996* (Lawrence: University Press of Kansas, 1998), 49, citing Walter O. Jacobson, "A Study of President Taft's Commission on Economy and Efficiency" (master's thesis, Columbia University, 1941), 69–70.
9. The best overview of the "New Freedom" is still Arthur S. Link, *Wilson: The New Freedom* (Princeton, N.J.: Princeton University Press, 1956). On the founding of

2. THE ELITE REFORMERS IN EXILE: 1913-1918

the Fed, see Peter Conti-Brown, *The Power and Independence of the Federal Reserve* (Princeton, N.J.: Princeton University Press, 2016), 15–23. On the development of the tax system in this era, see Ajay K. Mehrotra, *Making the Modern American Fiscal State: Law, Politics, and the Rise of Progressive Taxation, 1877–1929* (New York: Cambridge University Press, 2013), and W. Elliot Brownlee, *Federal Taxation in America: A Short History* (New York: Cambridge University Press, 2004), 52–57. On the Federal Trade Commission, see Laura Phillips Sawyer, *American Fair Trade: Proprietary Capitalism, Corporatism, and the "New Competition," 1890–1940* (New York: Cambridge University Press, 2017), 129–132.

10. William Dudley Foulke, *Fighting the Spoilsmen* (New York: G. P. Putnam's Sons, 1919), 228–229.
11. Foulke, *Fighting the Spoilsmen*, 234.
12. Stephen Skowronek, *Building a New American State: The Expansion of National Administrative Capacities, 1877–1920* (New York: Cambridge University Press, 1982), 195–196. Foulke, *Fighting the Spoilsmen*, 233–238.
13. "Politics," *Crisis* 6, no. 2 (June 1913): 60.
14. Foulke, *Fighting the Spoilsmen*, 226.
15. On the founding of the USCC, see Laura Phillips Sawyer, "Trade Associations, State-Building, and the Sherman Antitrust Act: The U.S. Chamber of Commerce, 1912–25," in *Capital Gains: Business and Politics in Twentieth-Century America*, ed. Richard R. John and Kim Phillips-Fein (Philadelphia: University of Pennsylvania Press, 2017), 25–42; and Laura Phillips Sawyer, *American Fair Trade: Proprietary Capitalism, Corporatism, and the "New Competition," 1890–1940* (New York: Cambridge University Press, 2017), 135–137. On the USCC referendum, see "Some Unfinished Business for the Next Congress," *Nation's Business*, April 15, 1915, 10. The vote was 573 for and 10 against. See also William Franklin Willoughby, *The Problem of a National Budget* (New York: D. Appleton and Company, 1918), 154; Harvey S. Chase, "National Expenditures Presented in Budget Form," *Nation's Business*, May 15, 1914, 5–6. Chase delivered essentially the same text in a speech on February 2, 1915, at the annual meeting of the USCC in Washington, D.C. See Harvey S. Chase, "Why Should We Have a National Budget? What a Government Budget is and How it Serves the Nation's House Keeping," *Nation's Business*, April 15, 1915, 12–13.
16. See Greene to Charles Van Hise, August 31, 1914, box 26, folder 294, RG 1.1, Ser. 200, Rockefeller Foundation Records, RAC. On the founding of the IGR, see James A. Smith, *The Idea Brokers: Think Tanks and the Rise of the New Policy Elite* (New York: Free Press, 1991), 52–55; James A. Smith, *Brookings at Seventy-Five* (Washington, D.C.: Brookings Institution, 1991), 9–14; and Donald T. Critchlow, *The Brookings Institution: Expertise and the Public Interest in a Democratic Society* (DeKalb: Northern Illinois University Press, 1985), 17–40.
17. See Critchlow, *The Brookings Institution*, 33.
18. Philip C. Jessup, *Elihu Root* (New York: Dodd, Mead, and Company, 1938), 122–123, 183–184.
19. See George C. Herring, *From Colony to Superpower: U.S. Foreign Relations since 1776* (New York: Oxford University Press, 2008), 348–350; Skowronek, *Building a New American State*, 212–222.

2. THE ELITE REFORMERS IN EXILE: 1913-1918

20. Elting E. Morison, *Turmoil and Tradition: A Study of the Life and Times of Henry L. Stimson* (Boston: Houghton Mifflin, 1960); Henry L. Stimson and McGeorge Bundy, *On Active Service in Peace and War* (New York: Harper and Brothers, 1948).
21. Skowronek, *Building a New American State*, 222–227.
22. The idea of "responsible government" emerged from scholars' analyses of public administration in the United Kingdom. For an account of the impact of this idea on the development of presidential administration in the United States, see Noah Rosenblum, "The Antifascist Roots of Presidential Administration," *Columbia Law Review* 122 (forthcoming), available at https://ssrn.com/abstract=3635821.
23. Henry L. Stimson and McGeorge Bundy, *On Active Service in Peace and War* (New York: Harper and Brothers, 1948), 56–81; Elting Elmore Morison, *Turmoil and Tradition: A Study of the Life and Times of Henry L. Stimson* (Boston: Houghton Mifflin, 1960), 213–229.
24. Henry L. Stimson, "The Principle of Responsibility in Government," in *The Revision of the State Constitution*, part 1, *General Principles and Mechanics of Revision; the Structure of State Government* (Albany: New York State Constitutional Convention Commission, 1915), 23, https://nysl.ptfs.com/data/Library1/Library1/pdf/13985474_p1.pdf.
25. See Morison, *Turmoil and Tradition*, 216–224; William F. Willoughby, *The Movement for Budgetary Reform in the States* (New York: D. Appleton and Company, 1918), 152–167, 211–217.
26. William H. Taft, "Economy and Efficiency in the Federal Government: II," *Saturday Evening Post*, February 13, 1915, 15.
27. William H. Taft, "Economy and Efficiency in the Federal Government," *Saturday Evening Post*, February 6, 1915, 4.
28. The starting point for understanding the U.S. government's mobilization for the war remains Robert D. Cuff, *The War Industries Board: Business-Government Relations During World War I* (Baltimore: Johns Hopkins University Press, 1973). For an astute analysis of the accumulated literature on mobilization, see Mark R. Wilson, "Economic Mobilization," in *A Companion to Woodrow Wilson*, ed. Ross A. Kennedy (Maldon, Mass.: Wiley-Blackwell, 2013), 287–307. For a still-valuable guide to the impact of the war at home, see David M. Kennedy, *Over Here: The First World War and American Society* (New York: Oxford University Press, 1980).
29. Arnold, *Making the Managerial Presidency*, 49, 52; Cuff, *The War Industries Board*; Skowronek, *Building a New American State*.
30. I thank Robert Post for bringing Taft's argument to my attention. See Robert Post, *The Ambivalent Construction of Modernity, 1921–1930*, vol. 10 of *The Oliver Wendell Holmes Devise History of the Supreme Court of the United States* (New York: Cambridge University Press, forthcoming), where Post cites William H. Taft, "The Administration Coordination Bill (February 14, 1918)" and "The Overman Bill (May 2, 1918)," in *William Howard Taft: Collected Editorials, 1917–1921*, ed. James F. Vivian (New York: Praeger, 1990), 35, 56–57.
31. Robert D. Cuff, "Creating Control Systems: Edwin F. Gay and the Central Bureau of Planning and Statistics, 1917–1919," *Business History Review* 63, no. 3 (Autumn 1989): 588–613.

2. THE ELITE REFORMERS IN EXILE: 1913-1918

32. Cuff, "Creating Control Systems."
33. Cuff.
34. On the Great Migration generally, see Isabel Wilkerson, *The Warmth of Other Suns: The Epic Story of America's Great Migration* (New York: Penguin, 2010). For an early, contemporary analysis, see W. E. B. Du Bois, "The Migration of Negroes," *Crisis* 14, no. 2 (June 1917): 63–66.
35. Francis, *Civil Rights and the Making of the Modern American State*, 52–56.
36. On Watson and his role in the Frank case, as well as his influence on the founding of the second Klan, see C. Vann Woodward, *Tom Watson: Agrarian Rebel* (New York: Macmillan, 1938), 376–386, 389. On the second Klan, see Linda Gordon, *The Second Coming of the KKK: The Ku Klux Klan of the 1920s and the American Political Tradition* (New York: Liveright, 2017), and Thomas R. Pegram, *One Hundred Percent American: The Rebirth and Decline of the Ku Klux Klan in the 1920s* (Chicago: Ivan R. Dee, 2011).
37. Francis, *Civil Rights and the Making of the Modern American State*, 52–56.
38. Francis, 43–49.
39. Elliott M. Rudwick, *Race Riot at East St. Louis, July 2, 1917* (Carbondale: Southern Illinois University Press, 1964); Charles L. Lumpkins, *American Pogrom: The East St. Louis Race Riot and Black Politics* (Athens: Ohio University Press, 2008).
40. Wilson's message, in a telegram sent to every Democratic state and county chairman in the nation on November 5, 1916, was widely printed in newspapers. See, for instance, "Wilson Certain He Will Win; Warns of Fraud in Final Hour," *Chicago Examiner*, November 6, 1916.
41. "The Massacre at East St. Louis," *Crisis* 14, no. 5 (September 1917): 219–238; Rudwick, *Race Riot at East St. Louis*.
42. The delivery of the resolution and petition was widely reported throughout the African American press. See, for instance, "Pres. Wilson Asked to Speak," *Nashville Globe*, August 10, 1917.
43. "The Negro Silent Parade," *Crisis* 14, no. 5 (September 1917): 241–244; "Wilson Pledge to Negroes," *Washington Post*, August 17, 1917; Francis, *Civil Rights and the Making of the Modern American State*, 71–75.
44. Francis, *Civil Rights and the Making of the Modern American State*, 72–78.
45. Woodrow Wilson, "A Statement to the American People," July 26, 1918, in *PoWW*, 49:97–99.
46. Z. L. Potter, "The Central Bureau of Planning and Statistics," *Journal of the American Statistical Association* 16, no. 125 (March 1919): 285.

3. AFTER THE ARMISTICE: SPRING 1919

1. During the sixty-fifth Congress, Wilson had enjoyed margins of 65–55 in the Senate and 215–212 in the House (where 211 Democrats caucused with 3 Progressives and 1 Socialist).
2. On investor nationalism, see Julia C. Ott, *When Wall Street Met Main Street: The Quest for an Investor's Democracy* (Cambridge, Mass.: Harvard University Press, 2011). On the position of the United States within the global political

3. AFTER THE ARMISTICE: SPRING 1919

economy of the post-armistice moment, see Adam Tooze, *The Deluge: The Great War, America and the Remaking of the Global Order, 1916–1931* (New York: Viking, 2014).

3. Some of these discussions are described in John Pratt to Benjamin Strong, February 5, 1919, file 640.2.1, p. 1, BSP. On the activity of the IGR, See James A. Smith, *The Idea Brokers: Think Tanks and the Rise of the New Policy Elite* (New York: Free Press, 1991), 52–55; James A. Smith, *Brookings at Seventy-Five* (Washington, D.C.: Brookings Institution, 1991), 9–14; and Donald T. Critchlow, *The Brookings Institution: Expertise and the Public Interest in a Democratic Society* (DeKalb: Northern Illinois University Press, 1985), 17–40.

4. Jesse Tarbert, "Reconsidering Progressive Era Opposition to Foundation Activity: The Farm Demonstration Project Controversy," *HistPhil*, August 8, 2016, https://histphil.org/2016/08/08/reconsidering-progressive-era-opposition-to-foundation-activity-the-farm-demonstration-project-controversy/.

5. For an example of one such "Dear John" letter, see Pratt to Rockefeller Jr., August 12, 1920. For JDR Jr.'s reply, see Rockefeller Jr. to Pratt, August 30, 1920, both in box 40, folder 317, JDRP. On Pratt's life and career, see "John T. Pratt," *National Budget*, September 15, 1919; *Report of Proceedings of the National War Labor Conference, Washington, June 13–15, 1918* (Washington: U.S. Government Printing Office, 1918), 16; "John Teele Pratt, Financier, Is Dead," *New York Times*, June 18, 1927; "Mrs. Ruth B. Pratt Inherits $9,152,771," *New York Times*, June 18, 1929. In the mid-1920s, Pratt's estate was valued at about $9 million. While this was relatively small compared to Rockefeller's, as a share of GDP, this was equivalent to about $2.11 billion in 2019 dollar figures. See Samuel H. Williamson, "Seven Ways to Compute the Relative Value of a U.S. Dollar Amount, 1774 to present," *MeasuringWorth*, accessed June 14, 2021, www.measuringworth.com/uscompare/.

6. A copy of this pamphlet is in file 640.2.1, pp. 3, 11, 26, 27, BSP.

7. File 640.2.1, pp. 3, 11, 26, 27, BSP.

8. See Liaquat Ahamed, *Lords of Finance: The Bankers Who Broke the World* (New York: Penguin, 2009), 50.

9. Ahamed, *Lords of Finance*, 56; Ron Chernow, *The Warburgs: The Twentieth-Century Odyssey of a Remarkable Jewish Family* (New York: Random House, 1993).

10. Robert T. Swaine, *The Cravath Firm and Its Predecessors, 1819–1947*, vol. 1, *The Predecessor Firms, 1819–1906* (Clark, N.J.: Lawbook Exchange, 2007), 13. Cotton's skills are discussed in Stimson to Hoover, May 21, 1917, reel 49, pp. 75–76, HLSP. Cotton was considered by Joseph Beal to have been "the best man in the class" of 1900 at Harvard Law, and Learned Hand considered Cotton to be the best student of his "whole generation"; quoted in Elting Elmore Morison, *Turmoil and Tradition: A Study of the Life and Times of Henry L. Stimson* (Boston: Houghton Mifflin, 1960), 308.

11. See Herbert Hoover to Henry Stimson, May 16, 1917, reel 49, pp. 12–13, and Hoover to Stimson, May 20, 1917, reel 49, p. 66, HLSP.

12. For an overview of his career, see Morison, *Turmoil and Tradition*.

13. Minutes, March 4, 1919, reel 51, pp. 777–778, HLSP. See also "National Budget Committee Advocates Finance Reform," *National Budget*, September 1, 1919, and

3. AFTER THE ARMISTICE: SPRING 1919

Minutes, March 15, 1919, reel 51, pp. 898–902, HLSP; HSCB, *National Budget System*, 66th Cong., 1st sess. (1919), 148. On the BMR, see Bruce McDonald, "The Bureau of Municipal Research and the Development of a Professional Public Service," *Administration and Society* 42, no. 7 (2010): 815–835.

14. Stimson to John T. Pratt, April 12, 1919, reel 52, p. 138, HLSP.
15. *Thirty Years of Lynching in the United States, 1892–1918* (New York: NAACP, 1919); Megan Ming Francis, *Civil Rights and the Making of the Modern American State* (New York: Cambridge University Press, 2014), 51.
16. Root to Storey, February 24, 1919, box I:C-333, folder 2, NAACPP.
17. Hughes to Storey, February 21, 1919, box I:C-333, folder 1, NAACPP.
18. Moton to Shillady, March 4, 1919, box I:C-333, folder 2, NAACPP.
19. The details of this incident are described in Cameron McWhirter, *Red Summer: The Summer of 1919 and the Awakening of Black America* (New York: Henry Holt, 2011), 1–11.
20. McWhirter, *Red Summer*, 1–11.
21. "National Conference on Lynching," *Crisis* 18, no. 1 (May 1919): 23–24.
22. For a useful account of Hughes's career and a critical discussion of its historical importance, see James A. Henretta, "Charles Evans Hughes and the Strange Death of Liberal America," *Law and History Review* 24, no. 1 (2006): 115–171; Daniel T. Rodgers, "Living without Labels," *Law and History Review* 24, no. 1 (2006): 173–178; William E. Forbath, "The Long Life of Liberal America: Law and State-Building in the U.S. and England," *Law and History Review* 24, no. 1 (2006): 179–192; William J. Novak, "The Not-So-Strange Birth of the Modern American State: A Comment on James A. Henretta's 'Charles Evans Hughes and the Strange Death of Liberal America,'" *Law and History Review* 24, no. 1 (2006): 193–199; Risa L. Goluboff, "Deaths Greatly Exaggerated," *Law and History Review* 24, no. 1 (2006): 201–208; and James A. Henretta, "In Defense of Traditional Stories and Labels," *Law and History Review* 24, no. 1 (2006): 209–213.
23. W. E. B. Du Bois, "Lynching," *Crisis* 18, no. 2 (June 1919): 59; "Hughes Condemns Lynching of Negro," *New York Times*, May 6, 1919; "The Anti-Lynching Conference," *Crisis* 18, no. 2 (June 1919): 92; NAACP, *Tenth Annual Report of the National Association for the Advancement of Colored People for the Year 1919* (New York: NAACP, 1920), 30–31; Jeffery A. Jenkins, Justin Peck, and Vesla M. Weaver, "Between Reconstructions: Congressional Action on Civil Rights, 1891–1940," *Studies in American Political Development* 24. no. 1 (April 2010): 66; Mark Robert Schneider, *We Return Fighting: The Civil Rights Movement in the Jazz Age* (Boston: Northeastern University Press, 2002), 14–16; McWhirter, *Red Summer*, 33–40, 57.
24. "The Anti-Lynching Conference," *Crisis* 18, no. 2 (June 1919): 92.
25. NAACP, *Tenth Annual Report*, 94–100.
26. Story to Hughes, May 9, 1919, box 5, Charles Evans Hughes Papers, CUL.
27. See McWhirter, *Red Summer*.
28. W. E. B. Du Bois, "Shillady and Texas," *Crisis* 18, no. 6 (October 1919): 283–284; the *Austin News* interview with Pickle is quoted in "The Case of Mr. Shillady," *Crisis* 18, no. 6 (October 1919): 300–301; NAACP, *Tenth Annual Report*, 27–28, 33. The NAACP published a detailed narrative in pamphlet form: *Mobbing of John Shillady* (New York: NAACP, 1919).

4. THE BUDGET DEBATE: 1919-1920

1. On Jones, see Scott M. Cutlip, *The Unseen Power: Public Relations: A History* (Hillsdale, N.J.: Lawrence Erlbaum Associates, 1994), 237.
2. "Congress to Act on Budget Bills," *National Budget*, September 1, 1919, 1, 4.
3. Henry L. Stimson, "A National Budget System: An Analysis of Our Present Wasteful Financial Methods," *World's Work*, August 1919, 371–375, and Henry L. Stimson, "A National Budget System, II: The Advantages and Need of the Budget System for National Expenditures," *World's Work*, September 1919, 528–536.
4. Stimson, "A National Budget System," 371–375; Stimson, "A National Budget System, II," 528–536.
5. Stimson, "A National Budget System," 372.
6. Stimson, "A National Budget System: II," 529.
7. Stimson, "A National Budget System: II," 533.
8. "Congress to Act on Budget Bills," *National Budget*, September 1, 1919, 1, 4.
9. Willoughby's role in arranging the hearings is mentioned in Donald T. Critchlow, *The Brookings Institution: Expertise and the Public Interest in a Democratic Society* (DeKalb: Northern Illinois University Press, 1985), 37, and in Brookings to John D. Rockefeller Jr., October 20, 1919, box 40, folder 315, JDRP. Lindsay's role is mentioned in "Budget Committees Named in Congress," *National Budget*, September 15, 1919.
10. HSCB, *National Budget System*, 66th Cong., 1st sess. (1919), 620.
11. HSCB, *National Budget System*, 285.
12. HSCB, 285.
13. U.S. Congress, *Journal of the House of Representatives of the United States*, 66th Cong., 1st sess. (October 21, 1919), 522.
14. Willoughby's authorship of the Good Bill is mentioned in Brookings to John D. Rockefeller Jr., October 20, 1919, box 40, folder 315, JDRP. Glass's role in developing the McCormick Bill is noted in "Congress to Get New Budget Bill: Senator McCormick's Measure Puts Bureau Under Secretary of Treasury," *New York Times*, November 28, 1919.
15. Glass lacks a modern biography. See James T. Patterson, *Congressional Conservatism and the New Deal: The Growth of the Conservative Coalition in Congress, 1933–1939* (Lexington: University Press of Kentucky, 1967), 18.
16. HSCB, *National Budget System*, 513. On Glass's part in the turn-of-the-century Virginia disfranchisement campaign, see Michael Perman, *Pursuit of Unity: A Political History of the American South* (Chapel Hill: University of North Carolina Press, 2009), 175, 215.
17. "Congress to Get New Budget Bill," *New York Times*, November 28, 1919.
18. HSCB, *National Budget System*, 216.
19. Stimson to Pratt, November 10, 1919, reel 53, p. 621, HLSP.
20. HSCB, *National Budget System*, 572–573. In contrast to his antagonistic performance at the House hearings, Allen was quite congenial in the Senate hearings. See SCCNB, *National Budget: Hearings on H.R. 9783*, 66th Cong., 2nd sess. (1920), 63–70. For more on Allen's exit from the BMR, and the ensuing controversy, see his testimony and the "Allen Exhibit" in Commission on Industrial Relations, *Industrial Relations: Final Report and Testimony*, Vol. IX, 64th Cong., 1st sess. (1916), S. Doc. 415, 8327–8342, 8462–8480.

21. "Congress to Get New Budget Bill," *New York Times*, November 28, 1919.
22. "Paul M. Warburg Not After Budget Office," *Budget*, December 1, 1919. (Starting with the issue of December 1, 1919, the name of this publication was shortened from the *National Budget* to the *Budget*.)
23. The committee's willingness to consider the McCormick Bill was emphasized in the January 1 issue of the *Budget*. See "Major Budget Witnesses Uphold National Committee's Contentions," *Budget*, January 1, 1920.
24. Heffernan Report, January 16, 1920, reel 54, pp. 302–305, HLSP.
25. For an overview of Collins's career, see Joseph E. Lowndes, *From the New Deal to the New Right: Race and the Southern Origins of Modern Conservatism* (New Haven, Conn.: Yale University Press, 2008), 11–39. See also Ira Katznelson, *Fear Itself: The New Deal and the Origins of Our Time* (New York: Norton, 2013), 139–141, 143–144, 187.
26. On Leffingwell's career, see Robert T. Swaine, *The Cravath Firm and Its Predecessors, 1819–1947*, vol. 2, *The Cravath Firm since 1906* (New York: Ad Press, 1948), 13, 17–18; Ron Chernow, *The House of Morgan: An American Banking Dynasty and the Rise of Modern Finance* (New York: Atlantic Monthly Press, 1990). Leffingwell's service to Kuhn, Loeb and Co. is mentioned in Paul D. Cravath to William G. McAdoo, May 7, 1917, box 6, folder 119, Russell Leffingwell Papers, YALE.
27. Heffernan Report, January 16, 1920, reel 54, pp. 302–305, HLSP.
28. Pratt to Stimson, February 18, 1920, reel 54, p. 579, HLSP. For McCormick's initial plan, see "McCormick Has Budget System Ready for G.O.P.," *Chicago Tribune*, May 19, 1919. For the final form of his bill, see Medill McCormick, *National Budget System*, 66th Cong., 2nd sess. (1920), S. Rep. 524. For a useful narrative focusing on the creation of the independent auditing function, see Roger R. Trask, *Defender of the Public Interest: The General Accounting Office, 1921–1966* (Washington, D.C.: U.S. Government Printing Office, 1996), 23–36.
29. On Cleveland and the founding of the IGR, see James A. Smith, *The Idea Brokers: Think Tanks and the Rise of the New Policy Elite* (New York: Free Press, 1991), 52–55; James A. Smith, *Brookings at Seventy-Five* (Washington, D.C.: Brookings Institution, 1991), 9–14; and Donald T. Critchlow, *The Brookings Institution: Expertise and the Public Interest in a Democratic Society* (DeKalb: Northern Illinois University Press, 1985), 17–40.
30. Frederick A. Cleveland and Arthur Eugene Buck, *The Budget and Responsible Government* (New York: Macmillan, 1920), 362–363. *The Budget and Responsible Government* is often cited as a founding document in the academic field of public administration. Scholars have relied on this volume to describe the supposed postwar consensus in favor of budget reform. However, previous scholars have not noticed that the book presents evidence of the intense contest between advocates of the Good Bill and the McCormick Bill, and it shows that Cleveland had clearly taken a side in these debates. Cleveland's critique of the Good Bill continues on pp. 372–378.
31. Cleveland to Samuel McCune Lindsay, June 23, 1919, reel 52, p. 722, HLSP.
32. Cleveland and Buck, *Budget and Responsible Government*, xv.
33. Cleveland and Buck, xvi–xvii.
34. Cleveland and Buck, ix–x. This disagreement between Cleveland and Taft in 1920, although not noted by her, supports Irene Rubin's contention that Taft himself had

5. THE DARK HORSE: 1920-1921

dictated the preferences of his namesake commission, and that Cleveland's endorsement of a presidential budget in his work on the Taft Commission reflected Taft's views rather than Cleveland's. See Irene Rubin, "Early Budget Reformers," *American Review of Public Administration* 24, no. 3 (1994): 244–245. By this time, the board had been expanded with the inclusion of Taft, New York banker Manny Strauss, and Nicholas Murray Butler, the president of Columbia University.

35. For a useful timeline of the various votes and committee schedules, see Charles Wallace Collins, "Historical Sketch of the Budget Bill in Congress," *Congressional Digest* 2, no. 2 (November 1922): 37–38.
36. Stephen Skowronek, *Building a New American State: The Expansion of National Administrative Capacities, 1877–1920* (New York: Cambridge University Press, 1982), 206–207; Collins, "Historical Sketch of the Budget Bill in Congress," 37–38.
37. David Franklin Houston to Joseph Patrick Tumulty, June 3, 1920, in *PoWW*, 65:358. For Houston's own explanation of his reasoning, see David F. Houston, *Eight Years with Wilson's Cabinet, 1913 to 1920: With a Personal Estimate of the President* (New York: Doubleday, Page, 1926), 2:82–90.
38. See *PoWW*, 65:361–363.
39. Wilson's embrace of the Treasury budget seems to provide a good example of what Stephen Skowronek has called "Wilson's method of embracing new principles of government so as to redirect and defuse their transformative implications." Stephen Skowronek, "The Reassociation of Ideas and Purposes: Racism, Liberalism, and the American Political Tradition," *American Political Science Review* 100, no. 3 (August 2006): 393.

5. THE DARK HORSE: 1920-1921

1. On Lowden's record in Illinois, see Thomas R. Pegram, *Partisans and Progressives: Private Interest and Public Policy in Illinois, 1870–1922* (Urbana: University of Illinois Press, 1992), 188–210.
2. Henry Stimson's papers contain a voluminous correspondence between Stimson and Wood in late 1919 and 1920. See HLSP, reels 53–56.
3. W. E. B. Du Bois, "Presidential Candidates," *Crisis* 20, no. 2 (June 1920): 69.
4. On Harding generally, the best scholarly treatment remains Robert K. Murray, *The Harding Era: Warren G. Harding and His Administration* (Minneapolis: University of Minnesota Press, 1969). Also useful is John W. Dean, *Warren G. Harding* (New York: Times Books, 2004). For a more positive reappraisal, see Dylan Matthews, "Secret Love Child Aside, Warren Harding Was a Solid President," *Vox*, August 13, 2015, https://www.vox.com/2014/7/9/5881009/in-defense-of-warren-harding. On the possibly apocryphal attribution of the term "founding fathers," see Jill Lepore, *The Whites of Their Eyes: The Tea Party's Revolution and the Battle over American History* (Princeton, N.J.: Princeton University Press, 2011), 16, 182n29.
5. Warren Harding, "Back to Normal," in *Rededicating America: Life and Recent Speeches of Warren G. Harding*, ed. Frederick E. Schortemeier (Indianapolis, Ind.: Bobbs-Merrill, 1920), 223–229.
6. "Harding Nominated for President on the Tenth Ballot at Chicago; Coolidge Chosen for Vice President," *New York Times*, June 12, 1920.

5. THE DARK HORSE: 1920-1921

7. On Parsons, see Henry Stimson, "The Late Herbert Parsons," *New York Times*, September 25, 1925; "Text of Republican Platform as Adopted by Chicago Convention Last Night," *New York Times*, June 11, 1920.
8. The first two items on Harding's list were budget reform and executive reorganization. Schortemeier, *Rededicating America*, 56–57. For the antilynching plank in the Republican platform, see Randolph Downes, "Negro Rights and White Backlash in the Campaign of 1920," *Ohio History Journal* 75, nos. 2–3 (1966): 87.
9. "The Political Conventions," *Crisis* 20, no. 4 (August 1920): 176.
10. Charles H. Brough to James B. A. Robertson, September 16, 1920, box 3, folder 16, RG 8-D-1-3, Oklahoma Governors' Papers, Oklahoma State Archives Division, Oklahoma City, Okla., http://digitalprairie.ok.gov/cdm/ref/collection/race-riot/id/243 (emphasis in original). On Brough, see Foy Lisenby, *Charles Hillman Brough: A Biography* (Fayetteville: University of Arkansas Press, 1996).
11. Downes, "Negro Rights and White Backlash in the Campaign of 1920," 101.
12. Downes, 100–107. Harding's Sons of the American Revolution application can be found at Ancestry.com; interested readers can use the search field under "U.S., Sons of the American Revolution Membership Applications, 1889–1970," available at https://www.ancestry.com/search/collections/2204/. See also "New York in the Revolution," in *Documents Relating to the Colonial History of the State of New York*, ed. Berthold Fernow (Albany, N.Y.: Weed, Parsons and Company, 1887), 15:291; Mrs. Amos G. Draper, "Revolutionary Ancestry of the Presidents of the United States," *Daughters of the American Revolution Magazine*, March 1921, 136.
13. On Harding generally, see Murray, *The Harding Era*.
14. Pratt's use of the phrase is noted in his obituary, "John Teele Pratt, Financier, Is Dead," *New York Times*, June 18, 1927.
15. Warren G. Harding, "Less Government in Business and More Business in Government," *World's Work*, November 1920, 25–27. Harding's lessons from Professor Lindsay, as well as Page's account of the article's production, are mentioned in a letter from *World's Work* editor Arthur W. Page to Henry Stimson. Page describes the article's publication as an attempt to force the senator to commit himself publicly to Page and Stimson's shared agenda. Page to Stimson, September 17, 1920, reel 56, p. 179, HLSP. For Pratt's meeting with Harding, see Pratt to Members, September 1, 1920, file 640.2.1, BSP. Lindsay makes reference to his work with Harding in Lindsay to Harding, December 8, 1920, box 9, Samuel McCune Lindsay Papers, CUL.
16. "League Men Explain Support of Harding," *New York Times*, October 15, 1920.
17. "Presidential Election of 1920: A Resource Guide," LoC, accessed June 16, 2021, https://www.loc.gov/rr/program/bib/elections/election1920.html.
18. The literature on these questions is of course extensive. See, for example, Ellen Carol DuBois, *Woman Suffrage and Women's Rights* (New York: New York University Press, 1998), and Lynn Dumenil, *The Modern Temper: American Culture and Society in the 1920s* (New York: Hill and Wang, 1995). On public opinion in this era, see Walter Lippmann, *Public Opinion* (New York: Harcourt, Brace and Company, 1922), and Brian Balogh, "'Mirrors of Desires': Interest Groups, Elections, and the Targeted Style in Twentieth-Century America," in *The Associational State:*

5. THE DARK HORSE: 1920-1921

American Governance in the Twentieth Century (Philadelphia: University of Pennsylvania Press, 2015), 66–88.
19. Gustavus A. Weber and Laurence F. Schmeckebier, *The Veterans' Administration: Its History, Activities, and Organization* (Washington, D.C.: Brookings Institution, 1934), 154–155. On the formation of the veterans care system generally, see Jessica L. Adler, *Burdens of War: Creating the United States Veterans Health System* (Baltimore: Johns Hopkins University Press, 2017).
20. Theda Skocpol, *Protecting Soldiers and Mothers: The Political Origins of Social Policy in the United States* (Cambridge, Mass.: Harvard University Press, 1992), details the creation and operation of the scandal-ridden Civil War pension system but does not follow the development of federal veterans policy beyond 1920.
21. Kathleen J. Frydl, *The GI Bill* (New York: Cambridge University Press, 2009), 47.
22. Parkhurst L. Whitney, "A Preliminary Report Including a Consideration of Possible Future Activities," reel 56, pp. 200–214, HLSP.
23. Stimson to Henry M. Sage, October 5, 1920, reel 56, p. 324, HLSP.
24. Whitney, "A Preliminary Report Including a Consideration of Possible Future Activities."
25. Stimson to W. W. Warwick, September 10, 1920, reel 56, pp. 132–133, HLSP.
26. NBC, *A Proposal for Government Reorganization, Published in the Interest of National Economy* (New York: NBC, 1921), 47–48.
27. See Earl D. Bond (with the collaboration of Paul O. Komora), *Thomas W. Salmon: Psychiatrist* (New York: Norton, 1950). For a discussion of the methods developed by Salmon and their relation to methods adopted by the army in the 1990s, see Franklin D. Jones, "The Psychiatric Lessons of War," in *Textbook of Military Medicine*, vol. 4, *War Psychiatry*, ed. Franklin D. Jones, Linette R. Sparacino, Victoria L. Wilcox, Joseph M. Rothberg, and James W. Stokes (Washington, D.C.: Office of the Surgeon General at TMM Publications, 1995), 9–10. Salmon outlined his theories and methods in "General View of Neuropsychiatry," in *The Medical Department of the United States Army in the World War*, vol. 10, *Neuropsychiatry*, ed. Pearce Bailey, Frankwood E. Williams, Paul O. Komora, Thomas W. Salmon, and Norman Fenton (Washington, D.C.: U.S. Government Printing Office, 1929), 273–302.
28. Quoted in Bond, *Thomas W. Salmon*, 77.
29. Thomas W. Salmon, "The Insane Veteran and a Nation's Honor: The Better Way Out of the Present Deplorable Situation Involves a Lapse of Time; the Worse Way Out Is Merely Barefaced Shirking of Public Duty," *American Legion Weekly*, January 28, 1921, 5–6, 18.
30. The *American Legion Weekly* editor introduced Salmon as "the man who can discuss with the most unimpeachable authority the situation of the neuro-psychiatric veteran of the World War"; see Salmon, "The Insane Veteran and a Nation's Honor," 5–6, 18.
31. Rosemary Stevens, *A Time of Scandal: Charles R. Forbes, Warren G. Harding, and the Making of the Veterans Bureau* (Baltimore: Johns Hopkins University Press, 2016), 36–37.
32. The activities of the consultants are discussed in Rosemary A. Stevens, "Can the Government Govern? Lessons from the Formation of the Veterans Administration,"

5. THE DARK HORSE: 1920-1921

Journal of Health Politics, Policy and Law 16, no. 2 (Summer 1991): 281–305. For the connections between Mellon and White, see Mellon Institute of Industrial Research, "Outline of the Smoke Investigation," *Smoke Investigation Bulletin* 1, no. 1 (August 1912): 7, and David Cannadine, *Mellon: An American Life* (New York: Random House, 2006), 46–49.

33. *Report of the Consultants on Hospitalization, Appointed by the Secretary of the Treasury to Provide Additional Hospital Facilities under Public Act 384* (Washington, D.C.: U.S. Government Printing Office, 1923), 8–9.
34. *Report of the Consultants on Hospitalization*, 7–8.
35. See HCIFC, *Hearings on Consolidation of Government Agencies for the Benefit of Disabled Ex-service Men*, 67th Cong., 1st sess. (1921), 44.
36. Lamont to Gary, December 8, 1915, and Lamont to Henry M. Dawes, January 8, 1918, box 91, folder 9, Thomas Lamont Papers, Baker Library, Harvard Business School, Boston, Mass.
37. Dawes to Milton J. Foreman, April 25, 1921, box 277, folder 3, CGDP.
38. HCIFC, *Consolidation of Government Agencies*, 43. The report is quoted in Weber and Schmeckebier, *The Veterans' Administration*, 218.
39. HCIFC, *Consolidation of Government Agencies*, 14. For Laporte's association with Mellon, see, for instance, "Mellons Seen Behind McNair: Campaign Treasurer Is Ally of Powerful Family, Opponent Says," *Pittsburgh Press*, August 9, 1933.

6. EARLY SUCCESS: SPRING AND SUMMER 1921

1. *Address of Warren G. Harding, President of the United States, Delivered at a Joint Session of the Two Houses of Congress, April 12, 1921* (Washington, D.C.: U.S. Government Printing Office, 1921).
2. *Address of Warren G. Harding, April 12, 1921*, 3.
3. *Address of Warren G. Harding, April 12, 1921*, 6.
4. *Address of Warren G. Harding, April 12, 1921*, 8.
5. *Address of Warren G. Harding, April 12, 1921*, 10.
6. *Address of Warren G. Harding, April 12, 1921*, 11.
7. *Address of Warren G. Harding, April 12, 1921*, 12.
8. *Address of Warren G. Harding, April 12, 1921*, 12–13; "Harding Rejects League Outright ... Tells Congress of Policy," *New York Times*, April 13, 1921.
9. *Address of Warren G. Harding, April 12, 1921*, 13; Megan Ming Francis, *Civil Rights and the Making of the Modern American State* (New York: Cambridge University Press, 2014), 86.
10. "Tells Congress of Policy," *New York Times*, April 13, 1921.
11. Brookings to John D. Rockefeller Jr., April 12, 1921, box 40, folder 315, JDRP.
12. W. E. B. Du Bois, "President Harding," *Crisis* 22, no. 2 (June 1921): 68; Francis, *Civil Rights and the Making of the Modern American State*, 88.
13. See Jeffery A. Jenkins, Justin Peck, and Vesla M. Weaver, "Between Reconstructions: Congressional Action on Civil Rights, 1891–1940," *Studies in American Political Development* 24, no. 1 (April 2010): 67, and William B. Hixson Jr., "Moorfield Storey and the Defense of the Dyer Anti-Lynching Bill," *New England Quarterly* 42, no. 1 (March 1969): 65–81.

6. EARLY SUCCESS: SPRING AND SUMMER 1921

14. Francis, *Civil Rights and the Making of the Modern American State*, 103–104.
15. For the Storey-Wickersham correspondence (cited in Francis, *Civil Rights and the Making of the Modern American State*, 104n18), see box I:C80, folder "Wickersham, George, 1921–1922," NAACPP.
16. Francis, *Civil Rights and the Making of the Modern American State*, 88–89; Scott Ellsworth, *Death in a Promised Land: The Tulsa Race Riot of 1921* (Baton Rouge: Louisiana State University Press, 1982); John Hope Franklin and Scott Ellsworth, eds., *The Tulsa Race Riot: A Scientific, Historical and Legal Analysis* (Oklahoma City: Tulsa Race Riot Commission, 2000); Eddie Faye Gates, *They Came Searching: How Blacks Sought the Promised Land in Tulsa* (Austin, Tex.: Eakin Press, 1997).
17. "Harding Exhorts Negroes to Study," *New York Times*, June 7, 1921; Francis, *Civil Rights and the Making of the Modern American State*, 89.
18. See the NBC letterhead in Pratt to Members, May 17, 1921, file 640.2.1, p. 45, BSP.
19. See "Constitutional and Legal Phases of President's Veto of the Budget Bill, December 1920," series 1, box 5, folder 8, Charles Wallace Collins Papers, University of Maryland Library, College Park, Md.
20. Stephen Skowronek notes that the final version of the budget act that was passed in 1921 "actually made the removal of the Comptroller General even more difficult." See Stephen Skowronek, *Building a New American State: The Expansion of National Administrative Capacities, 1877–1920* (New York: Cambridge University Press, 1982), 207. The differences in the two versions can be seen by comparing HSCB, *National Budget System: Conference Report to Accompany H.R. 9783*, 66th Cong. 2nd sess. (1920), 1, 3, 5–6, and SCCNB, *National Budget System: Conference Report to Accompany S. 1084*, 67th Cong. 1st sess. (1921), H. Rep. 96, 1, 3–5.
21. Dawes to Harding, January 25, 1921, Dawes to Harding, January 26, 1921, and Harding to Dawes, January 31, 1921, box 277, folder 3, CGDP.
22. Harding to Dawes, June 9, 1921, box 277, folder 3, CGDP.
23. Dawes to John T. McCutcheon, July 13, 1921, box 101, folder 46, CGDP; Charles G. Dawes, *The First Year of the Budget of the United States* (New York: Harper and Brothers, 1923), 121–132.
24. Dawes, Memorandum for the President, July 11, 1921, box 112, folder 10, CGDP, printed in Dawes, *First Year of the Budget*, 27.
25. Dawes to George H. Lorimer, April 29, 1922, box 112, folder 112, CGDP. This point is made by Peri Arnold, who writes that "Dawes's organization of the budget bureau aimed at making it a centralizing, presidential staff. In particular, he meant the bureau to counteract the autonomy of the agencies." See Peri E. Arnold, *Making the Managerial Presidency: Comprehensive Reorganization Planning, 1905–1996* (Lawrence: University Press of Kansas, 1998), 55.
26. Robert S. Brookings to John D. Rockefeller Jr., March 27, 1919, box 40, folder 315, JDRP.
27. See James R. Garfield to Herbert Hoover, July 7, 1925, box 514, Reorg. of Govt. Depts., Hoover Speech (5-21-25) Reactions B-H, HH-CP.
28. Pratt to John D. Rockefeller Jr., August 12, 1920, box 40, folder 317, JDRP.
29. Pratt to Members, September 1, 1920, file 640.2.1, pp. 33–34, BSP.
30. NBC, *A Proposal for Government Reorganization, Published in the Interest of National Economy* (New York: NBC, 1921), 14.
31. NBC, *Proposal for Government Reorganization*, 21–39.

6. EARLY SUCCESS: SPRING AND SUMMER 1921

32. NBC, 14–16, 39.
33. Fosdick to John D. Rockefeller Jr., March 24, 1921, box 40, folder 315, JDRP.
34. The committee members were as follows: from the House, C. Frank Reavis (R., Neb.), Henry Temple (R., Pa.), and Robert Walton Moore (D., Va.); and from the Senate, Reed Smoot (R., Utah), James Wadsworth (R., N.Y.), and Pat Harrison (D., Miss.). See Arnold, *Making the Managerial Presidency*, 57–58.
35. Arnold, *Making the Managerial Presidency*, 58–59.
36. Elihu Root, "National Expenditures and Public Economy," *Proceedings of the Academy of Political Science in the City of New York* 9, no. 3 (July 1921): 428.
37. Warren G. Harding, "Business in Government and the Problem of Governmental Reorganization for Greater Efficiency," *Proceedings of the Academy of Political Science in the City of New York* 9, no. 3 (July 1921): 429–433.
38. Arnold, *Making the Managerial Presidency*, 59; "Filibuster Blocks Harding Dictation," *New York Times*, July 27, 1921; Harding to Brown, March 22, 1921, box 1, folder 3, WFPB; Cong. Rec., 67th Cong. 1st sess. (1921), 61, pt. 5: H4320.
39. "Veterans' Bureau Plan in Congress," *New York Times*, May 26, 1921; "Passes Bill Merging Veteran Relief Boards," *New York Times*, June 11, 1921; "For Soldier Relief Unity," *New York Times*, July 21, 1921; Weber and Schmeckebier, *The Veterans' Administration: Its History, Activities, and Organization* (Washington, D.C.: Brookings Institution, 1934), 218–19; HCIFC, *Consolidation of Government Agencies for the Benefit of Disabled Ex-Service Men*, 67th Cong., 1st sess. (1921), 43.

7. EQUAL PROTECTION UNDER LAW: 1921–1923

1. "Says Harding Plays While Veterans Suffer," *New York Times*, September 22, 1921.
2. Charles H. Brough to James B. A. Robertson, September 16, 1920, box 3, folder 16, RG 8-D-1-3, Oklahoma Governors' Papers, Oklahoma State Archives Division, Oklahoma City, Okla., http://digitalprairie.ok.gov/cdm/ref/collection/race-riot/id/243.
3. See Magdalene Zier, "Crimes of Omission: State-Action Doctrine and Anti-Lynching Legislation in the Jim Crow Era," *Stanford Law Review* 73, no. 3 (March 2021): 777–819; Jeffery A. Jenkins, Justin Peck, and Vesla M. Weaver, "Between Reconstructions: Congressional Action on Civil Rights, 1891–1940," *Studies in American Political Development* 24, no. 1 (April 2010): 67; Claudine L. Ferrell, *Nightmare and Dream: Antilynching in Congress, 1917–1922* (New York: Garland, 1986), 150–187; and William B. Hixson Jr., "Moorfield Storey and the Defense of the Dyer Anti-Lynching Bill," *New England Quarterly* 42, no. 1 (March 1969): 65–81. On Taft's confidential opinion, see Megan Ming Francis, *Civil Rights and the Making of the Modern American State* (New York: Cambridge University Press, 2014), 103–104, 158, and Johnson to Villard, August 1, 1921, White to Marshall, August 2, 1921, Johnson to Walling, August 3, 1921, in the Anti-Lynching File, NAACPP. The Storey-Wickersham correspondence is preserved in box I:C80, folder "Wickersham, George, 1921–1922," NAACPP.
4. House Committee on the Judiciary, *Anti-Lynching Bill: Report to Accompany H.R. 13*, 67th Cong., 1st sess. (1921), H. Rep. 452. The average manufacturing worker's expected earnings is based on fifty weeks earning $22.18 per week. See "Gross Hours and Earnings of Productive Workers in Manufacturing, 1919 to Date," in

7. EQUAL PROTECTION UNDER LAW: 1921–1923

U.S. Bureau of Labor Statistics, *Employment and Earnings, Including the Monthly Report on the Labor Force* 7, no. 2 (August 1960): 29.
5. House Committee on the Judiciary, *Anti-Lynching Bill*, 7–16.
6. "Stamp Advertising the Semicentennial of Birmingham in October 1921," Bhamwiki.com, accessed June 21, 2021, https://www.bhamwiki.com/w/File:Semicentennial_stamp.jpg.
7. "President Harding's Democratic Friend," *New York Times*, September 18, 1921.
8. *Address of the President of the United States at the Celebration of the Semicentennial of the Founding of the City of Birmingham, Alabama, October 26, 1921* (Washington, D.C.: U.S. Government Printing Office, 1921), 11.
9. *Address of the President of the United States at the Celebration of the Semicentennial of the Founding of the City of Birmingham*, 7–8.
10. *Address of the President of the United States at the Celebration of the Semicentennial of the Founding of the City of Birmingham*, 8.
11. *Address of the President of the United States at the Celebration of the Semicentennial of the Founding of the City of Birmingham*, 9.
12. *Address of the President of the United States at the Celebration of the Semicentennial of the Founding of the City of Birmingham*, 10.
13. *Address of the President of the United States at the Celebration of the Semicentennial of the Founding of the City of Birmingham*, 10.
14. *Address of the President of the United States at the Celebration of the Semicentennial of the Founding of the City of Birmingham*, 11.
15. *Address of the President of the United States at the Celebration of the Semicentennial of the Founding of the City of Birmingham*, 6–7.
16. "Harding Says Negro Must Have Equality in Political Life," *New York Times*, October 27, 1921.
17. W. E. B. Du Bois, "President Harding and Social Equality," *Crisis* 23, no. 2 (December 1921): 54–55.
18. Lewis Houston was lynched at the park (formerly named "Central Park," now named "Linn Park") on November 24, 1883. His was the first of thirty lynchings in Jefferson County between 1883 and 1940. See John Hammontree, "Could a New Monument Heal Jefferson County's Racial Divide?," *Birmingham Magazine*, July 2019. The reactions of prominent white southern leaders to Harding's speech are compiled in "The Looking Glass," *Crisis* 23, no. 3 (January 1922): 127–132.
19. "Praise and Assail Harding Negro Talk," *New York Times*, October 28, 1921.
20. "Praise and Assail Harding Negro Talk."
21. Cong. Rec., 67th Cong. 1st sess. (1921), 61, pt. 5: H4320.
22. Cong. Rec., 67th Cong. 3rd sess. (1921), 62, pt. 1: H548; "Southern Men Fight Anti-Lynching Bill," *New York Times*, December 20, 1921.
23. "Filibuster Blocks Anti-Lynching Bill," *New York Times*, December 21, 1921.
24. Cong. Rec., 67th Cong. 3rd sess. (1922), 62, pt. 2: H1721 (statement of Thomas Sisson); Francis, *Civil Rights and the Making of the Modern American State*, 116.
25. Cong. Rec., 67th Cong., 2nd sess. (1922), 62, pt. 2: H1774 (statement of Hatton W. Sumners). The mechanics of the filibuster are explained in Jenkins, Peck, and Weaver, "Between Reconstructions," 70; U.S. House of Representatives, Office of the Historian, "Anti-Lynching Legislation Renewed," *Black Americans in Congress, 1870–2007* (Washington, D.C.: U.S. Government Printing Office, 2008).

7. EQUAL PROTECTION UNDER LAW: 1921-1923

26. U.S. Congress, *House Journal*, 67th Cong., 2nd sess. (January 26, 1922), 100.
27. Harding's remarks were conveyed by Martin B. Madden, "'I'll Sign Dyer Bill'—Harding," *Chicago Defender*, February 18, 1922.
28. W. E. B. Du Bois, "The Dyer Bill in the Senate," *Crisis* 23, no. 6 (April 1922): 248 (emphasis in original). On the support of northern Democrats in the House, see Jenkins, Peck, and Weaver, "Between Reconstructions," 70–71.
29. Jenkins, Peck, and Weaver, 72; Francis, *Civil Rights and the Making of the Modern American State*, 118–121. For a useful account of Borah's role in the antilynching debate, see Jill Gill, "Borah, Lynching and the Wrong Side of History: How States' Rights Aligned Idaho and the South on Race," *Blue Review*, August 26, 2013, https://wayback.archive-it.org/8092/20190724182847/https://thebluereview.org/william-borah-lynching-history/.
30. Jenkins, Peck, and Weaver, "Between Reconstructions," 72; Francis, *Civil Rights and the Making of the Modern American State*, 118–121; Zier, "Crimes of Omission," 805; Gill, "Borah."
31. The most detailed discussion of the bill's constitutionality is in Ferrell, *Nightmare and Dream*, 150–187. See also Zier, "Crimes of Omission."
32. "Filibuster Blocks Anti-Lynching Bill," *New York Times*, December 21, 1921. In a self-serving attempt to cast himself as a true friend willing to dispense tough love and straight talk to African Americans, Borah later claimed, in a 1926 letter to W. E. B. Du Bois, that all but one of the Republicans on the Judiciary Committee agreed with him that the bill was unconstitutional, and he charged that his fellow Republicans had "played politics with the negro" by voting in favor of the bill. See Borah to Du Bois, July 17, 1926, W. E. B. Du Bois Papers, University of Massachusetts, Amherst, Mass., cited in Zier, "Crimes of Omission," 805n153.
33. Charles H. Brough to James B. A. Robertson, September 16, 1920, box 3, folder 16, RG 8-D-1-3, Oklahoma Governors' Papers, Oklahoma State Archives Division, Oklahoma City, Okla.
34. On Curtis's career, see Jennifer Davis, "Charles Brent Curtis, First Native American Congressional Member," *In Custodia Legis*, January 26, 2018, https://blogs.loc.gov/law/2018/01/charles-brent-curtis-first-native-american-congressional-member/, and William E. Unrau, *Mixed-Bloods and Tribal Dissolution: Charles Curtis and the Quest for Indian Identity* (Lawrence: University Press of Kansas, 1989).
35. Report of James Weldon Johnson, quoted in "Dyer Anti-Lynching Bill," *Crisis* 25, no. 1 (November 1922), 24–26.
36. "Statistics of the Congressional Election of November 7, 1922," U.S. House of Representatives, accessed June 21, 2021, https://history.house.gov/Institution/Election-Statistics/1922election/.
37. "Democrats Open Finish Fight on Anti-Lynch Bill," *New York Tribune*, November 29, 1922.
38. "Senate Democrats Start Filibuster, Stop All Business," *New York Times*, November 29, 1922.
39. "Filibuster Menaces Ship Subsidy Bill," *New York Times*, December 1, 1922.
40. "Harding Favors Dyer Bill," *New York Times*, December 2, 1922.
41. "Filibuster Kills Anti-Lynching Bill," *New York Times*, December 3, 1922.
42. Jenkins, Peck, and Weaver, "Between Reconstructions," 75; Francis, *Civil Rights and the Making of the Modern American State*, 121–124.

43. Francis, *Civil Rights and the Making of the Modern American State*, 158.
44. Francis, 132.
45. Francis, 132–133.
46. Francis, 127–163.
47. Walter White, *A Man Called White: The Autobiography of Walter White* (New York: Viking Press, 1948), 48–51.
48. Walter White, "Massacring Whites in Arkansas," *Nation*, December 6, 1919, 715–716; Francis, *Civil Rights and the Making of the Modern American State*, 142–144.
49. Moore v. Dempsey, 261 U.S. 86 (1923); Francis, *Civil Rights and the Making of the Modern American State*, 127–163.
50. Francis, *Civil Rights and the Making of the Modern American State*.
51. Pete Daniel, "Black Power in the 1920s: The Case of Tuskegee Veterans Hospital," *Journal of Southern History* 36, no. 3 (August 1970): 368–388.
52. *Report of the Consultants on Hospitalization, Appointed by the Secretary of the Treasury to Provide Additional Hospital Facilities under Public Act 384* (Washington, D.C.: U.S. Government Printing Office, 1923), 18.
53. For discussion of the role of race in the creation of the veterans' hospital system, see Mark Robert Schneider, *We Return Fighting: The Civil Rights Movement in the Jazz Age* (Boston: Northeastern University Press, 2002); Vanessa N. Gamble, *Making a Place for Ourselves: The Black Hospital Movement, 1920–1945* (New York: Oxford University Press, 1995), 70–104; and Daniel, "Black Power in the 1920s," 368–388.
54. Transcript of conference between the CoH and the National Committee of Negro Veteran Relief, November 1, 1921, box 20, Records of the Board of CoH, Record Group 121.5.1, NA2.
55. Two useful accounts of this episode can be found in Gamble, *Making a Place for Ourselves*, 70–104, and Daniel, "Black Power in the 1920s," 368–388.
56. Harding to Hines, April 19, 1923, box 71, USVB-DF, quoted in Daniel, "Black Power in the 1920s," 373.
57. *Address of the President of the United States at the Celebration of the Semicentennial of the Founding of the City of Birmingham*.
58. Daniel, "Black Power in the 1920s," 380–388.
59. "Veterans' Bureau Plan in Congress," *New York Times*, May 26, 1921; "Passes Bill Merging Veteran Relief Boards," *New York Times*, June 11, 1921; "For Soldier Relief Unity," *New York Times*, July 21, 1921; Gustavus A. Weber and Laurence F. Schmeckebier, *The Veterans' Administration: Its History, Activities, and Organization* (Washington, D.C.: Brookings Institution, 1934), 218–219; HCIFC, *Consolidation of Government Agencies for the Benefit of Disabled Ex-Service Men*, 67th Cong. 1st sess., 1921, 43.

8. BACKLASH: SPRING AND SUMMER 1923

1. JCR, *Reorganization of the Executive Departments*, 67th Cong., 4th sess. (1923), S. Doc. 302, p. 1.
2. Walter F. Brown, "Memorandum Describing the Reorganization Plan Recommended by the President and His Cabinet," WFBP.
3. Brown, "Memorandum," 22.

8. BACKLASH: SPRING AND SUMMER 1923

4. Brown, 23.
5. JCR, *Reorganization of the Executive Departments*, 3.
6. William F. Willoughby, *Principles of Public Administration: With Special Reference to the National and State Governments of the United States* (Baltimore: Johns Hopkins University Press, 1927), 99; Peri E. Arnold, *Making the Managerial Presidency: Comprehensive Reorganization Planning, 1905–1996* (Lawrence: University Press of Kansas, 1998), 69–70.
7. Brown, "Memorandum," 83–84; Arnold, *Making the Managerial Presidency*, 71–73.
8. See, for instance, William F. Willoughby to Herbert Hoover, March 12, 1923, box 515, "Reorganization of Government Depts., 1922–1923," HH-CP.
9. JCR, *Reorganization of the Executive Departments*, 1.
10. "Congress Is a Nest of Cowards, Says Dawes in Speech," *New York Times*, October 14, 1922.
11. George H. Nash, "The 'Great Humanitarian': Herbert Hoover, the Relief of Belgium, and the Reconstruction of Europe after World War I," *Tocqueville Review* 38, no. 2 (2017): 55–70.
12. For an evenhanded and thorough overview of Hoover's career, see William E. Leuchtenburg, *Herbert Hoover* (New York: Henry Holt, 2009).
13. Arnold, *Making the Managerial Presidency*, 64–68.
14. "Harding 'Voyage of Understanding' Trip Itinerary," Ohio History Connection, Warren G. Harding Collection, accessed June 22, 2021, https://ohiomemory.org/digital/collection/p16007coll100/id/561/.
15. "President Warren G. Harding's Visit to Southern Utah, June 27, 1923," Washington County Historical Society (Washington County, Utah), accessed June 22, 2021, http://wchsutah.org/miscellaneous/warren-g-harding.php.
16. "Calls Harding Martyr to 24-Hour-Day Job; W. F. Brown Blames Faulty Federal System," *New York Times*, August 4, 1923.
17. "Harding's Death Revives Plans for Easing Burden," *New York Times*, August 5, 1923.
18. "$2,000,000,000 Spent for Aid, but War Veterans Suffer," *New York Times*, February 25, 1923.
19. Rosemary A. Stevens, *A Time of Scandal: Charles R. Forbes, Warren G. Harding and the Making of the Veterans Bureau* (Baltimore: Johns Hopkins University Press, 2016), 161–163.
20. On the "Ohio Gang," see Stevens, *A Time of Scandal*, 231–233, 283.
21. "Half Hours with the Government," *Washington Post*, August 28, 1921.
22. "Veterans' Bureau at Work: Colonel Forbes Clearing up the Tangle of Service Men's Relief Claims," *New York Times*, September 25, 1921, quoted in Rosemary A. Stevens, "The Invention, Stumbling, and Reinvention of the Modern U.S. Veterans Health Care System, 1918–1924," in *Veterans' Policies, Veterans' Politics: New Perspectives on Veterans in the Modern United States*, ed. Stephen R. Ortiz (Gainesville: University Press of Florida, 2012), 54.
23. Marquis James, "What's Wrong in Washington?," *American Legion Weekly*, March 9, 1923, 11, 18–22.
24. "Worried by Critics, Cramer Takes Life," *New York Times*, March 15, 1923.
25. "Mortimer Swears Forbes Was Bribed," *New York Times*, December 2, 1924; Associated Press, "Payment of $5,000 Bribe Charged," *New York Times*, January 31, 1925.

26. Stevens, *A Time of Scandal*, 201–221.
27. Stevens, 153–156, 193–194.
28. Stevens, 243–266.
29. Forbes, in fact, eventually married Mortimer's ex-wife. Stevens, *A Time of Scandal*, 273–274.
30. "Legion Demands Ousting of Sawyer," *New York Times*, October 20, 1922.
31. Stevens, *A Time of Scandal*, 306.
32. "General Hines Resigns," *New York Times*, July 29, 1920; "Personal Mention," *Marine Engineering*, September 1920, 779–80; "Ask Bolling to Testify in Shipping Inquiry Today," *New York Times*, November 30, 1920.
33. "Gen. Hines Charges Fraud and Waste in Veterans' Relief," *New York Times*, October 23, 1923.
34. Hines to Reed, February 11, 1924, box 170, USVB-DF.
35. McInerny to Hines, April 18, 1923, box 220, USVB-DF.
36. McInerny to Hines, April 20, 1923, box 220, USVB-DF.
37. On Sawyer's covetousness toward the materiel at the Perryville depot, see Stevens, *A Time of Scandal*, 155–156.
38. Smith to Hines, May 26, 1923, box 220, and Hines to Reed, February 11, 1924, box 170, USVB-DF.
39. My argument here follows that made by Rosemary A. Stevens, who—in the most exhaustive and authoritative study of the Veterans Bureau scandal to date—concludes: "When all aspects of the case are considered, it is reasonable to conclude from the evidence that Forbes was found guilty of a crime he did not commit." Stevens argues that the Veterans Bureau scandal tells us less about the supposed corruption of the Harding administration than about "the disruptions that were necessary in establishing the Veterans Bureau" and "the risks that exist for anyone who takes on the thankless task of consolidating diverse, established pieces of government into a single agency." Stevens, *A Time of Scandal*, 308–311.
40. In the March 9 story in the *American Legion Weekly*, Ijams is the only Veterans Bureau official described in complimentary terms: "Ijams is a sort of professional stop-gapper about the Bureau," and "Ijams is competent." See Marquis James, "What's Wrong in Washington?," *American Legion Weekly*, March 9, 1923, 11. For Ijams's role in attempting to undermine Harding's policy at Tuskegee, see Pete Daniel, "Black Power in the 1920s: The Case of Tuskegee Veterans Hospital," *Journal of Southern History* 36, no. 3 (August 1970): 371, 372, 374, 381, 385.

9. SOUTHERN STRENGTH: 1923-1924

1. Calvin Coolidge, *Annual Message of the President of the United States, December 6, 1923* (Washington, D.C.: U.S. Government Printing Office, 1923), 11.
2. Lynn Dumenil, "'The Insatiable Maw of Bureaucracy': Antistatism and Education Reform in the 1920s," *Journal of American History* 77, no. 2 (September 1990): 500.
3. On Catholic education-policy advocacy, see Douglas J. Slawson, *The Department of Education Battle, 1918–1932: Public Schools, Catholic Schools, and the Social Order* (Notre Dame, Ind.: University of Notre Dame Press, 2005).

9. SOUTHERN STRENGTH: 1923-1924

4. On the KKK's support for the bill, see Thomas Pegram, *One Hundred Percent American: The Rebirth and Decline of the Ku Klux Klan in the 1920s* (Chicago: Ivan R. Dee, 2011), 116–118. On southern opposition, see Dumenil, "'The Insatiable Maw of Bureaucracy,'" 501–502.
5. NEA, *The Towner-Sterling Bill* (Washington, D.C.: NEA, 1922), 13.
6. NEA, *The Towner-Sterling Bill*, 104–112.
7. *Address of Warren G. Harding, President of the United States, Delivered at a Joint Session of the Two Houses of Congress, April 12, 1921* (Washington, D.C.: U.S. Government Printing Office, 1921), 8.
8. See Walter F. Brown, "Memorandum Describing the Reorganization Plan Recommended by the President and the Cabinet: As Outlined in Senate Document No. 302, 67th Congress, 4th Session" (December 14, 1923), 63, WFBP.
9. *Annual Message of the President of the United States, December 6, 1923.*
10. NAACP, *Memorandum on the Sterling-Towner Bill* (H.R. 7), 1919, W. E. B. Du Bois Papers, University of Massachusetts, Amherst, Mass.
11. In April 1922, after acknowledging an error in referring to the Towner-Sterling Bill by its previous name, "Smith-Towner," Du Bois explained that "we have become used to looking to Hoke Smith of Georgia for every anti-Negro atrocity introduced in Congress." W. E. B. Du Bois, "The Sterling-Towner Bill," *Crisis* 23, no. 6 (April 1922): 248.
12. W. E. B. Du Bois, "Mississippi," *Crisis* 24, no. 3 (July 1922): 104.
13. Florence Kelley, "The Denial of Education," *World Tomorrow* 5, no. 3 (March 1922): 78.
14. Florence Kelley, "The Sterling Discrimination Bill," *Crisis* 26, no. 6 (October 1923): 252–255. This article is partially quoted in Dumenil, "The Insatiable Maw of Bureaucracy," 520.
15. HCE, *To Create a Department of Education and to Authorize Appropriations of Money to Encourage the States in the Promotion and Support of Education: Hearings on H.R. 3923*, 68th Cong., 1st sess. (1924), 354. The USCC's report is a curious document. Portions contain an almost verbatim copy of the introduction to a pamphlet issued by the NEA. Compare the following two sources: HCE, *To Create a Department of Education*, 412–413, and NEA, *The Towner-Sterling Bill*, 5.
16. James Weldon Johnson, Memorandum [1924 ?], W. E. B. Du Bois Papers, University of Massachusetts, Amherst, Mass.
17. HCE, *To Create a Department of Education*.
18. HCE, 508–559; John Randolph Tucker and Henry St. George Tucker, eds., *The Constitution of the United States: A Critical Discussion of its Genesis, Development, and Interpretation* (Chicago: Callaghan and Co., 1899). In an 1884 essay in the *North American Review*, the elder Tucker used dozens of population tables from census data to argue that the federal government should leave southerners to solve the problem of race relations. See John Randolph Tucker, "Race Progress in the United States," *North American Review* 138, no. 3 (February 1884): 163–177.
19. HCE, *To Create a Department of Education*, 293.
20. HCE, 294.
21. HCE, 468, 472; Slawson, *The Department of Education Battle*, 141.
22. HCE, *To Create a Department of Education*, 602. The racial slur appears unredacted in the record of the hearings.

23. The rationale for the Curtis-Reed Bill is described in "Statement of Dr. William M. Davidson, Superintendent of Schools, Pittsburgh, Pa., and Chairman Legislative Commission, NEA," in HCE, *Proposed Department of Education: Hearings on H.R. 7*, 70th Cong., 1st sess. (1928), 5.
24. HCE, *To Create a Department of Education*, 347–348.

10. CONGRESSIONAL COUNTEROFFENSIVE: SPRING 1924

1. Frederick Jackson Turner, "The Significance of the Section," *Wisconsin Magazine of History*, March 1925, 255–280. The quote appears on 278.
2. A detailed play-by-play of the Bonus battles is beyond the scope of this chapter; it would also stand little chance of improving upon several excellent treatments of this episode. The best recent analysis of this early phase of the Bonus issue can be found in Stephen R. Ortiz, *Beyond the Bonus March and GI Bill: How Veteran Politics Shaped the New Deal Era* (New York: New York University Press, 2010), 22–28. Any account of the Bonus must rely heavily on William Pencak, *For God and Country: The American Legion, 1919–1941* (Boston: Northeastern University Press, 1989), and William Pyrle Dillingham, *Federal Aid to Veterans, 1917–1941* (Gainesville: University of Florida Press, 1952).
3. "Fight Against Bonus Planned by Veterans," *New York Times*, May 17, 1920.
4. "Defer Bonus Action, Speed Tax Revision, the President Urges," *New York Times*, July 13, 1921.
5. "Says Harding Plays as Veterans Suffer," *New York Times*, September 22, 1921.
6. "The Bonus Swindle," *Nation*, March 1, 1922, 238.
7. Charles G. Dawes to Warren G. Harding, July 26, 1922, box 277, folder 3, CGDP. By "the past," Dawes was alluding to the scandals surrounding the payment of Union Army pensions after the Civil War. See Theda Skocpol, *Protecting Soldiers and Mothers: The Political Origins of Social Policy in the United States* (Cambridge, Mass.: Harvard University Press, 1992), which details the scandal-ridden Civil War pension system, but which does not follow the development of federal veterans policy beyond 1920.
8. "Soldiers' Adjusted Compensation: Message of the President of the United States," Congressional Serial Set, 67th Cong., H. doc. 396, pp. 2–3, 5. See also "Bonus Killed in Senate," *New York Times*, September 21, 1922; Gustavus A. Weber and Laurence F. Schmeckebier, *The Veterans' Administration: Its History, Activities and Organization* (Washington, D.C.: Brookings Institution, 1934), 185–193; Ortiz, *Beyond the Bonus March and GI Bill*, 25–27.
9. Marquis James, "Big Business Trains Its Guns on Adjusted Compensations," *American Legion Weekly*, November 16, 1923, 9–10, 24–26.
10. Payments to veterans who saw no service overseas were limited to $500. For a full explanation of the rules, see Weber and Schmeckebier, *Veterans' Administration*, 186.
11. In 1924, a forty-hour-per-week production worker could expect to earn that sum in about seven and a half months. This was computed assuming a forty-hour week and using data from Lawrence H. Officer and Samuel H. Williamson, "Annual Wages in the United States, Unskilled Labor and Manufacturing Workers

1774–Present," *MeasuringWorth*, accessed June 21, 2021, https://www.measuringworth .com/datasets/uswage/. Thanks to inflation, the real value of the $625 certificates would have been halved by 1945. When the Bonus was actually paid, however—in 1936, after Congress overrode Franklin D. Roosevelt's veto—real wages had also declined thanks to the Depression. The average payment of $581 was equivalent to about six and a half months of production labor. On the enactment of the immediate Bonus payment in 1936, see Ortiz, *Beyond the Bonus March and GI Bill*, 165–176.

12. Mae M. Ngai, *Impossible Subjects: Illegal Aliens and the Making of Modern America* (Princeton, N.J.: Princeton University Press, 2004), 21–55.
13. Adam Hochschild, "When America Tried to Deport its Radicals," *New Yorker*, November 4, 2019.
14. Sadao Asada, "Between the Old Diplomacy and the New, 1918–1922: The Washington System and the Origins of Japanese-American Rapprochement," *Diplomatic History* 30, no. 2 (April 2006): 211–230.
15. Masayo Duus, *The Japanese Conspiracy: The Oahu Sugar Strike of 1920* (Berkeley: University of California Press, 1999), 303–307.
16. George C. Herring, *From Colony to Superpower: U.S. Foreign Relations since 1776* (New York: Oxford University Press, 2008), 467–468.
17. Cited in David Burner, *Herbert Hoover: A Public Life* (New York: Alfred A. Knopf, 1979), 197.
18. U.S. Congress, *Senate Journal*, 68th Cong., 1st sess., May 15, 1924, 352; U.S. Congress, *House Journal*, 68th Cong., 1st sess., May 15, 1924, 533.
19. W. E. B. Du Bois, *Dusk of Dawn: An Essay Toward an Autobiography of a Race Concept* (New York: Oxford, 2007), 133.
20. JCR, *Reorganization of the Executive Departments*, 68th Cong., 1st sess. (1924), S. Doc. 128.
21. Peri E. Arnold, *Making the Managerial Presidency: Comprehensive Reorganization Planning, 1905–1996* (Lawrence: University Press of Kansas, 1998), 79–80. JCR, *Reorganization of the Executive Departments*.
22. JCR, *Reorganization of the Executive Departments*, 32. Arnold, *Making the Managerial Presidency*, 77–78.
23. SCIUSVB, *Report*, 68th Cong., 1st sess. (1924), S. Rept. 103, pt. 2: 3, 6–9.
24. SCIUSVB, *Report*, 1. (Note: This report contains a "part 2"—cited above and below—but no section formally labeled "part 1." The present citation refers to page 1 of the first, unnumbered portion of the report.)
25. SCIUSVB, *Report*, pt. 2: 27.
26. SCIUSVB, *Report*, pt. 2: 8.
27. The changes at DuPont and General Motors are described in Alfred D. Chandler Jr., *Strategy and Structure Chapters in the History of the Industrial Enterprise* (Cambridge, Mass: MIT Press, 1962).
28. This is a clear example of a phenomenon noted by the political scientist John Kingdon, where policy makers and policy analysts define a policy problem to fit a preexisting policy solution. In this case, the preexisting solution was administrative consolidation. See John W. Kingdon, *Agendas, Alternatives, and Public Policies* (Boston: Harper Collins, 1984).
29. "Coolidge and Dawes Nominated," *New York Times*, June 13, 1924.

11. LOW EXPECTATIONS: 1924-1927

30. "Democrats Nominate Davis and C. W. Bryan," *New York Times*, July 10, 1924. For a thorough debunking of the idea that the 1924 Democratic National Convention was commonly called the "Klanbake" by contemporaries, see Jennifer Mendelsohn and Peter A. Shulman, "How Social Media Spread a Historical Lie," *Washington Post*, March 15, 2018.
31. See Walter Lippmann, Chester Rowell, and Herbert Croly, "Why I Shall Vote for— I. Davis; II. Coolidge; III. La Follette," *New Republic*, October 29, 1924, 218–223, reprinted in John L. Shover, *Politics of the Nineteen Twenties* (Waltham, Mass.: Ginn-Blaisdell, 1970), 56–78.

11. LOW EXPECTATIONS: 1924-1927

1. The first (and still useful) account is Peter Odegard, *Pressure Politics: The Story of the Anti-Saloon League* (New York: Columbia University Press, 1928). The theme of business organizational methods is emphasized in K. Austin Kerr, *Organized for Prohibition: A New History of the Anti-Saloon League* (New Haven, Conn.: Yale University Press, 1985). For an analysis of the league's rise to power and its relation to earlier temperance activism, see Thomas Pegram, *Battling Demon Rum: The Struggle for a Dry America, 1800–1933* (Chicago: Ivan R. Dee, 1998), 109–135. Journalist Daniel Okrent provides an entertaining and illuminating survey in *Last Call: The Rise and Fall of Prohibition* (New York: Scribner, 2010). Historian Lisa McGirr makes a forceful argument for viewing alcohol Prohibition as a seedbed for the modern American carceral state in *The War on Alcohol: Prohibition and the Rise of the American State* (New York: Norton, 2015).
2. On the wartime regulations, see Laurence F. Schmeckebier, *The Bureau of Prohibition: Its History, Activities and Organization. Institute for Government Research* (Washington, D.C.: Brookings Institution, 1929), 4–5; Okrent, *Last Call*, 99–100; Pegram, *Battling Demon Rum*, 146–147.
3. McGirr, *The War on Alcohol*; Okrent, *Last Call*; Pegram, *Battling Demon Rum*.
4. On the authorship of the Volstead Act, see Okrent, *Last Call*, 110.
5. Schmeckebier, *The Bureau of Prohibition*, 4–5; Okrent, *Last Call*, 99–100; Pegram, *Battling Demon Rum*, 146–147.
6. On this lack of formal organization, see Schmeckebier, *The Bureau of Prohibition*, where he notes that the unit "was never established by law, all the powers exercised by it being vested in the Commissioner of Internal Revenue. Not even the appropriation acts recognized the Unit, all the appropriations being for the purpose of enforcing the law" (7–8).
7. For a careful examination of this symbiotic relationship, see Thomas R. Pegram, "Hoodwinked: The Anti-Saloon League and the Ku Klux Klan in 1920s Prohibition Enforcement," *Journal of the Gilded Age and Progressive Era* 7, no. 1 (January 2008): 89–119.
8. Root to Lewis L. Clarke, December 20, 1919, box 137, folder "1919 C-F," Elihu Root Papers, LoC. The recipient was president of the American Exchange National Bank.
9. Okrent, *Last Call*, provides several valuable vignettes illustrating this theme: on Taft, see 108; on Hoover's pre-1920 view, see 99; on Root's Supreme Court appearance, see 121.

11. LOW EXPECTATIONS: 1924-1927

10. Felix Frankfurter, "A National Policy for Enforcement of Prohibition," *Annals of the American Academy of Political Science* 109 (September 1923): 193–195.
11. NBC, *A Proposal for Government Reorganization, Published in the Interest of National Economy* (New York: NBC, 1921), 60.
12. William F. Willoughby, *The Reorganization of the Administrative Branch of the National Government* (Baltimore: Johns Hopkins University Press, 1923), 253.
13. For Mellon's opinion, see David Cannadine, *Mellon: An American Life* (New York: Random House, 2006), 294, 317.
14. Schmeckebier, *The Bureau of Prohibition*, 19.
15. Schmeckebier, 19–20.
16. Charles Lee Reese to John J. Raskob, November 26, 1924, file 1936, John J. Raskob Papers, Hagley Library, Wilmington, Del.
17. Schmeckebier, *The Bureau of Prohibition*, 9.
18. Cannadine, *Mellon*, 317; Schmeckebier, *The Bureau of Prohibition*, 9–13; *Annual Report of the Commissioner of Internal Revenue* (Washington, D.C.: U.S. Government Printing Office, 1925), 26; *Annual Report of the Secretary of the Treasury* (Washington, D.C.: U.S. Government Printing Office, 1926), 139. For an account of the contemporary decentralization at firms such as DuPont and General Motors, see Alfred D. Chandler Jr., *Strategy and Structure Chapters in the History of the Industrial Enterprise* (Cambridge, Mass: MIT Press, 1962).
19. This is noted in Schmeckebier, *The Bureau of Prohibition*, 10.
20. See Schmeckebier, 20.
21. Jesse Tarbert, "The Quest to Bring 'Business Efficiency' to the Federal Executive: Herbert Hoover, Franklin Roosevelt, and the Civil Service Reformers in the Late 1920s," *Journal of Policy History* 31, no. 4 (October 2019): 512–532. Herbert Hoover, "200 Bureaus, Boards and Commissions! The Administrative Branch of the Government Needs Complete Overhauling. As Important as Civil Service Reform and the Budget," *Nation's Business*, June 5, 1925, 9–10. Drafts of the speech can be found in box 514, "Reorganization of Government Departments, 1925," HH-CP. Hoover arranged for the speech to be printed in booklet form with the title *Reduction of Waste in Government by Reorganization of Executive Departments*. Receipts in Hoover's papers show that he printed and distributed (at his own expense) at least fifteen thousand copies. See box 41, "(2) 486 (1) Chamber of Commerce of U.S. Address 13th Annual Meeting May 21, 1925," Hoover Statements-Background, HHPL.
22. Hoover, "200 Bureaus, Boards and Commissions!," 9.
23. Hoover, 9.
24. Harry Marsh to Harold Phelps Stokes, May 22, 1925, box 7, folder AAb7, NCSRLP-C.
25. This amounted to 411,898 out of 515,772 total employees. See U.S. Bureau of the Census, *Historical Statistics of the United States, 1789-1945* (Washington, D.C.: U.S. Government Printing Office, 1949), 294.
26. William Dudley Foulke to Harold Phelps Stokes, July 30, 1923, box 3, folder 69, Harold Phelps Stokes Papers, YALE.
27. The members were Arthur W. Procter (age 36), a New York attorney and accountant with experience in administrative reform organizations; Robert Wood Johnson (age 32), a vice president at Johnson & Johnson; and Catesby L. Jones (age 35), a

11. LOW EXPECTATIONS: 1924-1927

Wall Street attorney originally from Savannah, Georgia. Proctor had published a well-regarded book, *Principles of Public Personnel Administration* (New York: D. Appleton and Company, 1921), and had served as a staff member for the IGR, the BMR, and the Taft Commission.

28. Harry Marsh to George McAneny, December 30, 1927, box 7, folder 1927, GMcAP; Harry Marsh to Harold Phelps Stokes, May 22, 1925, box 7, folder AAb7, NCS-RLP-C; Robert Wood Johnson, Catesby L. Jones, and Arthur W. Procter, "Brief Report," June 30, 1925, box 429, "National Civil Service Reform League, 1924–1928," HH-CP. In addition to Hoover, the young men also met with William F. Willoughby of the IGR; Luther Steward, president of the National Federation of Federal Employees; Treasury Secretary Andrew Mellon; Herbert Brown, director of the Bureau of Efficiency; and former assistant secretary of the navy Franklin D. Roosevelt.
29. Harold Phelps Stokes to Harry W. Marsh, June 10, 1925, box 7, folder AAb7, NCSRLP-C.
30. See "Statement of Purposes of the NCSRL with Respect to Simplification of the Administrative Branch of Federal Government," box 7, folder 1926, GMcAP; also in box 7, folder AAb7, NCSRLP-C.
31. Harold Phelps Stokes to Harry W. Marsh, May 20, 1926, box 7, folder AAb7, NCSRLP-C.
32. They were invited by NCSRL executive committee member Samuel H. Ordway, who was a New York State Supreme Court justice.
33. See Robert Chiles, *The Revolution of '28: Al Smith, American Progressivism, and the Coming of the New Deal* (Ithaca, N.Y.: Cornell University Press, 2018), 64–67.
34. Harry Marsh to Robert McCurdy Marsh, June 2, 1926, and Marsh to Burlingham, July 16, 1926, box 7, folder AAb7; and Harry W. Marsh, "Chronological Steps to be Taken in Organization of Activities on Government Reorganization," December 22, 1926, box 7, folder AAb7, NCSRLP-C.
35. See letters from Thomas W. Swan to Norman Davis, Franklin D. Roosevelt, John T. Pratt, Walter S. Gifford, James F. Curtis, Edward Bok, Richard Hooker, Julius Rosenwald, and Mary Burnham, October 29, 1926, box 7, folder AAb7, NCSRLP-C; Thomas W. Swan to George McAneny, November 10, 1926, box 7, folder 1926, GMcAP.
36. See "Aim to Fight Waste in Federal Bureaus," *New York Times*, May 12, 1927.
37. The three without significant business experience were Charles Francis Adams III (treasurer of Harvard and a noted yachtsman), Archibald B. Lovett (a private lawyer and judge from Savannah, Georgia), and Matthew Woll (vice president of the American Federation of Labor. The four with executive experience were Robert S. Brookings, John V. Farwell, Herbert Hoover, and Franklin D. Roosevelt. The four publishing executives were Edward W. Bok, Edwin F. Gay, George McAneny, and Edwin T. Meredith. The four corporate lawyers were John W. Davis, Charles Evans Hughes, Frank L. Polk, and Henry L. Stimson. James F. Curtis was not a corporate lawyer, but he was a law partner of Raymond Fosdick. Norman H. Davis was a diplomat and member of the Council on Foreign Relations.
38. For FDR's 1919 budget committee testimony, see HSCB, *National Budget System*, 66th Cong., 1st sess. (1919), 654. See also "Harvard Union Speech" (speech file 114), February 26, 1920, Franklin D. Roosevelt, Master Speech File, 1898–1945, Franklin D. Roosevelt Presidential Library and Museum, quoted in Frank Freidel,

Franklin Roosevelt: The Ordeal (Boston: Little, Brown, 1954), 16; Roosevelt to R. Walton Moore, quoted in "Would Americanize Government First," *New York Times*, March 9, 1920. Typescripts of this letter can be found in box 34, folder Na-11, NCSRLP-W, and in the R. Walton Moore Papers at FDRPL. The NCSRL committee's meeting with Roosevelt is mentioned in Marsh to Stokes, May 22, 1925, box 7, folder AAb7, NCSRLP-C.

39. On the proposed budget, see memorandum enclosed in Harry W. Marsh to George McAneny, March 21, 1927, box 7, folder 1927, GMcAP, also in box 7, folder AAb7, NCSRLP-C.
40. Kaplan to McAneny, January 9, 1929, box 8, folder 1929, GMcAP.
41. Report on National Civil Service Reform League, November 23, 1926, box 6, folder 31, JDRP.
42. See Jesse Tarbert, "Reconsidering Progressive Era Opposition to Foundation Activity: The Farm Demonstration Project Controversy," *HistPhil*, August 8, 2016, https://histphil.org/2016/08/08/reconsidering-progressive-era-opposition-to-foundation-activity-the-farm-demonstration-project-controversy/.
43. For Rockefeller's response to the farm demonstration controversy, see Jerome Greene to Charles Van Hise, August 31, 1914, box 26, folder 294, RFR. See also Senate Select Committee, *Industrial Relations: Final Report and Testimony, Vol. IX*, 64th Cong., 1st sess. (1916), S. Doc. 415.
44. Rockefeller gave the NCSRL $1,000 a year from 1922 through 1930, when his contribution decreased to an annual $500. See Kaplan to McAneny, December 6, 1928, and McAneny to Rockefeller Jr., December 29, 1928, box 7, folder 1928; Thomas Appleget to McAneny, January 18, 1929, box 8, folder 1929; Arthur Packard to McAneny, February 4, 1930, box 8, folder 1930; and Packard to McAneny, January 15, 1931, box 8, folder 1931, GMcAP.
45. The bureau's bylaws stipulated that its five-man advisory board would include one representative of the NCSRL. On the bureau's founding, see Rockefeller to William F. Willoughby, July 24, 1922, box 40, folder 316, JDRP; "Memorandum of Mr. John D. Rockefeller, Jr.'s gifts to the IGR," February 7, 1923, box 40, folder 315, JDRP; and IGR, "A Descriptive History of the Bureau of Public Personnel Administration," March 17, 1925, box 40, folder 316, JDRP.
46. On the bureau's move to Chicago, see Guy Moffett to Beardsley Ruml, Memorandum on "Civil Service Assembly of the United States and Canada," September 16, 1929, box 44, folder 552, FA063 Spelman Fund of New York, RAC. On the formation of the Public Administration Clearing House, see "Memorandum to the Members of the Board of the Public Administration Clearing House," December 26, 1930, box 65, folder 695, FA063 Spelman Fund of New York, RAC, and Frank O. Lowden to Beardsley Ruml, December 31, 1930, box 65, folder 695, FA063 Spelman Fund of New York, RAC.
47. Barry Karl and Stanley Katz gave a preliminary assessment of these developments in two oft-cited essays: "The American Private Philanthropic Foundation and the Public Sphere 1890–1930," *Minerva* 19, no. 2 (Summer 1981): 236–270, and "Foundations and Ruling Class Elites," *Daedalus* 116, no. 1 (Winter 1987): 1–40. For more recent interpretations that explore the complexities of the foundations' evolving role, see Elisabeth S. Clemens and Doug Guthrie, "Introduction: Politics and Partnerships," in *Politics and Partnerships: The Role of Voluntary Associations in*

12. THE GREAT ENGINEER: 1929-1931

America's Political Past and Present, ed. Elisabeth S. Clemens and Doug Guthrie (Chicago: University of Chicago Press, 2010), 1–24; and David C. Hammack and Helmut K. Anheier, *A Versatile American Institution: The Changing Ideals and Realities of Philanthropic Foundations* (Washington, D.C.: Brookings Institution Press, 2013).
48. Report on National Civil Service Reform League, February 26, 1932, box 6, folder 31, JDRP.

12. THE GREAT ENGINEER: 1929-1931

1. Robert Catherwood to Harry W Marsh, April 3, 1925, box 46, folder Yb-3, NCSRLP-W.
2. Louisa Lee Schuyler to FDR, June 2, 1923; "Correspondence, American Construction Council," box 7, FDR Family, Business, and Personal Papers, FDRL.
3. "History of Hoover-Ball," HHPL, accessed June 30, 2021, https://hoover.archives.gov/hoovers/history-hoover-ball.
4. For an analysis of Lily-Whiteism in the 1928 primaries, see Donald J. Lisio, *Hoover, Blacks, and Lily-Whites: A Study of Southern Strategies* (Chapel Hill: University of North Carolina Press, 1985). For an entertaining and informative exploration of the motivations of Black advocates of Lily-Whiteism, see John Jeremiah Sullivan and Joel Finsel, "Though the Heavens Fall, Part 1," *Oxford American,* February 26, 2015, https://main.oxfordamerican.org/item/541-editor-love. For an analysis of Lily-Whiteism in relation to the evolution of the Republican Party in the South, see Boris Heersink and Jeffrey A. Jenkins, *Republican Party Politics and the American South, 1865–1968* (New York: Cambridge University Press, 2020).
5. W. E. B. Du Bois, "Is Al Smith Afraid of the South?," *Nation,* October 17, 1928, 392–394.
6. Du Bois, "Is Al Smith Afraid of the South?"
7. Herbert Hoover, "Inaugural Address. March 4, 1929," in *Public Papers of the Presidents of the United States: Herbert Hoover, 1929* (Washington, D.C.: U.S. Government Printing Office, 1976), 6.
8. Theresa Johnston, "The Doctor-President Who Made Stanford Better," *Stanford Magazine,* January 6, 2016, https://stanfordmag.org/contents/the-doctor-president-who-made-stanford-better.
9. NACE, *Federal Relations to Education* (Washington, D.C.: National Capital Press, October 1931), 1.
10. Lisio, *Hoover.*
11. Douglas J. Slawson, *The Department of Education Battle, 1918–1932: Public Schools, Catholic Schools, and the Social Order* (Notre Dame, Ind.: University of Notre Dame Press, 2005), Lynn Dumenil, "'The Insatiable Maw of Bureaucracy': Antistatism and Education Reform in the 1920s," *Journal of American History* 77, no. 2 (September 1990): 512–514.
12. Davis and Johnson, graduates of Morehouse College, had both pursued graduate study at the University of Chicago in the 1910s. Johnson's career is well-known. For details on Davis, see Hugh M. Gloster, "John W. Davis," *Journal of Negro History* 66, no. 1 (Spring 1981): 78–80. On the protest over the delayed appointments, see

Louis L. Athey, "Florence Kelley and the Quest for Negro Equality," *Journal of Negro History* 56, no. 4 (October 1971): 261; and David A. Lane Jr., "The Report of the National Advisory Committee on Education and the Problem of Negro Education," *Journal of Negro Education* 1, no. 1 (April 1932): 5–15.

13. NACE, *Federal Relations to Education*, 25.
14. NACE, 25.
15. NACE, 25.
16. NACE, 93–94.
17. NACE, 25–26.
18. NACE, 25–26.
19. The members of the committee voted 43–8 in favor of the majority report. A separate vote was held on the committee's recommendation for a department of education. The results of that vote were 38 for, 11 against, 2 abstaining. Among the "nays" was the IGR's William F. Willoughby. No record has been discovered explaining his opposition, but he likely opposed the plan not because he opposed consolidation, but because it conflicted with his own pet reorganization plan. NACE, *Federal Relations to Education*, 99–100.
20. NACE, 105–106.
21. NACE, 105–106.
22. NACE, 108.
23. NACE, 109.
24. NACE, 110–112.
25. NACE, 103.
26. PRCST, *Recent Social Trends in the United States: Report of the President's Research Committee on Social Trends*, 2 vols. (New York: McGraw-Hill, 1933); Barry Karl, "Presidential Planning and Social Science Research: Mr. Hoover's Experts," *Perspectives in American History* 3 (1969): 347–409.
27. Herbert Hoover, "Forward by the President of the United States," in PRCST, *Recent Social Trends*, 1:v.
28. Thomas Jackson Woofter, *Races and Ethnic Groups in American Life* (New York: McGraw-Hill, 1933).
29. For his earlier approach, see Charles H. Judd, "The Federal Department of Education," *School and Society*, June 5, 1920, 662–663.
30. See Charles H. Judd, "Education," in PRCST, *Recent Social Trends*, 1:332. The full report was published as Charles H. Judd, *Problems of Education in the United States* (New York: McGraw-Hill, 1933).
31. Judd, "Education," 365.
32. Existing accounts highlight the role of DuPont associates without noting that this same group was behind opposition to earlier efforts to reorganize national enforcement of Prohibition. See Daniel Okrent, *Last Call: The Rise and Fall of Prohibition* (New York: Scribner, 2010), 294–299, and Lisa McGirr, *The War on Alcohol: Prohibition and the Rise of the American State* (New York: Norton, 2015).
33. See "Statement Presented Before the House Judiciary Committee," February 27, 1930, box 4, NCLOEP.
34. *Annual Report of the President of the AAPA for the Year 1932* (Washington, D.C.: AAPA, 1932), AAPA Papers, LoC.

13. DASHED HOPES: 1930-1933

35. David Farber, *Everybody Ought to Be Rich: The Life and Times of John J. Raskob, Capitalist* (New York: Oxford University Press, 2013), 229–233.
36. The letter was excerpted and summarized in "Hoover for Prohibition; Would Rigidly Enforce the 'Great Experiment,'" *New York Times*, February 24, 1928.
37. See Hoover to Hughes, March 25, 1929, and Hoover to William H. Taft, April 7, 1929, box 236, Subject File: "NCLOE—Corresp.," HH-PP; Memo, May 20, 1929, box 236, Subject File: "NCLOE—Corresp." HH-PP.
38. On the subject of Wickersham's Washington retainers, see Charles C. Burlingham to Felix Frankfurter, February 7, 1924, box 4, folder 8, Charles C. Burlingham Papers, Harvard Law Library, Cambridge, Mass. On Wickersham's reputation generally, see Phillips Wyman to Lawrence Ritchie, July 17, 1929, box 33, "Wickersham Hon George W 1929," NCLOEP.
39. "Hoover Names 10 Lawyers and One Woman Educator to Study Law Enforcement," *New York Times*, May 21, 1929.
40. Herbert Hoover, *Proposals to Improve Enforcement of Criminal Laws of the United States*, 71st Cong., 2nd sess. (1930), H. Doc. 252, pp. 2, 8.
41. Hoover, *Proposals to Improve Enforcement of Criminal Laws*, 2.
42. Herbert Hoover, "Special Message to the Congress Proposing a Study of the Reorganization of Prohibition Enforcement Responsibilities. June 6, 1929," in *Public Papers of the Presidents of the United States*, 178.
43. See "Progress Report, October 25, 1929," box 26, "Reports of Commission," NCLOEP; and Robert A. Taft to Wickersham, June 12, 1929, box 28, NCLOEP. The meeting minutes of December 3, 1929, announce that the commission had finally secured Prohibition researchers. Minutes of Meeting Held December 3 and 4, 1929, box 1, NCLOEP.
44. The bureau's chief counsel sent a draft to Hoover on October 23; see James J. Britt to Walter H. Newton, October 23, 1929, box 197, Subject File: "Govt. Depts., Reorg. of," HH-PP. For the mid-November delivery to the Wickersham Commission, see Max Lowenthal to Roscoe Pound, November 16, 1929, box 24, NCLOEP. The timeline for the securing of researchers, approval of a plan, and the exchange of draft bills is established in "Minutes of Meeting Held December 3 and 4, 1929," and "Minutes of Meeting Held January 7 and 8, 1930," box 1, NCLOEP.
45. Robert A. Taft to Wickersham, June 12, 1929, box 28, NCLOEP.
46. See "Notes for Chairman's Progress Report, February 5," box 26, "Reports of Commission," NCLOEP; and HCEED, *Transfer the Bureau of Prohibition to the Department of Justice: Report to Accompany H.R. 8574*, 71st Cong., 2nd sess., House Rep. 594, 2.
47. HCEED, *Transfer the Bureau of Prohibition*, 2.
48. "Dry Enforcement in Mitchell's Hands; Shift of Prohibition Bureau to Department of Justice Effected at Midnight," *New York Times*, July 1, 1930.

13. DASHED HOPES: 1930-1933

1. NBC, *A Proposal for Government Reorganization, Published in the Interest of National Economy* (New York: NBC, 1921), 47–48.

13. DASHED HOPES: 1930-1933

2. "Heads of 5 Great Veterans' Groups Ask Preparedness," *Washington Post*, February 19, 1927. For more about the Pension Bureau, see Gustavus A. Weber, *The Bureau of Pensions: Its History, Activities and Organization* (Washington, D.C.: Brookings Institution, 1924). For a useful account of the National Soldiers' Home, see Judith G. Cetina, "A History of Veterans' Homes in the United States, 1811–1930" (PhD diss., Case Western Reserve University, 1977).
3. Frank T. Hines, *Annual Report of the Director, United States Veterans' Bureau, for the Fiscal Year Ended June 30, 1928* (Washington, D.C.: U.S. Government Printing Office, 1928), 2.
4. On the American Medical Association's opposition to the Veterans' Administration, see Rosemary Stevens, "Can the Government Govern? Lessons from the Formation of the Veterans Administration," *Journal of Health Politics, Policy and Law* 16, no. 2 (Summer 1991): 281–305.
5. See Colonel Campbell Blackshear Hodges to Hoover, Memorandum on "Coordination of Veterans' Activities," May 17, 1929; Hoover to Hines, May 23, 1929; and Memo, May 23, 1929, box 195, Subject File: "Govt. Depts., Coord. of Veterans Affairs," HH-PP.
6. HCEED, *Consolidation of Veterans' Activities: Hearings on H.R. 6141*, 71st Cong., 1st sess. (1930), 1.
7. HCEED, *Consolidation of Veterans' Activities*, 1.
8. HCEED, 42–62.
9. HCEED, 46.
10. HCEED, 75.
11. HCEED, 77, 81.
12. HCEED, 114.
13. HCEED, 117.
14. HCEED, 123.
15. HCEED, 178.
16. HCEED, 190.
17. Donald J. Lisio notes that Interior Secretary Wilbur, "as a trusted cabinet member and old friend of the President . . . apparently felt confident of convincing Hoover to reorganize veterans' affairs within the Interior Department. To his surprise, however, Hines had expertly usurped his favored position." Lisio describes Hines as "a master bureaucrat" who "enjoyed overwhelming his listeners with his vast knowledge of the intricate laws governing veterans' benefits." See Donald J. Lisio, *The President and Protest: Hoover, MacArthur, and the Bonus Riot*, 2nd ed. (New York: Fordham University Press, 1994), 9–13.
18. "Veterans' Bureaus United by Hoover," *New York Times*, July 9, 1930; Charles A. and William Beard, *The American Leviathan: The Republic in the Machine Age* (New York: Macmillan, 1930), 779.
19. HCEED, *Transfer the Bureau of Prohibition to the Department of Justice: Report to Accompany H.R. 8574*, 71st Cong., 2nd sess. (1930), House Rep. 594, p. 2.
20. David Farber, *Everybody Ought to Be Rich: The Life and Times of John J. Raskob, Capitalist* (New York: Oxford University Press, 2013), 299–311.
21. A commonly cited example of this criticism, and one that reveals how even the most informed observers were disinterested in organizational questions, is Walter Lippmann, "The Great Wickersham Mystery," *Vanity Fair*, April 1931, 41–42.

13. DASHED HOPES: 1930-1933

22. This is spelled out in "Conclusions and Recommendations," number 9, in NCLOE, *Report on the Enforcement of the Prohibition Laws of the United States, January 7, 1931* (Washington, D.C.: U.S. Government Printing Office, 1931), 146.
23. On Baker, see Douglas B. Craig, *Progressives at War: William G. McAdoo and Newton D. Baker, 1863-1941* (Baltimore: Johns Hopkins University Press, 2013).
24. "Conclusions and Recommendations," number 9, in NCLOE, *Report on the Enforcement of the Prohibition Laws of the United States*, 146.
25. Max Freedman, ed., *Roosevelt and Frankfurter: Their Correspondence, 1928-1945* (Boston: Little, Brown, 1967), 457.
26. This is spelled out in "Conclusions and Recommendations," number 10, in NCLOE, *Report on the Enforcement of the Prohibition Laws of the United States*, 146; see also p. 263 in the same report; Felix Frankfurter, "A National Policy for Enforcement of Prohibition," *Annals of the American Academy of Political and Social Science* 109 (September 1923): 193-195.
27. NCLOE, *Report on the Enforcement of the Prohibition Laws of the United States*, 283.
28. See Wickersham to James M. Beck, November 1, 1932, box 8, folder 9, James M. Beck Papers, PUL.
29. *The Negroes' Relation to Law Observance* study was led by an African American scholar, Ira De A. Reid, director of research for the National Urban League. See Mary van Kleeck to George Wickersham, March 25, 1930, box 29, folder "Vankleeck Mary May 1930," NCLOEP; for Dyer's speech, see "Address of Congressman Dyer to the National Law Observance and Enforcement Commission, Wednesday, March 12, 1930," box 37, folder "House Representatives: Dyer L C," NCLOEP.
30. A useful summary of the reorganization movement during Hoover's presidency, and an analysis of its relation to the New Deal's Brownlow Committee, can be found in Bryant Putney, "Reorganization of Federal Administrative Agencies," in *Editorial Research Reports 1936, Vol. II* (Washington, D.C.: CQ Press, 1936), 187-204.
31. "Statistics of the Congressional Election of November 4, 1930," U.S. House of Representatives, accessed June 25, 2021, https://history.house.gov/Institution/Election-Statistics/1930election/.
32. See, for instance, Theodore Joslin to Albert Shaw, February 19, 1932, box 198, Subject File: "Govt. Depts., Reorg. of," HH-PP.
33. These letters can be found in several folders labeled "Reorganization of Government Depts., Hoover Speech (5-21-25) Reactions" in box 514, HH-CP. Among the handful of exceptions mentioned are James R. Garfield to Hoover, July 7, 1925; Charles Nagel to Hoover, July 16, 1925; and Samuel McCune Lindsay to Hoover, August 31, 1925, all in box 514, HH-CP. See also, Paul Cravath to Hoover, May 22, 1925, box 41, folder "(4) 486 (3)," Hoover Statements—Background, HHPL; and Robert S. Brookings to Hoover, June 25, 1925, box 41, folder "(3) 486 (2)," Hoover Statements—Background, HHPL.
34. "Hoover Opposes Centralization at Washington," *New York Herald-Tribune*, December 9, 1926.
35. Herbert Hoover, "The President's News Conference of December 29, 1931," and "Statement on Economy in Government. December 29, 1931," in *Public Papers of the Presidents of the United States, Herbert Hoover, 1931* (Washington, D.C.: U.S. Government Printing Office, 1976), 650.

36. Hoover, "The President's News Conference of December 29, 1931," and "Statement on Economy in Government," 650.
37. Hoover, "The President's News Conference of December 29, 1931," and "Statement on Economy in Government," 649–654.
38. "Bureau Reform," *New York Times*, January 3, 1932.
39. Among the changes he suggested were creation of the following positions: "Public Works Administrator (new office)"; "Personnel Administrator (change from chairman of Civil Service Commission)"; "Assistant Secretary for Public Health (new)"; "Assistant Secretary for Education (change from commissioner)"; "Assistant Secretary for Merchant Marine (new office)"; "Assistant Secretary for Conservation (new office)"; "Assistant Secretary for Agricultural Research (change from present Assistant Secretary)"; "Assistant Secretary for Agricultural Economics (change from director)"; and "The establishment of an Assistant Secretary for Merchant Marine." See Herbert Hoover, "Special Message to the Congress on the Reorganization of the Executive Branch. February 17, 1932," in *Public Papers of the Presidents of the United States, Herbert Hoover, 1932–33* (Washington, D.C.: U.S. Government Printing Office, 1976), 56–61.
40. See Arthur Krock, "Hoover Asks Power to Unite Bureaus; Democrats Opposed," *New York Times*, February 18, 1932; William Starr Myers and Walter H. Newton, *The Hoover Administration: A Documented Narrative* (New York: Charles Scribner's Sons, 1936), 177–178.
41. Arthur Krock, "Further Economies Urged by President," *New York Times*, March 9, 1932.
42. Putney, "Reorganization of Federal Administrative Agencies."
43. Herbert Hoover, "Special Message to the Congress on the Reorganization of the Executive Branch. December 9, 1932," in *Public Papers of the Presidents of the United States, Herbert Hoover, 1932–33*, 882–891; "House Lines Form to Block President on Reorganization," *New York Times*, January 9, 1933; "Democrats Decide to Bar Regrouping," *New York Times*, January 14, 1933; Putney, "Reorganization of Federal Administrative Agencies."
44. Leonard D. White, "Public Administration," chapter 27 in PRCST, *Recent Social Trends in the United States: Report of the President's Research Committee on Social Trends* (New York: McGraw Hill, 1933), 2:1425.
45. White, "Public Administration," 1410.
46. White, 1421.
47. Herbert Hoover, "Forward by the President of the United States," in PRCST, *Recent Social Trends in the United States*, 1:v.
48. Barry Karl, "Presidential Planning and Social Science Research: Mr. Hoover's Experts," *Perspectives in American History* 3 (1969): 347–409.
49. Emphasis in original. Frederic Delano to FDR, February 26, 1932, Papers as Governor, 1928–1933, box 20, FDRPL. Hoover remains an enigma. Here I have emphasized his record on administrative reform while avoiding analysis of his record on economic and social policy. A judicious assessment of Hoover's career can be found in William E. Leuchtenburg, *Herbert Hoover* (New York: Henry Holt, 2009). For a provocative-yet-nuanced reassessment of Hoover's economic policy that retains a historiographical edge after three decades, see Stuart Bruchey, *Enterprise: The Dynamic Economy of a Free People* (Cambridge, Mass.: Harvard University

Press, 1990), 442–472. For a no-nonsense riposte to those who would attempt to cast Hoover as a political liberal or progressive, see Eric Rauchway, *Winter War: Hoover, Roosevelt, and the First Clash Over the New Deal* (New York: Basic Books, 2018).

CONCLUSION

1. This is a topic for another book. See Robert D. Schulzinger, *The Wise Men of Foreign Affairs: The History of the Council on Foreign Relations* (New York: Columbia University Press, 1984).
2. On the development of the Liberty League, see Daniel Okrent, *Last Call: The Rise and Fall of Prohibition* (New York: Scribner, 2010), 361–364; George Wolfskill, *The Revolt of the Conservatives: A History of the American Liberty League, 1933–1940* (Boston: Houghton Mifflin, 1962); David Farber, *Everybody Ought to Be Rich: The Life and Times of John J. Raskob, Capitalist* (New York: Oxford University Press, 2013), 299–311; Lisa McGirr, *The War on Alcohol: Prohibition and the Rise of the American State* (New York: Norton, 2015), 248; James T. Patterson, *Congressional Conservatism and the New Deal* (Lexington: University Press of Kentucky, 1967), 251–253; and Kim Phillips-Fein, *Invisible Hands: The Businessmen's Crusade Against the New Deal* (New York: Norton, 2009).
3. Herbert Hoover, *The Memoirs of Herbert Hoover: The Great Depression, 1929–1941* (New York: Macmillan, 1952), 219–232, 454–455.
4. See especially Phillips-Fein, *Invisible Hands*. The classic study is Patterson, *Congressional Conservatism and the New Deal*.
5. This point cuts against the traditional emphasis on the differences between FDR and his Republican predecessors. While those differences were real, especially on questions of economic policy and labor relations, it remains noteworthy (and perhaps instructive) that FDR's views on budget reform and executive reorganization were quite similar to those of Herbert Hoover. See Jesse Tarbert, "The Quest to Bring 'Business Efficiency' to the Federal Executive: Herbert Hoover, Franklin Roosevelt, and the Civil Service Reformers in the Late 1920s," *Journal of Policy History* 31, no. 4 (October 2019): 512–532. For a thoughtfully provocative account of the 1932–1933 interregnum that avoids many of the shortcomings of earlier treatments, see Eric Rauchway, *Winter War: Hoover, Roosevelt, and the First Clash Over the New Deal* (New York: Basic Books, 2018).
6. See Ira Katznelson, *Fear Itself: The New Deal and the Origins of Our Time* (New York: Liveright, 2013).
7. See Barry Karl, "Constitution and Central Planning: The Third New Deal Revisited," *Supreme Court Review* 1988, no. 1 (1988): 163–201. On reorganization efforts during the New Deal, see Peri E. Arnold, *Making the Managerial Presidency: Comprehensive Reorganization Planning, 1905–1996* (Lawrence: University Press of Kansas, 1998), 81–117. The classic monographs are Barry D. Karl, *Executive Reorganization and Reform in the New Deal* (Cambridge, Mass.: Harvard University Press, 1963), and Richard Polenberg, *Reorganizing Roosevelt's Government* (Cambridge, Mass.: Harvard University Press, 1966).
8. See Arnold, *Making the Managerial Presidency*, 81–117.

9. On the Hoover Commissions, see Arnold, *Making the Managerial Presidency*, 118–227, and Joanna L. Grisinger, *The Unwieldy American State: Administrative Politics Since the New Deal* (New York: Cambridge, 2014).
10. Arnold, *Making the Managerial Presidency*, 118–227, and Grisinger, *The Unwieldy American State*.
11. On the continuities between the NAACP's legal activism in the 1920s and the *Brown v. Board of Education* case, see Megan Ming Francis, *Civil Rights and the Making of the Modern American State* (New York: Cambridge University Press, 2014), 27–28.
12. In a sense, this book serves as a sort of prequel to several recent studies of racism and political realignment, including Eric Schickler, *Racial Realignment: The Transformation of American Liberalism, 1932–1965* (Princeton, N.J.: Princeton University Press, 2016); Robert Mickey, *Paths Out of Dixie: The Democratization of Authoritarian Enclaves in America's Deep South, 1944–1972* (Princeton, N.J.: Princeton University Press, 2015); and Angie Maxwell and Todd Shields, *The Long Southern Strategy: How Chasing White Voters in the South Changed American Politics* (New York: Oxford University Press, 2019). For a provocative account of modern conservatism that emphasizes the importance of Republicans from the Far West, see Kathryn S. Olmsted, *Right Out of California: The 1930s and the Big Business Roots of Modern Conservatism* (New York: New Press, 2015). On the civil rights legislation of the mid-1960s, see Julian E. Zelizer, *The Fierce Urgency of Now: Lyndon Johnson, Congress, and the Battle for the Great Society* (New York: Penguin, 2015), 85–130. For a general overview of the political history and realignments of the past half century, see Kevin M. Kruse and Julian E. Zelizer, *Fault Lines: A History of the United States Since 1974* (New York: Norton, 2017).
13. See Noah Rosenblum, "The Antifascist Roots of Presidential Administration," *Columbia Law Review* 122 (forthcoming), available at https://ssrn.com/abstract=3635821.
14. My argument about the timing of the evolution of the Republican Party before 1933 contradicts the standard narrative, which emphasizes the 1920 election as an inflection point and blames business interests for the GOP's abandonment of Black voters. See Heather Cox Richardson, *To Make Men Free: A History of the Republican Party* (New York: Basic Books, 2014), 171–220.
15. In a sense, my argument here can be viewed as an inversion of Gabriel Kolko's argument about the decidedly non-radical nature of many of the reforms enacted during the so-called Progressive Era in *The Triumph of Conservatism: A Reinterpretation of American History, 1900–1916* (New York: Free Press, 1963), and *Main Currents in Modern American History* (New York: Harper and Row, 1976).
16. My general argument here joins that of other scholars who emphasize the importance of an illiberal "third tradition" in American history. What to call that tradition is a contested question in the United States in 2021. Is it populist? Fascist? Nationalist? White nationalist? Or merely conservative? For the purposes of this book, I have referred to this tradition variously as racist, antigovernment, and antidemocratic rather than wade further into murkier waters. On illiberal traditions in America, see Gary Gerstle, *American Crucible: Race and Nation in the Twentieth Century* (Princeton, N.J.: Princeton University Press, 2001), and Rogers Smith, "Beyond Tocqueville, Myrdal, and Hartz: The Multiple Traditions in

CONCLUSION

America," *American Political Science Review* 87, no. 3 (September 1993): 549–566. For work that may perhaps prove useful for christening this tradition, see Federico Finchelstein, *From Fascism to Populism in History* (Berkeley: University of California Press, 2019); Jason Stanley, *How Fascism Works: The Politics of Us and Them* (New York: Penguin, 2018); and Toni Morrison, "Racism and Fascism," *Journal of Negro Education* 64, no. 3 (1995): 384–385.

INDEX

Academy of Political Science (New York), 46, 89–90
Adams, Charles Francis, III, 233n37
administrative reform. *See* budget; executive reorganization
air travel, regulation of, 80–81
alcohol, industrial users of. *See* DuPont Company: and Prohibition enforcement
alcohol, prohibition of. *See* Prohibition
Alien Property Custodian, U.S., 139
Allen, William H., 58, 215n20
American exceptionalism, 190–191
American Legion, 75–76, 115, 130, 171
American Legion Weekly, 114, 131–132
American Liberty League, 185–186
American Medical Association, 172–173
American Mining Congress, 178
American Political Science Association, 154
Anderson, Henry W., 167
Andrews, Lincoln C., 146
Anti-Saloon League, 140–143, 145, 166
antidemocratic politics, 9, 16–17, 186, 242n16. *See also* Jim Crow: disfranchisement
antigovernment politics, 9, 178, 189, 242n16. *See also* filibuster
antilynching: and election of 1920, 67–69, 72; and election of 1928, 157; and elite reformers, 5, 7; and Harding, 81–82; NAACP campaign, 47–51; post-1933 efforts, 188; and Wickersham Commission, 176–177. *See also* Dyer Bill; National Conference on Lynching
antistatism. *See* antigovernment politics
Appleget, Thomas, 152
Army Corps of Engineers, 108–109
Asiatic Barred Zone, 133
Association Against the Prohibition Amendment (AAPA), 165–166, 174, 185
Association of the Bar of the City of New York, 47
associative state, 203n9
Attorney General, U.S., 39, 63, 93–94, 139

Baker, Newton D., 167, 175
Bank of America, 73
Beard, Charles A., 174
Beck, James M., 174, 176
big government, 1–2, 53, 117–118, 201n2

INDEX

Birth of a Nation, The (1915 film), 27
Bok, Edward W., 233n37
Bonus: agitation for, 129–130; Bonus Act (1924), 132, 229n11; Bonus Bill (1921), 130; Bonus Bill (1922), 131; Dawes on, 131; federal power, relationship to, 201n4
Borah, William, 99–100, 128–129, 138, 166
Brandeis, Louis, 27–28
Brookings Institution, 30n, 153, 158. *See also* Institute for Government Research
Brookings, Robert S., 82, 178, 233n37
Brough, Charles, 69, 92, 100, 103
Brown v. Board of Education, 188
Brown, Walter F.: appointment to reorganization committee, 89–91; on Harding's death, 112; as postmaster general, 177; reorganization plan of, 107–112, 122, 135–136
Brownlow Committee, 186–187, 189
Brownlow, Louis, 153, 187
Brownsville (Texas) Affair: 19–22
Bruere, Henry, 27–28
Buck, Arthur E., 61
budget: Budget and Accounting Act (1921), 85–86, 130; Congress's role in system, 31–32, 53; corporate governance as model, 3–4, 6, 32–33, 44–45, 53–55; historical significance of, 154, 182, 204n12; independent audit, role of in system, 44, 56, 60, 62–64; managerial rationalization as reform rationale, 87; and National Budget Committee, 52–64; national system before 1921, 2, 44; proposals for auditing function, 44–45, 53–54, 56, 60, 62–64; relationship to executive reorganization and civil service reform, 147; state-level reform, 30–31; and Taft administration, 13–16; and United States Chamber of Commerce, 29. *See also* Budget Bureau, U.S.
Budget and Responsible Government, The (Cleveland and Buck), 60–62, 216n30
Budget Bureau, U.S.: creation and early operation, 85–87; location within federal administration, 109, 135, 187, 189–190. *See also* Good Bill; McCormick Bill
bureaucracy, 2–3, 31, 36–37, 91, 172
Bureau of Efficiency, U.S., 90
Bureau of Municipal Research, 14–15, 20, 27–28, 30, 46, 58, 187
Bureau of Prohibition, U.S.: creation of, 147, 166, 231n6; transfer to Department of Justice, 167–169, 174. *See also* Prohibition
Bureau of Public Personnel Administration, 152–153
business efficiency, 87, 146, 151, 204n11
business-government analogy, 3–4; and budget, 32–33, 44–45, 53–55, 63, 86–87; and executive reorganization, 80, 148, 151–152; and veterans agencies, 114, 173
Butler, Nicholas Murray, 71
Byrns, Joseph, 180

cabinet, role of in administration, 87, 110
capitalism, 4, 59, 190
Carnegie Corporation, 153
Catholic political activism, 7, 120–121, 126–127
Central Bureau of Planning and Statistics, U.S., 36–37, 151
Chamber of Commerce. *See* United States Chamber of Commerce
Chandler, Alfred D., Jr., 202n6, 204n12
Chase, Harvey, 29, 210n15
Church, Earl D., 172
Civil Rights Act (1964), 9, 188–189
Civil Service Act (1883), 11
Civil Service Commission, U.S., 2, 11
civil service reform, 10–12; decline in popularity, 148–149; and executive reorganization, 147, 149–150; and National Soldiers Homes, 173; and Prohibition, 142–143, 145, 176; and Wilson, 28–29. *See also* National Civil Service Reform League
Clayton Act (1914), 28
Cleveland, Frederick: and Academy of Political Science, 89; background of, 207n13; and IGR, 30, 60–61; and

INDEX

Stimson, 33; and Taft Commission, 15, 30, 207n14, 216n34; and *The Budget and Responsible Government*, 60–62, 216n30; and Willoughby, 61
Collins, Charles Wallace, 56–57, 59–60, 85
Commercial Economy Board, U.S., 36
Commission on Organization of the Executive Branch of the Government. *See* Hoover Commissions
Committee for Aid to Disabled Veterans, 73–74, 130–132
Committee on Department Methods. *See* Keep Commission
Comptroller General, U.S.: provisions for removal of, 63, 85, 221n20; role as independent auditor in budget system, 63–64
Comstock, Ada, 167
Congress, U.S.: administrative role of, 13, 31–32, 45, 53, 55–56, 64, 173, 184; control of military expenditures, 109; and executive reorganization, 89–90, 108–110, 135–136, 148, 177, 180–181; and Taft Commission, 14, 16, 23
conservatism, 4–5, 24, 66, 93, 100n, 186, 190, 192, 202n8, 242n16
Constitution, U.S.: and debates on education policy, 124; and executive reorganization, 35; and lynching, 40, 49–50, 83, 93, 97–99, 102, 176, 224n32; and Prohibition, 7, 141–144, 165–166, 175; and removal power, 63–64. *See also specific amendments*
Consultants on Hospitalization, 75, 77–78, 105
Coolidge, Calvin: election of 1924, 138–139; and executive reorganization, 119, 136; and Harding scandals, 139; and Immigration Act (1924), 132–134; and proposed department of education and welfare, 122; reputation of among elite reformers, 155–156; succession to presidency, 112; and Veterans Bureau scandal, 139; veto of Bonus Bill, 132; and western Republicans, 128–129
corporate governance. *See* business-government analogy

Cotton, Joseph, 45–46, 213n10
Council of National Defense, U.S., 35–36
Council on Foreign Relations, 134, 185, 233n37
Cox, James, 71
Cramer, Charles, 114
Cravath, Paul, 71
Crisis (NAACP publication): circulation of, 37; coverage of lynching, 38–40, 51; on Dyer Bill, 98–99; on election of 1920, 67, 69; on Harding, 82, 96; on Towner-Sterling Bill, 123; on Wilson, 29
Curtis, Charles, 50, 100, 100n, 126–127
Curtis, James F., 233n37

Dallinger, Frederick, 126
Daugherty, Harry, 93–94
Davis, John W. (attorney and politician), 138–139, 150, 233n37
Davis, John W. (educator), 160, 162–163
Davis, Norman H., 233n37
Dawes Committee, 76–79, 81, 91, 105
Dawes, Charles G.: background, 76; on Bonus, 131; as budget director, 86–87, 221n25; and Dawes Committee, 76–78; and executive reorganization, 110; nomination for vice-presidency, 138
decentralization, administrative consolidation described as, 137, 146
Delafield, Edward C., 73
Delano, Frederic, 183
Democratic Party: and Association Against the Prohibition Amendment, 166, 174, 185; and immigration policy, 134; and NAACP, 22–23, 25; National Convention (1924), 138–139. *See also* southern Democrats
Defense, U.S. Department of: creation of, 187; proposals for, 108–109
Dixon, Thomas, 26
dollar-a-year men, 35–36, 41, 46
Douglass, Frederick, 126
Du Bois, W. E. B.: on Dyer Bill, 98–99, 135; on East St. Louis Massacre, 39; on Harding, 82, 95–96; on Hoover in 1928, 158; on Immigration Act (1924), 135; on Republican candidates in

Du Bois, W. E. B. (*continued*)
1920, 67; and Republican Party, 20;
on Shillady, 51; on Smith in 1928, 158;
on Towner-Sterling Bill, 123, 228n11;
on Washington, 21–22; on Wilson in
1912, 22–23
DuPont, Pierre, 165, 174
DuPont Company: and AAPA, 165, 174,
185, 236n32; and American Liberty
League, 185; organizational structure
of, 137; and Prohibition enforcement,
145–146
Dyer Bill: in Congress, 50, 82–83, 92–94,
97–102; constitutionality of, 83, 92,
99–100; filibuster (House), 97–98;
filibuster (Senate), 101–102; passage in
House, 98; provisions of, 93; relation
to Bonus Bill, 131; significance of
defeat, 184, 188
Dyer, Leonidas, 50, 82, 92–93, 176–177

Economy Act (1932), 181–182
education: for African Americans, 95,
160–163; and Catholic policy
advocates, 120, 126–127, 159–160, 163;
National Advisory Committee on,
159–163; proposals for federal
department of, 109, 119, 127–127,
228n15; role of federal government in,
158–165; Social Trends project on,
163–165. *See also* Towner-Sterling Bill
Education, U.S. Bureau of, 120–122,
126–127
education and welfare, proposal for
federal department of: and Coolidge,
122; and Harding-Brown plan, 108–109,
119, 171, 188; southern opposition to,
125–127; and Towner-Sterling Bill,
119, 122
efficiency: as goal for reform, 5–6, 13–15,
23, 87, 90, 176, 179; Hoover's views on,
110–111, 148, 170, 177–179; managerial
versus fiscal, 108, 170, 189; and
Prohibition enforcement, 146, 174;
and Roosevelt, Franklin, 151–152;
Taft's views on, 13–14; and veterans
agencies, 76–78, 116, 137–138, 169,

173–174; and wartime mobilization,
34–37. *See also* business efficiency
Eighteenth Amendment, 141–143.
See also Prohibition
Eisenhower, Dwight, 187–188
elections, U.S.: of 1908, 20–21; of 1910, 16;
of 1912, 22–25; of 1916, 39; of 1918, 42;
of 1920, 65–72; of 1922, 101–102; of
1924, 128–129, 138–139; of 1928, 155,
157–158, 165–166; of 1930, 177; of 1932,
181, 185–186; of 1934, 186; of 1936, 186
Electoral College, 72, 157
elite reformers, 3–9, 23, 202n5
Emergency Immigration Act (1921), 133
Ex-Service Men's Anti-Bonus League, 131
Executive Office of the President, U.S., 187
executive reorganization, 6; Congress-
centered version, 15, 89, 135, 177; as
corollary to budget reform, 88; and
education policy, 108–109, 119, 171,
188; and Harding, 88–90; Harding-
Brown proposal, 89–91, 107–113, 122,
127; and Hoover, 147–148, 177–182,
240n39; and IGR, 88–89; National
Budget Committee proposal, 87–88;
NCSRL committee, 147–152; and
Prohibition enforcement, 165–169;
and Taft Commission, 15; and
veterans agencies, 91, 170–174; and
Wilson, 28
executive-professional reform coalition,
202n5

Farm Bloc, 8, 100, 129, 157, 177. *See also*
southern Democrats; western
Republicans
Farwell, John V., 233n37
federal agencies, reorganization of.
See executive reorganization
Federal Board for Vocational Education,
U.S., 73–74, 171
Federal Board of Hospitalization, U.S.,
86, 115
Federal Elections Bill (1890), 16, 69, 100,
189
Federal Liquidation Board, U.S., 86
federal motor transport agent, U.S., 86

INDEX

federal power, 2, 5, 8, 184–186, 192; and Collins, 59; and Dawes, 131; expansion in mid-twentieth century, 5, 8, 189; and Harding, 80; and Hoover, 148, 182; and incremental change, 140; and Prohibition, 146; and Taft, Robert, 168
Federal Purchasing Board, U.S., 86
Federal Real Estate Board, U.S., 86
Federal Reserve Board, U.S., 28, 45, 57
Federal Specialization Board, U.S., 86
Federal Trade Commission, U.S., 28
Federal Traffic Board, U.S., 86
Federal Works Agency, U.S., 187
Fifteenth Amendment, 16, 21
filibuster: of Brown's salary in 1921, 90–91; of Dyer Bill, 97–98, 101–102, 135, 184; of Federal Elections Bill (1890), 16, 69, 100, 189; threat of, 104
Food Administration, U.S., 35, 45–46
Forbes, Charles: allegations against, 114–115, 137–139; background, 113; early tenure at Veterans Bureau, 113–114; questions about guilt, 116–117, 139, 227n39; and Tuskegee Hospital, 106
foreign policy establishment, 185
Fortune, T. Thomas, 20
Fosdick, Raymond, 88–89, 233n37
Foulke, William Dudley, 28–29, 148–149
founding fathers, 67
Four-Power Treaty (1921), 133
Frank, Leo, 37–38, 121n
Frankfurter, Felix, 4, 144, 175, 202n8
Frear, James, 61
Fuel Administration, U.S., 35

Garfield, James A., 11
Garfield, James R., 88
Garner, John Nance, 180–181
Garrett, Finis J., 90, 97
Gay, Edwin, 36, 151, 233n37
Gebhart, John, 166
General Motors, 137, 185
Glass, Carter, 56–61, 142
Good Bill: authorship of, 54, 56, 61; and Cleveland, 61; and Taft, 61–62; hearings on 54–56; passage in 1919, 55; passage in 1921, 85; Wilson administration opposition to, 57–59; and Wood, 66
Good government: and administrative reform, 1–3, 10–13, 23, 42, 87, 139, 147; and anticorruption, 1, 10, 42, 139; and Bonus, 131; and law, 7, 144; as method to undercut radical reform, 1, 201n1; and Roosevelt, Theodore, 11; and Taft, 12–13, and Wilson, 24, 28. *See also* civil service reform
Good, James W., 54
Goodnow, Frank, 32–33
Great Depression, 170
Great Migration, 37, 95–96
Greene, Jerome, 30
Gregory, Thomas, 39
Grubb, William, 167
Gruening, Martha, 39
Gulick, Luther, 187

Haiti, 67
Hamilton, Alexander, 61, 67, 124
Hanihara, Masanao, 134
Harding, Warren: agenda of, 184; and antilynching legislation, 81–82, 102; background of, 67–68; and Bonus Bill, 130–131; Birmingham speech (1921), 94–97; and budget reform, 71, 79–80; death, 111–112; and election of 1920, 65–72; and executive reorganization, 89–90, 107–111; on federal expenditures in the states, 80; first hundred days, 79–91; genealogy, 70; and immigration, 133–143; on racism and lynching, 66–69; 71–72; relationship with cabinet, 110; scandals, 70, 117–118, 138–139, 227n39; on Tulsa massacre, 84–85; and veterans agencies, 76
Harrison, Benjamin, 11
Harrison, Pat: and Bonus, 130–131; filibuster of Dyer Bill, 101–102; and Harding, 92, 96–97; and Harding-Brown reorganization proposal, 108, 136
Harvard Endowment Fund, 53
Health, Education, and Welfare, U.S. Department of, 188

Heffernan, William, 59
Hines, Frank T., 115–117, 138, 171, 178, 238n17
Holmes, Oliver Wendell, 104
Hooverball, 156
Hoover Commissions, 187–188
Hoover, Herbert: and American Liberty League, 186; and anti-Asian racism, 134; and anti-Black racism, 157–158; approach to presidency, 156, 169; background, 110–111; on education, federal role in, 159; election in 1928, 155; and executive reorganization, 110–111, 147–152, 177–183, 233n37; as Food Administrator, 45–46; and Harding, 72, 110–111; and Prohibition, 166–169; reputation as Secretary of Commerce, 156; and Roosevelt, Franklin, 241n5; shortcomings of, 182–183, 240n49; and social science, 158
Houston, David Franklin, 59–60, 63
Howard University, 105
Hughes, Charles Evans: background, 48–49; and lynching, 47–50; as elite reformer, 3; and executive reorganization, 150, 233n37; and Harding, 71; and Immigration Act (1924), 133–134; as presidential nominee in 1916, 66

Ijams, George, 117, 227n40
Immigration Act (1917), 133
Immigration Act (1924), 132–135
Immigration Act (1924), 189
Immigration and Nationality Act (1965), 188
Immigration Restriction Act (1921), 95–96, 133
independent establishments, within executive branch, 108
influenza pandemic of 1918–1919, 109, 112, 112n
Institute for Government Research (IGR): and budget reform, 43, 54; creation, 30; and executive reorganization, 87, 89, 107–109; merger to form Brookings Institution, 153; and Prohibition enforcement, 145; in World War I, 35; and veterans agencies, 73
Institute of Public Administration, 187
Interdepartmental Board of Contracts, 86
interparty alliances. *See under* southern Democrats; western Republicans

James, Marquis, 132n, 227n40
Jim Crow, 16–19; as constraint on national policymaking, 7, 104, 186; disfranchisement, 21, 56, 69, 188–189; and election of 1920, 67; executive branch, segregation of, 25–26; and Harding, 95; and Hoover, 157; and Republican Party, 37; and Supreme Court, 50; and Taft, 23; and veterans hospitals, 104–106; and Wilson, 25–27
Johnson, Albert, 133
Johnson, George, 163
Johnson, Hiram, 66–68, 129, 138
Johnson, James Weldon, 124
Johnson, Lyndon B., 188
Johnson, Mordecai, 160, 162–163
Johnson, Robert Wood, 232n27
Joint Committee for Aid to Disabled Veterans, 73–74, 130–132
Joint Committee on the Reorganization of Government Departments, 89, 107–111, 135–136
Jones, Catesby L., 232n27
Jones, John Price, 52–53
J. P. Morgan and Co., 43, 45, 60, 76
Judd, Charles H., 164–165

Keep Commission, 14, 88
Kelley, Florence, 123
Kenyon, William S., 167
Kingdon, John, 230n28
Knox, Philander, 84
Krock, Arthur, 180–181
Ku Klux Klan: and *The Birth of a Nation*, 26–27; and Democratic Party, 138; formation of second Klan, 38; and immigration, 133; and Prohibition, 143, 145; and Towner-Sterling Bill,

INDEX

120–121; and Tuskegee hospital, 106;
  and Wilson, 27
Kuhn, Loeb, and Co., 45

La Follette, Robert, 129, 138
Lamont, Thomas, 76
Lane, Franklin, 73
Laporte, Ewing, 78
law firms: Cadwalader, Wickersham,
  and Taft, 12, 49–50; Carter, Ledyard,
  and Milburn, 49; Cravath, 45, 60;
  Davis, Polk and Wardwell, 150;
  Winthrop and Stimson, 45
League of Nations, 57, 66, 71–72, 79, 81, 129
Leffingwell, Russell, 60
Lemann, Monte, 167, 175
L'Engle, Madeleine, 59n
liberalism, 5, 192, 202n8
Liberty Loan, 46, 53
Lily-White Republicans. See Republican
  Party: Lily-White delegations
Lincoln University, 84–85
Lindsay, Samuel McCune: and Hoover,
  178; and Harding, 71, 218n15; and
  National Budget Committee, 46,
  53–54, 62
Lippmann, Walter, 238n21
Lodge Bill. See Federal Elections Bill
Lodge, Henry Cabot, 16, 69, 102
Loesch, Frank J., 167
Lovett, Archibald B., 233n37
Lowden, Frank, 66–68
Lowenthal, Max, 168
Lowrey, Bill G., 126
lynching, 7, 17; of Frank, 37–38; and
  Harding, 68–69, 81–82; and Hoover,
  158; of Houston, in Birmingham, 96,
  223n18; in Jenkins County, Georgia,
  47–48; NAACP campaign against,
  38, 47; Red Summer, 50–51; and
  Republican platform (1920), 68–69;
  role of newspapers, 17; and Roosevelt,
  Theodore, 19; and Wickersham
  Commission, 176; and Wilson,
  40–41. See also Dyer Bill; National
  Conference on Lynching

Mackintosh, Kenneth, 167
managerial revolution, 3, 202n6
Marsh, Harry W., 148–149
Maurice and Laura Falk Foundation, 153
McAdoo, William, 138–139
McAneny, George, 20, 233n37
McCann advertising firm, 53
McCormick Bill, 55–58, 62, 66, 85, 128
McCormick, Medill, 55, 57–58, 60–61
McCormick, Paul J., 167
McKinley, William, 11
Mellon, Andrew, 75–76, 145–147
Mellon Institute, 75
Meredith, Edwin T., 233n37
merit system, 11–12, 28–29, 143, 148
Merriam, Charles, 187
Milburn, John, 49
Moore v. Dempsey, 102–104, 188
Moore, R. Walton, 136, 151
Mortimer, Elias, 114–115
Moton, Robert Russa, 37, 47, 160, 162–163

National Association for the
  Advancement of Colored People
  (NAACP): antilynching campaign,
  38–39; and Bar Association of
  New York, 46–51; creation, 22; and
  Democratic Party, 22; endorsement
  of Wilson (1912), 22–24; growth
  during Wilson years, 37; and Harding,
  68–69; legal strategy, 188; lobbying
  Wilson on lynching, 40–41; and *Moore
  v. Dempsey*, 103–104; and Republican
  National Convention (1920), 67;
  response to Wilson racism, 25–26;
  Silent Parade, 39–40; and Towner-
  Sterling Bill, 122–123. See also *Crisis*
  (NAACP publication); Dyer Bill;
  National Conference on Lynching
Nagel, Charles, 50
Nation (publication), 25n, 131, 158
National Advisory Committee on
  Education, 159–163
National Budget Committee: budget
  reform campaign of, 52–64; creation,
  42–46; and executive reorganization,

National Budget Committee (*continued*)
87–88, 107–109, 186; and Harding, 71, 85; and Prohibition enforcement, 144–145, 166; and veterans agencies, 74, 76, 171; and Wilson administration, 57–60, 62–64
National Bureau of Economic Research, 153
National Capital Park and Planning Commission, U.S., 183
National Catholic Welfare Council, 126, 159–160
National Civil Service Reform League (NCSRL), 11; and Calvin Coolidge, 155–156; and executive reorganization, 148–152; and McAneny, 20; and social science and philanthropy, 152–154; and Wilson, 28–29
National Commission on Law Observance and Enforcement. *See* Wickersham Commission
National Committee for Mental Hygiene, 74–75
National Committee of Negro Veteran Relief, 105
National Conference on Lynching (1919), 47–51, 66–67, 93
National Consumers League, 123
National Education Association, 120–122, 124
National Home for Disabled Soldiers, 172–173
National Institute of Public Administration, 153–154
National Security Act (1947), 187
National Tuberculosis Association, 74
nationalism, 205n15
Negro Silent Parade (1917), 39–40
New Deal, 5, 181, 185–187, 189,
New Freedom, 28
New York State Constitutional Convention (1915), 30–33, 45
New York Times, 12, 70n, 71, 82, 96, 97–98, 101–103, 110, 112, 113–114, 151, 161, 179, 180
New York Tribune, 101
Newton, Walter H., 172
Nineteenth Amendment, 72

normalcy, 41, 67–68, 190
Norton, Charles Dyer: background 14–15; death, 112n; and IGR, 30; and National Budget Committee, 43–44; and Stimson, 33; and Taft Commission, 14–15; testimony on Good Bill, 55

Ohio Gang, 113
Overman Act (1918), 35–36, 87–88, 180
Overman, Lee, 35

Pace, Edward, 163
Page, Arthur W., 53, 74
Paris Peace Conference, 49
Parsons, Herbert, 68
party factions. *See under* Democratic Party; Republican Party
party realignment, 242n12
Patterson, Robert U., 114
Pendleton Act. *See* Civil Service Act (1883)
Pension Bureau, U.S., 171–173
philanthropy: and education for African Americans, 160; and NAACP, 38, 104, 188; and social science, 152–154, 158; and Tuskegee, 18, 20. *See also specific foundations*
Poindexter, Miles, 67
Polk, Frank, 150, 233n37
Pound, Roscoe, 167
Post Office Department, U.S., 29, 108, 143, 177
Pratt, John T., 44–46, 57–60, 71, 88–89, 213n5
Pratt, Ruth Baker, 44n
presidency, U.S.: administrative role of, 13–16, 36–37, 53–57, 81–82, 87; reorganization authority, 109, 180; staff agency to assist, 54, 57, 86, 187–190, 221n25
President's Commission on Economy and Efficiency. *See* Taft Commission
President's Committee on Administrative Management. *See* Brownlow Committee
President's Research Committee on Social Trends: creation, 163–164; Hoover's vision for, 164; legacy of,

INDEX

182, 187; project on administration, 182; project on education, 163–165; publication of reports, 181–182; and race, 164
Procter, Arthur, 232n27
Progressive Party, 22, 66, 129
progressivism, 4–5, 24, 49, 66, 99, 128–129, 138, 202n8
Prohibition, 140–143; and civil service reform, 143, 145, 176; and election of 1928, 166; and elite reformers, 7, 143–144; Enforcement Act (1927), 147, 154; enforcement, proposals for reorganization of, 88, 145–147; Food and Fuel Control Act (1917), 141; movement to repeal, 165–166, 174, 185; and race, 142–143; Wartime Prohibition Act (1919), 141. See also Bureau of Prohibition, U.S.; Wickersham Commission
Public Administration Clearing House, 153, 158, 187
Public Health Service, U.S., 73
public works, proposals for department of, 88, 178–179, 181, 187–188

race riots and massacres: East St. Louis (1917), 38–39; Jenkins County, Georgia (1919), 47–48; Phillips County, Arkansas (1919), 103–104; Tulsa, Oklahoma (1921), 83–85. See also Red Summer
racism: and Collins, 59; and Democratic party, 7–8; and education, 121–126, 159–164; and Harding, 66–70, 81–82, 84–85, 94–97; and Hoover, 134, 157–158; and federal power, 191–192; and Prohibition, 142–143; and Roosevelt, Theodore, 18–20; and Social Trends project, 164; and Taft, 21–23; and veterans hospitals, 91, 104–106; and Wickersham Commission, 176–177; and Wilson, 22, 25–27; and woman suffrage, 72; and World War I, 37, 42. See also antilynching; Jim Crow; lynching
radio, regulation of, 80–81

Radio Bureau, U.S., 108
Rainey, Henry T., 180–181
Raskob, John, 165–166
Rayburn, Sam, 73, 78
Red Summer, 50–51
Reed, David Aiken, 133
Reed, David Alden, 126–127
Reese, Charles Lee, 145–146
Reorganization Act (1939), 187
Republican Party: and African American voters, 20–23, 66–69, 176–177, 190, 242n14; and elite reformers, 3, 10, 71–72, 185, 188–190; Lily-White delegations, 22, 157, 159, 235n4; margin of control in Congress, 16, 42, 72, 82, 102, 155, 157, 169, 177; Mugwumps, 83; National Convention (1900), 11; National Convention (1908), 12; National Convention (1912), 66; National Convention (1920), 65–68; National Convention (1924), 128–129, 134, 138–139; National Convention (1928), 157, 159, 166; in Ohio, 89; and Tuskegee Institute, 21–22. See also western Republicans
responsible government, 4, 32–34, 53–55, 211n22
Rockefeller Foundation, 30, 74–75, 153, 164
Rockefeller, John D., Jr., 43–44, 58, 88–89, 152–154
Roosevelt, Franklin D.: administration of, 185–187; and administrative reform, 151–152, 186–187, 233n37; election in 1932, 181; and Hoover, 151, 156, 182–183, 241n5; reelection in 1936, 186
Roosevelt, Theodore, 11–12, 18–22, 66
Root, Elihu: and administrative reform, 14, 190–191; and antilynching, 47, 49; background, 4–5, 30–31; and diplomacy with Japan, 133–134; and foreign affairs, 185; and Harding, 71, 89–90, 112–113, 117; and Prohibition, 143–144; pronunciation of forename, 30n2; and Stimson, 4–5, 32, 202n8; and Taft, 12–13, 31

Rosenberg Fund, 153
Russell Sage Foundation, 153

Salmon, Thomas, 74, 76–78, 219n27, 219n30
Sawyer, Charles, 112, 115–117
Scott, Hugh, 114
Sheppard-Towner Act, 81
Shillady, John, 47, 51
Shortridge, Samuel, 100–102, 135
Smith, Alfred E., 50, 138, 157–158, 166
Smith, Hoke, 120–121, 121n
Smoot, Reed, 89, 111–112, 135
social science, 152–154, 158
Social Science Research Council, 153–154, 158, 163, 166, 187
Social Trends. *See* President's Research Committee on Social Trends
soldiers bonus. *See* Bonus
southern Democrats, 7–8; and civil rights legislation, 188–189; and Dyer Bill, 97–98, 101–102; and federal education policy, 121, 123–127; and fiscal conservatism, 58; and Harding, 69–70, 92, 96–97; and immigration policy, 134–135; interparty alliance with western Republicans, 7–8, 16, 55, 69, 100, 134–135, 157, 177, 188–190; and Jim Crow, 16–17; and Lodge Bill, 16, 69–70, 100, 102; and New Deal, 186–187; political power of, 184, 190
Spanish Flu. *See* influenza, pandemic of 1918–1919
spoils system, 11–12, 21–22, 143
Standard Oil, 44
Sterling, Thomas, 121
Stimson, Henry L.: and administrative reform, 32–33, 190–191; and American Liberty League, 186; background, 31, 45; and big government, 4; and Bonus, 131; and budget reform, 31–34, 45–46, 53–57; and executive reorganization, 150, 233n37; and foreign affairs, 185; and Frankfurter, 4–5, 202n8; and Harding, 71; ideology of, 4–5, 202n8; as leader of elite reformers 3, 33–34; at New York Constitutional Convention, 31–34; and Page, 218n15; and Parsons, 68; as popularizer of responsible government, 32–33; and prohibition, 144; and Root, 4–5, 31; as Secretary of State, 179; and veterans issues, 73–74, 130; and Wood, 66
Stokes, Harold Phelps, 148–151, 179
Storey, Moorfield, 22, 47, 50 83, 99
Strong, Benjamin, 45, 57–60
Sweet, Burton, 91

Taft Commission: creation of, 14–16; defense, proposal for department of, 109; and Harding-Brown reorganization plan, 90; and Institute for Government Research, 30; legacy of, 23, 33; and National Budget Committee, 43, 60–61; and U.S. Chamber of Commerce, 29; and Wilson, 27–28; World War I mobilization, influence on, 35–36
Taft, Henry W., 12, 72
Taft, Robert A., 168
Taft, William H., 12–15; and Brownsville, 20–21; and budget reform, 13–15, 24, 33, 34, 43, 61–62; as chief justice, 92, 102–104; and Cleveland, 207n13, 216n34; and Dyer Bill, 92; and election of 1908, 20–21; and executive reorganization, 89; presidency of, 13–23; and Prohibition, 144; and Washington, 20–21
Teapot Dome scandal, 139
temperance, 140–141, 143–144
Thirty-One, the, 71–72
Towner-Sterling Bill: catholic opposition to, 159–160; elite reformers view of, 122, 127; hearings, 124–126; and NAACP, 122–124; provisions of, 121–122; southern opposition to, 121, 124–127; and United States Chamber of Commerce, 123, 127, 228n15
Towner, Horace, 121
Treasury, U.S. Department of: and Budget Bureau, 54–64, 86, 109, 135, 151, 187; nonfiscal functions, 108; and Prohibition enforcement, 88, 142–147,

INDEX

166–168, 174, 176; and veterans agencies, 73–78, 105–106
Trotter, William Monroe, 20
Truman, Harry, 187
Tucker, Henry St. George, III, 124–125
Tucker, John Randolph, 124, 228n18
Tulsa Massacre, 83–85
Tumulty, Joseph, 40
Turner, Frederick Jackson, 128
Tuskegee Institute, 18, 21–22, 37, 46–47, 49, 67, 105
Tuskegee Veterans Hospital, 105–106, 117
Twentieth Century Fund, 153
Twenty First Amendment, 185

Union Theological Seminary, 125
United States Attorney for the Southern District of New York, 31, 45
United States Chamber of Commerce: and Bonus, 132; creation of, 29; and Hoover, 147; on proposals for a department of education, 123, 127, 228n15
University of Chicago, 153, 187

veterans: adjusted compensation for (*See* Bonus); African American, 68–69, 105–106; hospital system, 104–106; of World War I, 72–78. *See also specific agencies and organizations*
Veterans Administration, U.S., 172–174, 177–179
Veterans Bureau, U.S.: creation of, 91; consolidation to create Veterans Administration, 171–174; and education and welfare, proposal for department of, 109, 122; scandal, 113–118, 227n39; Tuskegee Hospital, 104–106; World War Veterans Act (1924), 136–138
vetoes, presidential: Coolidge (Bonus, 1924), 132; Harding (Bonus, 1922), 131; Roosevelt, Franklin (Bonus,1936), 230n11; Wilson (Budget, 1920), 63–64, 66, 85; Wilson (Immigration, 1917), 134; Wilson (Volstead Act, 1919), 142
Villard, Oswald Garrison, 22, 25–26

Volstead Act (1919), 142–143
Voting Rights Act (1965), 9, 188–189

war debt, 42, 46
War Industries Board, 35–36
War Risk Insurance Bureau, 73–74, 171
Warburg, Paul, 45, 58
Washington and Lee University, 124–125
Washington Naval Conference (1921), 133
Washington Post, 113–114
Washington, Booker T., 17–18, 20–21, 23, 37, 46
Watson, Tom, 38, 121n
welfare, proposal for federal department of, 81, 108. *See also* education and welfare, proposal for federal department of
Wells, Ida, 37
western Republicans: and budget reform, 58; and civil rights, 188–189; and Coolidge, 128–129; and Dyer Bill, 99–100; and executive reorganization, 111; and Hoover, 157; and immigration, 134–135; interparty alliance with southern Democrats, 7–8, 16, 55, 69, 100, 134–135, 157, 177, 188–190; and Lodge Bill, 16; and New Deal, 185–186; and Progressive Party, 138; and Taft Commission, 16
Wheeler, Wayne, 142
White, Leonard D., 182
White, Walter, 103–104
White, William Charles, 75, 77–78
Wickersham Commission, 166–169, 174, 176–77
Wickersham, George: background, 166–167; and Dyer Bill, 83; and Harding 71; and lynching, 49; and Prohibition, 175–176; and Stimson, 32; and Taft, 12–13
Wilbur, Ray Lyman, 159, 172–173, 238n17
Williamson, William, 168–169, 172–173
Willoughby, William F.: background, 15; and education proposals, 236n19; and Good Bill, 54, 56, 61, 71; and Harding, 61; and Institute for Government

Willoughby, William F. (*continued*)
Research, 30, 43; and National Budget Committee, 43–45; and Prohibition enforcement, 145; and Taft Commission, 15

Wilson, Woodrow: academic writing, 27; background, 26; and *The Birth of a Nation*, 27; and budget reform, 58–59; and Carter Glass, 56; and civil service reform, 28–29; and East St. Louis massacre, 39; and election of 1912, 22–24; and elite reformers, 6, 24–25, 34–35, 184; and federal power, 27–29, 217n39; and lynching, 40–41, 49–50; New Freedom, 28; racism of, 25–27; segregation of executive branch, 25–26; and Taft Commission, 27–28; and veterans agencies, 75; veto of budget bill, 63–64, 66, 85

Woll, Matthew, 233n37

woman suffrage, 72

Wood, George H., 172–173

Wood, Leonard, 66–68

World Court, 111, 129

World War I, 34–37, 42

World War Veterans Act (1924), 136–138, 140, 146, 170

World's Work (magazine), 53, 71

GPSR Authorized Representative: Easy Access System Europe, Mustamäe tee
50, 10621 Tallinn, Estonia, gpsr.requests@easproject.com

www.ingramcontent.com/pod-product-compliance
Lightning Source LLC
Chambersburg PA
CBHW022046290426
44109CB00014B/1000